Security, With Care

Restorative Justice and Healthy Societies

Elizabeth M. Elliott

Fernwood Publishing • Halifax and Winnipeg

Editing and design: Brenda Conroy
Cover image: Gary Weaver
Cover design: John van der Woude
Printed and bound in Canada by Hignell Book Printing

Published in Canada by Fernwood Publishing
32 Oceanvista Lane
Black Point, Nova Scotia, B0J 1B0
and 748 Broadway Avenue, Winnipeg, Manitoba, R3G 0X3
www.fernwoodpublishing.ca

Fernwood Publishing Company Limited gratefully acknowledges the financial support of the
Government of Canada through the Canada Book Fund, the Canada Council for the Arts,
the Nova Scotia Department of Tourism and Culture and the Province of Manitoba,
through the Book Publishing Tax Credit, for our publishing program.

Library and Archives Canada Cataloguing in Publication

Elliott, Elizabeth M. (Elizabeth May), 1957-
Security, with care : restorative justice and healthy
societies / Elizabeth M. Elliott.

Includes bibliographical references and index.
ISBN 978-1-55266-425-4 (pbk.).--ISBN 978-1-55266-432-2 (bound)

1. Restorative justice. 2. Social values.
3. Interpersonal relations. 4. Social change. I. Title.

HV8688.E46 2011   364.6'8   C2010-908036-X

Contents

This book is dedicated to my first teachers
— my parents —
Albina Mihelich Elliott and Wallace Elliott

Human beings suffer,
They torture one another,
They get hurt and get hard.
No poem or play or song
Can fully right a wrong
Inflicted and endured.

The innocent in gaols
Beat on their bars together.
A hunger-striker's father
Stands in the graveyard dumb.
The police widow in veils
Faints at the funeral home.

History says, *Don't hope
On this side of the grave.*
But then, once in a lifetime
The longed-for tidal wave
Of justice can rise up
And hope and history rhyme.

So hope for a great sea-change
On the far side of revenge.
Believe that a further shore
Is reachable from here.
Believe in miracles
And cures and healing wells.

— Seamus Heaney, *The Cure at Troy,* 1961

It took me a long time and most of the world to learn what I know about love and fate and the choices we make, but the heart of it came to me in an instant, while I was chained to a wall and being tortured. I realised, somehow, through the screaming in my mind, that even in that shackled, bloodied helplessness, I was still free: free to hate the men who were torturing me, or to forgive them. It doesn't sound like much, I know. But in the flinch and bite of the chain, when it's all you've got, that freedom is a universe of possibility. And the choice you make, between hating and forgiving, can become the story of your life.

— Gregory David Roberts, *Shantaram*, 2003

Preface

I began my journey in the criminal justice world in 1981 as a young adult, recently out of university, freshly returned from some travelling adventures and ready for something completely different. Criminal justice was not even on my radar, so when I was hired by a non-profit society to do some research and writing, the idea of going to prison suddenly seemed like another exotic adventure. Until that time I had never given prison much thought. Once there, the thoughts that taxed my assumptions and the images that wouldn't go away compelled me into the world of social work. My habitat became courts, prisons, halfway houses and the offices of under-resourced community organizations. The work was never boring, but it became burdensome. Each human being — prisoner, victim, criminal justice professional and the people who care about them — was valuable and important, but there were so many of them, and most of them were struggling with terrible personal burdens. How could we help them all when there were so few of us willing to do the work?

The time to leave social work came in 1986, when the work had become too economically, ethically and personally exhausting. I understood my problem the following year, when in the first semester of my PhD program at the School of Criminology at Simon Fraser University I came across this passage in one of my theory course texts, Stanley Cohen's *Visions of Social Control* (1985: 236–37):

> I remember hearing… a parable which Saul Alinsky, the radical American community organizer used to tell. It went something like this. A man is walking by the riverside when he notices a body floating down stream. A fisherman leaps into the river, pulls the body ashore, gives mouth to mouth resuscitation, saving the man's life. A few minutes later the same thing happens, then again and again. Eventually yet another body floats by. This time the fisherman completely ignores the drowning man and starts running upstream along the bank. The observer asks the fisherman what on earth is he doing? Why is he not trying to rescue this drowning body? "This time," replies the fisherman, "I'm going upstream to find out who the hell is pushing these poor folks into the water."
>
> An impressive message to social workers: as long as you do nothing about original causes, you will continually just be pulling out

bodies, mopping up the casualties. Here lay the promise of sociology: to get at structure, power, history and politics — the real stuff of social problems. But Alinsky had a twist to his story: while the fisherman was so busy running along the bank to find the ultimate source of the problem, who was going to help those poor wretches who continued to float down the river?

My answer to the dilemma was to do a little of both. I continued my PhD studies and taught criminology courses in Kent and Matsqui Institutions for the now defunct Prison Education Program (PEP). I also became a mother of two children and worked as a sessional instructor at the university when the PEP was shut down. By the time I was finally working fulltime in the university, my kids were in school and my prison work became a volunteer vocation.

By now the imperfections of the criminal justice system had become the elephant in the room. The problem was that very few efforts to reform the system to make it less harmful and toxic to the people it affected were actually successful. In the early 1980s I was introduced to the concepts of victim-offender mediation and restitution, which were usually named in a longer list of alternatives to incarceration. The prison abolition movement, motivated by its members' intimate understanding of the harms produced by the prison itself, sought to reduce the use of incarceration. At the same time, victims of crime were beginning to voice their discontent with the criminal justice status quo, beginning with efforts from the feminist community to establish transition houses for women and children leaving violent relationships and sexual assault crisis centres. Ensuing political lobby groups for victims then sought relief in the only avenue available to them: longer prison sentences for offenders.

Then, in 1990, Howard Zehr's book, *Changing Lenses*, outlined preliminary ideas for a different paradigm — "restorative justice" (RJ). The concerns of all the people affected by crime seemed to be addressed in this new paradigm, and the ideas of the Norwegian criminologist Nils Christie in a 1974 article, "Conflicts as Property," now seemed more intriguing. The final catalyst was the marrying of these ideas to the teachings of the Aboriginal friends I had made through my work. From these teachers I learned that the problems were much deeper than a flawed criminal justice system and that our work needed to begin in our relationships with each other and the natural world and, most importantly, with ourselves. A new vista of possibilities opened up, and despite the enormity of the challenges everything seemed more hopeful.

The themes in *Security, With Care* emerged from my experiences in the past three decades in central Canada and on the West Coast, where I have been fortunate to engage with many wiser, more experienced and more passionate people on the same journey of healing and hope and have been introduced to their fellow travellers from other parts of the world. In no particular order, their contributions follow.

My first teachers in the field — Ruth Morris, Art Solomon and Claire Culhane — helped me and others to find our voices and encouraged our passion when the weight of the criminal justice system seemed too heavy; each of them has since passed away. Bob Gaucher, recently retired from the Department of Criminology at the University of Ottawa, has always pushed my intellectual thinking and continues to play an important role as a mentor and friend. Graham Stewart, formerly of the John Howard Society, was and continues to be a principled and intelligent mentor to my understanding of criminal justice policy. All of my friends, former colleagues and prisoner contacts in the criminal justice milieu in Toronto and Kingston taught me important lessons at the beginning of my travels, many of which helped me to develop my critical thinking around "conventional wisdom."

In British Columbia, the teachers seemed to multiply, particularly when my focus moved from criminal to restorative justice. I soon became enriched by the perspectives of former criminal justice leaders such as retired Judge Barry Stuart, who, in addition to innovating circle sentencing in the Yukon Territory, has been an enthusiastic supporter of community-based restorative justice and continues to serve as an important link between communities and the formal justice system since his relocation to Vancouver. Through Barry, came Kay Pranis in Minnesota and Molly Baldwin at Roca in Massachusetts, two women who combine humility, intellect, heart and passion to mobilize individuals and communities to act in accordance with values. Kay's and Molly's contributions continue to inspire many of us in this journey of change.

As luck would have it, a mere forty minutes drive from either work or my home was the Fraser Region's Community Justice Initiatives Association (CJI), home of the Mennonite community's contribution to conflict reconciliation. Co-directors Sandi Bergen and David Gustafson, after a decade of facilitating a victim-offender reconciliation program in the early 1990s, pioneered a sensitive process of victim-offender mediation in cases of severe violence. Their work, as evidenced by the testimonies of dozens of satisfied participants from the CJI process, has been significant to our understanding of the implications of trauma in RJ practices. This contact alerted me to Ottawa's Collaborative Justice Project (CJP) and its then-coordinator Jamie Scott, a United Church minister now working with the church's responsibilities emanating from Canada's Indian residential schools. The CJP continues to demonstrate the value of RJ processes within the courthouse, post-pleading and pre-sentencing.

The community-based RJ network in British Columbia, as creators of flexible processes that vary according to the community or situation, have been generous with stories and lessons from their experiences. Jacquie Stevaluk, now retired from North Shore Restorative Justice, offered many of us useful guidance on navigating the Scylla and Charybdis of deploying community-based RJ through the criminal justice system. Larry Moore and Cathie Douglas, formerly of the Kaslo Restorative Justice Society in the Kootenay region, continue to make enormous contributions through their knowledge of community-based RJ and their educational video-making skills. Larry and Cathie — apart from providing the best conversations about RJ before finishing the first cup of coffee in the morning — have been prolific contributors to RJ around the world and in my classrooms through their work as Heartspeak Productions. The coordinators and volunteers, past and present of myriad organizations — Communities Embracing Restorative Action, North Shore Restorative Justice, Vancouver Association for Restorative Justice, Abbotsford Restorative Justice Association, Restorative Justice Oak Bay, Vancouver Aboriginal Transformative Justice Services, Restorative Justice Victoria, Prince George Urban Aboriginal Justice Society and the Nanaimo Restorative Justice Program, to name only the few with which I have had contact over the years — have all continued through adversity and funding challenges to bring RJ philosophy and practices to the community level. The staff and volunteers of these organizations are the heart and soul of restorative justice in our neck of the woods. Special thanks to Darryl Gehlen and Mai Iverson of my home community RJ group, Mission Restorative Resolutions.

In no small measure has been the influence of prisoners and community volunteers in pockets of RJ sanctuary found in prisons. Over the past many years I have been privileged to participate in prison-based circles as part of the Alternatives to Violence Project, a talking circle called FAVOUR and many RJ workshops. In particular, local community contributors to my understanding of RJ in the prison context include Alana Abramson, Dan and Heather Basham, Deltonia "Malik" Cook, Carly Hoogeven, Carley Julien, Colleen McLeod, Marion Robinson, Robert Seto, Nicky Spires, Susan Underwood, and Mako Watanabe. Warren McDougall was especially helpful in giving the book manuscript a thorough read and offering many useful comments. Prisoner contributors from over the past ten years, from both Mission and Ferndale Institutions, were especially inspiring, and many have enriched my university courses by generously using precious prison escorted absences to speak to classes. With their permission, recent FAVOUR group contributors are Larry Bembin, Ron Caldwell, Yves Côté, Mark Jarman, Kirill Kovtchega, Roger Warren, Gary Weaver and Fred.

Academic colleagues have also been formidable sounding boards and supports over the years while this book was percolating. In the School of Criminology, I am indebted to its director, Robert Gordon, who believed in the value of the restorative justice approach and in 2002 helped to expedite the establishment of the Centre for Restorative Justice. More recently, I have been personally enriched by the presence of my new colleague, Brenda Morrison, whose work on RJ in schools, social-emotional learning and school violence has helped to flesh out other interesting areas of scholarly pursuit in the RJ domain both within the school and internationally. Jane Miller, who spent a few years with us at Simon Fraser as a restorative justice instructor, was a welcome colleague; our many conversations over the years have helped me to shape some of my thinking in different ways. Karlene Faith, now retired, co-authored one version of CRIM 315 with me for the university's Centre for Online and Distance Education, and continues to be a dear friend. I still pass on Karlene's advice to students: "Find out what you love to do. Learn to do it well. And do it in the service of the people." The university's Centre for Online and Distance Education, in particular John Whatley, were supportive sponsors of the first version of this book; Lynne Malcombe was a great editor. At Fernwood Publishing, much gratitude to Errol Sharpe, Brenda Conroy, Beverley Rach and Debbie Mathers. I also owe thanks to RJ scholar colleagues outside of Simon Fraser University and in other parts of the country and the world: Gordon Bazemore, Stephan Parmentier, Paul Redekop, Joao Salm, Dennis Sullivan, Juan Tauri, Elmar Weitekamp, and Howard Zehr.

My students over the years — as well as graduate student teaching assistants (TAs) — who have taken the School of Criminology's first RJ course (CRIM 315) with me, have made enormous contributions to this book by being both its first consumers and the editors of its content. (Thanks especially to one of our most enduring and stalwart TAs and friend, Melissa Roberts). Their own curiosity and courage in considering the paradigm shift between the more familiar retributive philosophy and restorative justice yielded many valuable questions and revealed many gaps. Their willingness to share their questions, doubts, agreements and stories, and to show up every week prepared to engage fully in the many experiential exercises and circle gatherings associated with the course was a gesture of trust and continues to be greatly appreciated. Teaching in a university is indeed a privilege, one that affords engagement with many young and motivated people who are inheriting the world we are passing on to them. I only hope they will forgive us.

While many of the folks acknowledged so far are also friends, there are friends outside of the ambit of the book's specific subject matter who have been supportive and caring during many trying times in this book's genesis. Thanks especially to David Antrobus, Carey Christiansen, Ron and Jeannette Cooney, Tom Crean, Carol Fissel, Heidi Graw, Merlyn Horton, Jay Jones, Barbara Roddick, David Snook, Jo Ann Turner and Jim Wilson. The book would never have been written at all if not for the astute attention and excellent work of Dr. Steve Mitchinson (family doctor) and Dr. Damien Byrne (surgeon), who detected and addressed my cancer when it first appeared. My oncologist, Dr. Robert Winston, has been both an exceptional professional and a compassionate human being. Thanks for their good work, their kindness, caring and giving me the gift of time, and for reminding me, in an unforgettable way, of the value of research in improving the results of any endeavour.

Finally, the biggest thanks go to my family, the primary community to which I belong: my partner, Milt Gluppe, who has weathered many storms with me both on and off the boat; my son Kristofor, who has taught me much about how to build community and being brave in the face of unexpected challenges; my daughter Maya, whose intellect and remarkable wisdom fuel my hope for the future; my parents, Albina and Wallace, to whom this book is dedicated; my amazing brother Peter — always there when I need him, even when thousands of kilometres away; sister-in-law Colleen and nieces Shannon and Megan, who have always been generous, kind and supportive.

Dineamaaganik.[1] Belonging to everything.

Note

1.   The meaning of this Ojibway word is explained by Chris Corrigan in a blog about an experience he had near Thunder Bay, Ontario, with a group of Ojibway elders at a gathering to work on traditional governance and Aboriginal rights and title. The term *dineamaaganik*, which Corrigan thought meant "all my relations," actually means "belonging to everything." For full story, see <http://chriscorrigan.com/parkinglot/?p=2015>.

Introduction

If blood will flow when flesh and steel are one
Drying in the colour of the evening sun
Tomorrow's rain will wash the stains away
But something in our minds will always stay
Perhaps this final act was meant
To clinch a lifetime's argument
That nothing comes from violence and nothing ever could
For all those born beneath an angry star
Lest we forget how fragile we are. (Sting, "Fragile," 1987)

Imagine the following scenario. You have just disembarked from a city bus around midnight and you immediately come upon a woman in distress on the ground, her anxious children gathered around her. You glance a fleeting shadow disappearing into an alleyway. What would be the first action you would take?

When presented with this thought experiment, most people's response is to attend to the needs of the woman on the ground. The second concern is to take care of the children and then, perhaps, to check out the person in the alley. Our sensibilities tend to have us focus first on the victim, then on those others affected by the harm and finally on the perpetrator. This is what we learn in our homes, in the schoolyard and in the community.

But this is not how our criminal justice system responds to harm. The first attention is paid to the perpetrator; indeed, later concerns of the system are also the perpetrator. When attention is paid to victims, it is usually in their capacity as witnesses, since in our system the state usurps the role of the victim. This is why *Criminal Code* offences in Canada are cited as "*R. vs John Smith*," with "R" representing "Regina" or "Rex" (Queen or King). The victim's and perpetrator's supporters and the communities they live in are usually not attended to at all.

The above thought experiment was presented by Dennis Maloney to demonstrate the disjuncture between what we want from a justice system and what we get. Until his death in 2007, Dennis spent sixteen years as the director of Deschutes County's community justice department in Oregon and was associate director of the Cascade Center for Community Governance. Like many people involved in restorative justice work, Dennis began his career working within the retributive criminal justice system. His

1

pull towards restorative justice began with his interest in how some of the Aboriginal communities he worked with handled problems we might categorize as crimes. Ultimately, he saw the community development possibilities of restorative justice and the crime prevention benefits derived from this holistic philosophy.

Maloney's appreciation for traditional Aboriginal ways of working through problems is echoed in this book, which uses primarily Canadian and American examples to illustrate themes germane to a fulsome expression of restorative justice. The Canadian emphasis is an obvious outcome of my own nationality and experience and is useful for its particular history of contact between settling Europeans and First Nations peoples. The Canadian intellectual John Ralston Saul, in his intriguing book *A Fair Country* (2008), challenges the Canadian historical premise that the nation was founded solely by the British and the French. Using historical records, he persuasively demonstrates that First Nations people heavily influenced the evolution of Canadian culture — as seen in our preference for negotiation over violence, our acceptance of diverse opinions between individuals and groups, and our belief in egalitarianism. Colonizing Europeans who arrived in the northern half of the continent were dependent on the hospitality and guidance of the indigenous people, who had lived successfully in the harsh climate. The French in particular engaged indigenous peoples on a personal level through marriage, resulting in the new cultural grouping known as Métis. Saul's assertion is that Canada is a Métis nation, a country informed by European and Aboriginal thought and ways.

The significance of this historical diversion is found in how Canadian approaches to restorative justice may differ from those of the U.S., the South Pacific and other pioneering nation sites of RJ. Most of what has been written about RJ has been directed by the cultural standpoint of the authors; this book is similar in that it reflects my own Canadian context and experiences. In establishing this from the outset, it is also necessary to note that Canada is a large country of ten provinces and three territories, delimited by three oceans and the forty-ninth parallel. Unique expressions of RJ pepper the country. In Nova Scotia, for example, RJ is deployed through governmental institutions down to the community. In British Columbia, where I reside, the RJ tradition has been primarily community-based.

Saul's assertion of the profound influence of Aboriginal ways on current Canadian culture has particular relevance to the British Columbia context. Community-based RJ groups have benefited from the teachings of their Aboriginal neighbours within the province and from the bordering Yukon Territory. We have been challenged through these relationships to deepen our understanding of what we call "restorative justice" to consider a more holistic context for conflict. This means that there is a tendency to see the promise of change as emerging from the grassroots of our society, rather than being institutionally driven.

Canadian expressions of RJ have also been informed by the valuable contributions of Mennonite organizations across the country. The first contemporary example of RJ globally came in 1974 from a small town in southern Ontario called Elmira, in which Mark Yantzi deployed a rudimentary version of victim-offender mediation in the case of two young men who had spent an evening vandalizing property. Yantzi's Mennonite background and consultation with elders in his community influenced his experimental approach; since then, the Mennonite-based Community Justice Initiatives (in both Waterloo, Ontario, and Langley, British Columbia) has emerged as a leader in the particular RJ approach of mediation. The Fraser Region Community Justice Initiatives Association in B.C. has also been of value for their internationally recognized violent offence mediation approach; the attention to trauma in this book was catalyzed by engagement with this organization.

A recent contribution to the literature by Jarem Sawatsky (2009), from a Mennonite community in the province of Manitoba, offers the case for a holistic approach to peace building that he calls "healing justice." In a portion of his argument, he questions RJ for its limitations of expression and its dependence on criminal justice institutions. Sawatsky's view of what is required to develop peaceful communities was partly influenced by his research with the First Nations community of Hollow Water. Using the medical framework of primary, secondary and tertiary care, Sawatsky argues that most RJ falls into the latter category, where it is deployed as a response to harm that has already occurred. Harm prevention targeted at people who are at higher risk of requiring tertiary intervention is the purview of secondary care; RJ in schools is an example of this. Primary care is that which is focused on changing the whole of society so that we are more likely to be out of harm's way. This offering challenges us again to think outside of the box RJ has found itself in — as a criminal justice add-on program.

In order to avoid the traps of co-optation and relegation to the criminal justice system's sidelines, RJ needs to be affirmed as something more than a program. In academic terms, it is more useful to conceptualize RJ as a paradigm — one that holds its own philosophical and theoretical framework — focusing on theories that purport to explain relevant phenomena and encouraging research that tests these propositions. In community development terms, RJ may be seen as a holistic approach that is grounded in core values that are helpful towards creating the kind of peaceful societies we say we want. On a more personal level, RJ is often described as a way of life, an approach to individual conduct that promises more peaceful relationships.

This book introduces several key concepts necessary for understanding the broader strokes and foundations of restorative justice. Its contents emerge from the basis of where we are in RJ currently, as an approach to conflict, and move into an appreciation of RJ as something fundamentally different from individualistic and retributive beliefs and processes.

In order to open up to the possibilities of restorative justice, it is first necessary to see where we are right now. This starting point entails not only an overview of the Canadian criminal justice system today but also a look at a road not yet committed to, although manifested, in the systems of our neighbours to the south. The United States is a large carceral experiment in the context of world systems, and what has been happening there offers us some insight into the consequences of particular penal policies. This is the subject of Chapter 1.

In order to better enable our critical analyses, we need to revisit familiar themes such as punishment and justice to consider what they mean and how they shape our beliefs about what should be a proper response to harm-doing. I use the term "harm-doing" instead of "crime" deliberately, since restorative justice is not merely about criminal justice but pertains to a wide terrain of social interaction, from parenting, schools and businesses to relationships in general. In Chapter 2 we unpack one of the heaviest pieces of baggage on this journey — punishment. The idea of punishment is axiomatic; we debate its implementation styles or intensity but rarely its utility. In this chapter we consider the views of many theorists about punishment — what it is, what it is for, how it works and whether it accomplishes what it promises — and review what works instead. In Chapter 3, our curiosity about punishment spills into the arena of justice; we ask: what is justice? Philosophers for eons have examined justice, as a feature of the democratic state, as the property of systems and as a character trait of individuals. Do we have a common understanding of justice, and to the extent that we differ, how does that play out in the criminal justice system and school and family disciplinary systems? We need to examine the meaning of justice so we are prepared to engage with a different framework for it, in the shift to a restorative justice paradigm.

At last, in Chapter 4, we engage directly with restorative justice itself. The concept of restorative justice, in its different expressions, is introduced as both a way of asking questions about harm and its effects and of focusing on certain phenomena. These key phenomena are addressed in more detail in Chapters 6, 7, 8, and 9, but in Chapter 4 I sketch their significance to the restorative justice lens overall, particularly in terms of healthy democratic societies. Restorative justice is about healing harms, which is not necessarily the mandate of the retributive system. Inevitably, this leads us to ponder the realistic possibilities for restorative justice within the context of our current systems, and many of us tend to think of criminal justice systems specifi- cally. There are some difficult yet intriguing consonances and contradictions between the retributive and restorative paradigms, and in Chapter 5 we take on some challenging ideas about the role of restorative justice in societies governed by the rule of law. Both in philosophy and practice, restorative justice asks what is necessary to live collectively and as our "best selves."

We pick up the phenomena outlined in Chapter 4 in Chapter 6, in which the theme is values and processes. Restorative justice is, if anything, about values in both thought and action. It also begins with each individual rather than being something "done" to someone else. Core values are those that seem to enjoy some universality, which helps in cross-cultural conflicts. But values require expression, and it is a goal of restorative justice that its values inform and embody the processes used to develop communities and work through conflicts. Conflicts are usually, although not always, the focus of restorative processes. And conflicts are about individuals who are not in "right relationship." In Chapter 7, we consider the individual and relationships within the paradigm of restorative justice. Individuals are autonomous, with their own agencies, and each is unique in their own way. Each person is on their own journey, and each carries with them their own varying life experiences. The following two chapters examine more closely two significant hotspots in the psychology of restorative justice that are manifested in individuals before or as a result of the harm being considered. These are also better understood when we see the individual in relationship with others. Restorative justice is often characterized as being *relational*, that the source of both harm and healing of individuals is found in relationships.

Chapter 8 reviews the concept of shame, which some theorists consider to be an innate affect. "Affect" is the biological portion of emotion. While the awareness of harm-doing is bound to generate some emotion, for those harmed, those committing the harmful act and those in the community containing everyone and beyond, our retributive systems of conflict resolution are not structured to manage the emotions antecedent to and generated by conflicts. Shame is a key emotion in this context, for both those harmed and those harming others. Restorative processes endeavour to create safe places for difficult conversations, which involves attention to shame management. The other psychological hotspot for restorative justice is trauma, the focus of Chapter 9. Trauma has been examined extensively since the 1970s, primarily due to therapeutic work with Viet Nam veterans and sexual assault victims. Knowledge of the effects of trauma helps us to better understand the behaviour of both those harmed and those committing the harm, which is particularly critical in cases involving violent crime or genocide. Early trauma is often a key factor in offending behaviour and a major hurdle in victim healing. Restorative justice not only opens our awareness of possible underlying implications of trauma but also reminds us that in responding to harm we should, at the very least, do no further harm.

In Chapter 10, we examine the critical component of the community in restorative justice. The idea of "community" has been critiqued for its idealistic connotations and often rightly so. This chapter entertains different definitions of community and considers ways in which communities constitute the web of relationships necessary for supporting healing efforts of parties to harm. But communities can also be built or reinvigorated when their members become involved in restorative processes, as individuals grow in their capacities to become more competent as citizens. Restorative processes can be opportunities to clarify community values. In this chapter, RJ opens up to its broader expression as a communal and individual way of being that cultivates more peaceful societies.

Our final chapter concludes with a look to what restorative justice might mean to us as individuals "doing what we can." Perhaps the most difficult aspect of restorative justice is that it asks us to begin with ourselves, to work towards "transforming the power-based self" (Sullivan and Tifft: 2005: 154–57). This requires us to think outside of the subject-object distinctions of the retributive justice paradigm, to move from beliefs that we "do" justice to others or "bring" them to justice towards the understanding that we must *be* just as individuals in our everyday lives. Restorative justice cannot be actualized merely through the implementation of new criminal justice or other system-based policies. If it isn't who we are, the policies will not be sustainable. In any event, the idea is to become more competent and engaged as citizens in our homes and communities, so that we need to rely less on formal government institutions to address our problems. Restorative justice is about *us*, how we are in the world in our everyday lives, how we conceptualize the problems with which we are confronted and how we respond to them. Its foundation is the belief that "we cannot get to a good place in a bad way — *ever*."[1]

Note

1. This phrase has been asserted often by Molly Baldwin, Executive Director of Roca, a "performance-based and outcomes-driven organization that helps young people to change their behavior and shift the trajectories of their lives through a High-Risk Youth Intervention Model." Roca serves very high-risk young people in Chelsea, Revere and East Boston, MA. See <www.rocainc.org>.

1

The March of Folly

State-Raised Convict

Jack Henry Abbott

He who is state-raised — reared by the state from an early age after he is taken from what the state calls a "broken home" — learns over and over and all the days of his life that people in society can do anything to him and not be punished by the law. Do anything to him with the full force of the state behind them.

As a child, he must march in lock-step to his meals in a huge mess hall. He can own only three shirts and two pairs of trousers and one pair of shoes.

People in society come to him through the state and injure him. Everyone in society he comes in contact with is in some capacity employed by the state. He learns to avoid people in society. He evades them at every step.

In *any* state in America someone who is state-raised can be shot down and killed like a dog by anyone, who has no "criminal record," with full impunity. I do not exaggerate this at all. It is a fact so ordinary in the minds of state-raised prisoners that it is a matter of common sense. If a prisoner were to show a skeptical attitude toward things of this nature, the rest of us would conclude that he is losing his mind. He is questioning what is self-evident to us: a practical fact of life....

My mind keeps turning toward one of the main aspects of prison that separates ordinary prisoners who, at some point in their lives, serve a few years and get out never to return — or if they do, it is for another short period and never again — and the convict who is "state-raised," i.e., the prisoner who grows up from boyhood to manhood in penal institutions....

Every society gives its men and women the prerogatives of men and women, of *adults*. Men are given their dues. After a certain age you are regarded as a man by society. You are referred to as "sir"; no one interferes in your affairs, claps your hands or ignores you. You are shown respect. Gradually your judgment is tempered because gradually you see it has real effects; it impinges on the society, the world. Your experience mellows your emotions because you are free to move about anywhere, work and play at anything. You are taught by the very terms of your social existence, by the objects that come and go from your intentions, the natures of your own emotions — and you learn about yourself, your tastes, your strengths and weaknesses. You, in other words, mature emotionally.

It is not so for the state-raised convict. As a boy in reform school, he is punished for being a little boy. In prison, he is punished for trying to be a man in the sense described above. He is treated as an adolescent in prison. Just as an adolescent is denied the keys to the family car for *any* disobedience, *any* mischief, I am subjected to the hole for *any* disobedience, *any* mischief....

Prison regimes have prisoners making extreme decisions regarding moderate questions, decisions that only fit the logical choice of either-or. No contradiction is allowed openly. You are not allowed to change. You are only allowed to submit; "agreement" does not exist (it implies equality). You are the rebellious adolescent who must obey and submit to the judgment of "grownups" — "tyrants" they are called when we speak of men.

A prisoner who is not state-raised tolerates the situation because of his social maturity prior to incarceration. He knows things are different outside prison. But the state-raised convict has no conception of any difference. He lacks experience and, hence, maturity. His judgment is untempered, rash; his emotions are impulsive, raw, unmellowed....

This thing I related above about emotions is the hidden, dark side of state-raised convicts. The foul under belly everyone hides from everyone else. There is something else. It is the other half — which concerns *judgment, reason* (moral, ethical, cultural). It is the mantle of pride, integrity, honor. It is the high esteem we naturally have for violence, force. It is what makes us *effective*, men whose judgment impinges on others, on the world: Dangerous killers who act alone and *without* emotion, who act with calculation and principles, to avenge themselves, establish and defend their principles with acts of murder that usually evade prosecution by law; this is the state-raised convicts' conception of manhood, in the highest sense. (Abbott 1981: 12–15)

☙ ☙ ☙

The above reflections — written by one of the U.S.'s best-known prisoners, Jack Henry Abbott, who came to public attention through his correspondence with the American writer Norman Mailer — paint a hostile view of the ability of state institutions to parent children. Abbott's resistance to the ideology of the prison seemed to follow his experiences of being a ward of the state. Most Canadians and Americans have never been in a prison, and most never will venture behind the razor-wired double-fences that surround the many prisons and jails in these countries. Our imaginings of the internal workings of the prison vary, from the brutal violence of everyday life depicted in television series such as *Oz*[1] to the leisurely existence of pampered prisoners opined by "tough on crime" politicians and journalists.[2] In contrast, James Blau's description of incarceration in a U.S. prison (at the end of this chapter) seems more reflective of the experience endured by the character of Phil Connors in the Harold Ramis movie *Groundhog Day* (1993) — the story of a man trapped in time in the same day, in the same routine, having the same conversations with the same people, over and over again.

The history of incarceration as a punishment for crime in Canada predates Confederation. From 1790 to 1825, the primary punishments meted out by the Criminal Assizes of Upper Canada (now known as Ontario) were corporal punishment, "burning on the hand," stock/pillory, banishment, fines, capital punishment and short periods of imprisonment, the latter being a secondary component to one of the other punishments.[3] During the 1820s, in a transition between the first and second halves of the decade, an interesting shift in the pattern of legal punishment began to occur. As the "shaming" punishments of hand burnings, corporal violence and stocks decreased in number (totally or by halves and two-thirds) and banishment reduced by half, records show that the number of people sentenced to prison tripled. As noted by Peter Oliver, this trend continued into subsequent decades: "Between 1836 and 1841 virtually all offenders convicted at the Assizes were sentenced to imprisonment" (1998: 14–15). By Confederation, in 1867, three penitentiaries existed: at Kingston, Halifax and Saint John. The latter two were turned over to provincial authorities in 1880. By that year, five penitentiaries spanned the country: near Kingston (1835), Montréal (St. Vincent de Paul, in 1872), Winnipeg (Stony Mountain, in 1875), New Westminster (B.C. Penitentiary, in 1878) and Moncton (Dorchester, in 1880) (Gosselin 1982: 71–74).[4] Today, 175 years later, there are fifty-three federal maximum, medium and minimum security penal institutions in Canada.

How do we explain the sudden enthusiasm for imprisonment as punishment in the late 1830s? One possibility is that the technology for such a punitive response — the hard edifice of the prison — became available in 1835 with the opening of the Portsmouth Penitentiary outside of what is now known as Kingston, Ontario (Curtis et al. 1985; Hennessy 1999). Portsmouth Penitentiary later became Kingston Penitentiary, which still operates as a maximum-security institution under the auspices of the Correctional Service of Canada. Current historians have many explanations for the emergence of Canada's first penitentiary (for examples, see Oliver 1998; Hennessy 1999; Gosselin 1982; Curtis et al. 1985); most agree that Upper Canadians in the 1830s saw crime as a topic of public interest. However, it has also been noted that the road of public opinion that led to acceptance of the penitentiary was a rocky one, marked by conflict between local residents and trades people on one side, and the ruling elites on the other (Smandych 1991).

Since then, imprisonment has maintained its primacy as a method of punishment, metaphorically as a "solution" to moral decay and instrumentally as a purposeful tool towards the goals of deterrence, rehabilitation, protection of society and punishment. Yet since its inception, there have been consistent public and political critiques of its efficacy in meeting these goals. Multiple periods of incarceration, which colour most federal prisoners' criminal records, defy notions such as that deterrence is affected by imprisonment or that rehabilitation strategies radically change the majority of individual prisoners. Although the incapacitation of persistently violent people offers some protection to society, better protection might be afforded by preventing or mitigating harm than by imposing punitive consequences after the act. To those who have lost their liberty to prison sentences, it's a given that prison is punishment, yet the belief that prisons are not punitive enough remains a common conservative critique.

Canada's current experience with incarceration, however, pales in comparison to the situation in the U.S., where the use of prisons accelerated with unprecedented and apparently unbridled enthusiasm from the 1980s to the present. Canadians should consider the example of our neighbours as a warning regarding the hazards of criminal justice policies predicated squarely in crime control rhetoric and the promise of "security." To see the manifestation of this phenomenon clearly, it is necessary to describe everything about it: what it looks like, what informs it, what makes it possible, who benefits from it and what effects it has on criminal justice policy as a whole.

The U.S. Situation

In the world of prisons, no country has embraced incarceration as effusively as the U.S. In early 2000, the number of people incarcerated in the U.S. passed the two million mark. One researcher noted that, in 2002, the global prison population rate was about 140 per 100,000 citizens, with the U.S. rate at about 700 per 100,000 (Walmsley 2003: 65); by mid-2008, the U.S. rate had increased to 740 (ICPS 2008). In stark contrast to Sweden, the country with the lowest rate of incarceration, which locks up one resident per 2,000, the U.S. incarcerates one in 150 people (Tonry 1999: 419). In Canada, the incarceration rate in 2007 was 116 per 100,000. At five times the average world rate, the U.S. earns the dubious title of "prison capital of the world."

This phenomenon — also referred to as mass imprisonment — is marked by two significant features: sheer numbers and the group targeted for incarceration. Garland notes: "Imprisonment becomes *mass imprisonment* when it ceases to be the incarceration of individual offenders and becomes the systematic imprisonment of whole groups of the population. In the case of the U.S., the group concerned is, of course, young black males in large urban centres" (2001: 6). This has developed, not as the result of carefully coordinated and cohesive social policy towards a collective goal but as a consequence of unchecked political, professional and economic opportunism.

The mass imprisonment phenomenon in the U.S. has become what Marc Mauer describes as a "race to incarcerate" (1999), specifically to incarcerate a disproportionate number of young African-American men. Based on today's incarceration rates, one in three African-American men can expect to be incarcerated at some time in their lives, as compared to one in seventeen of their white counterparts (Sentencing Project Website n.d.). African-American women do not fare much better, comprising 38 percent of women incarcerated in the U.S.; Latina women make up a further 17 percent of that population. The effects of this targeting of racial minorities, primarily through disproportionate drug charging practices, reach beyond prisons and into the communities of those targeted. The effects of incarceration are felt deeply by the children of prisoners and subsequent generations: in particular, the children of women prisoners suffer trauma as a result of family disintegration, dislocation and poverty (Radosh 2002).

Another salient feature of the U.S. situation is the proliferation of "supermax" prisons and the increased use of solitary total confinement, where conditions are characterized by isolation within incarceration — usually twenty-three hours a day of cell time. In the late twentieth century, prison psychologist Richard Korn raised serious concerns about the psychological effects of high security units such as the one at Lexington (1992). By the end of that century, approximately 20,000 prisoners were confined to these units in the U.S. (Human Rights Watch 2000). The problems with this practice are summarized by Craig Haney[5]: "There are few if any forms of imprisonment that appear to produce so much psychological trauma and in which so many symptoms of psychopathology are manifested" (2003: 125). The specific effects of this practice on prisoners incarcerated in supermax conditions include: negative attitudes and affect; insomnia; anxiety; panic; withdrawal; hypersensitivity; ruminations; cognitive dysfunction; hallucinations; loss of control; irritability, aggression and rage; paranoia; hopelessness; lethargy; depression; a sense of impending emotional breakdown; self-mutilation; and suicidal ideation and behaviour (Haney 2003: 130–31).

The Incarceration and Release Crime Control Model

The control units (twenty-three-hour lock-up) proliferating in the U.S. are a symptom of the swing in criminal justice policy toward the crime control model, as described by Herbert Packer (1964). This model, which stresses the apprehension and punishment of criminals on behalf of "law-abiding" citizens, works well as a tool of political expression in a "tough on crime" political culture. It follows that images of boot camps are also popular, despite research evidence showing that "the traditional, discipline-oriented boot camp model is ineffective in reducing recidivism" (Kempinen and Kurlychek 2003: 582). Politically, incarceration as a response to crime is no longer sufficient; of greater political concern today is that the conditions of confinement — rather than reflecting the civility of the nation itself, as Winston Churchill argued in the early twentieth century[6] — symbolize how tough on crime legislators are.

The effects of incarceration, however, do not remain contained within prison walls. Most imprisoned people are eventually released, and both the symbolic and actual effects of incarceration spill out into the streets, primarily of urban areas. If community safety is the main underpinning of mass and hyper-incarceration, how well is this interest served in the system's approaches to and mechanisms for eventual prisoner release? Questions about conditional release from custody have recently been re-energized, and the answers to them require some navigation through a sea of variables, most of which have to do with politics and the administration of correctional systems. Further, as James Austin wryly notes, "For those who have been toiling in the vineyards of prisons for many years, this newfound interest in prison releases is being met with a fair degree of skepticism and suspicion" (2001: 314).

A survey study of prison admission, release and community supervision practices in eight U.S. states[7] raises a number of considerations (Austin 2001). Across the sample, about 40 percent of prison admissions were parole violators; most of the remaining 60 percent of new court commitments related to people on probation who had violated technical conditions and/or accrued new criminal charges that resulted in them being incarcerated for the first time on their original warrants. Austin notes that continued prison growth not only forecasted both longer sentences for new prison admissions but also the recycling of former prisoners as parole violators (318). This suggests that any improvement in rates of parole and probation failure would likewise impact incarceration rates. Austin also notes that classification systems placed most prisoners in medium and minimum security institutions, indicating that prison populations are constituted mainly by low-risk prisoners, most of whom are not arrested or re-incarcerated regardless of any pre-release programming. Despite this, however, parole is used sparingly, with grant rates having dropped considerably over the years, from 70 percent in 1977 to 28 percent in 1997 (Seiter and Kadela 2003: 365).

Other researchers have investigated the effectiveness of different prisoner re-entry programs. Richard Seiter and Karen Kadela, for example, have noted that the "new penology" (Feeley and Simon 1992) has shifted the approach to release from "helping and counselling" parolees to risk management and surveillance (2003: 366). Their study suggests that the types of programs most likely to reduce recidivism include vocational training or work release programs, drug rehabilitation, education, halfway houses and programs focusing on pre-release issues (380). From the prisoners' perspective, securing employment is often the most pressing concern (367). The authors of one study note that although various problems made it difficult for them to determine the effects of imprisonment on subsequent employment, they could at least conclude that serving time diminishes the earnings of former prisoners by 10–30 percent (Western, Kling and Weiman 2001). At the same time, however, post-incarceration employment may be less affected by the imprisonment itself than by demographics. The latest spurt of growth in the U.S. prison population shows high concentrations of young, low-skill, minority men (Western, Kling and Weiman 2001: 411), whose employment prospects are poor even when they have not been imprisoned. This condition harkens back to neo-Marxist theories of the prison, which suggested the utility of the prison as a container for surplus labour.[8]

The overall decrease in early parole releases due to "truth in sentencing" initiatives, as well as the preponderance of lower-security (non-violent) prisoners, has meant that scarce resources are being vigorously deployed to dubious community-safety ends. More people are being locked up for longer periods of time as punishment for non-violent crimes, essentially as window displays for "tough on crime" political rhetoric. At the same time, this rhetoric leads to another practice that raises quite a different concern: the release of prisoners from segregated confinement in maximum-security prisons directly to the street. Austin notes: "The release of high-risk/high-custody inmates is common to all states" (2001: 327). Given the earlier discussion of the effects of solitary confinement on the individual's psychology, this is a serious situation indeed.

In the U.S., in any given year, about 40 percent of all prisoners will be released. In 1995, 460,000 people started parole. In 2005, 887,000 were released. The social costs of this can be nothing but tremendous. Struggling blue-collar areas and impoverished districts cannot sustain healthy neighbourhoods while re-absorbing such large numbers of people on parole, most of whom lack legal, marketable skills. There are few community agencies to assist them with reintegration. Their families have often been broken apart as a consequence of their incarceration. A criminal record automatically disenfranchises them from many social services, such as subsidized housing and welfare. Years of isolation, often including periods of solitary confinement, make adjustment to the outside world difficult, at best. In short, the social problems that lead so many individuals to imprisonment in the first place are exacerbated for those who return to life outside the prison.

Politics and Prisons in the U.S.

Former Pennsylvania state attorney general Ernie Preate was a prominent promoter of the "war on drugs" initiative who pledged to make Pennsylvania the country's leader in implementing tough mandatory drug sentences. Also a vigorous champion of the death penalty, Preate seemed well positioned to win the GOP nomination in his bid to be the governor of the state in 1993. However, his aspirations were derailed when the story broke that he was being investigated for mail fraud and nondisclosure of campaign contributions a decade earlier. Sentenced to fourteen months in prison, Preate found himself in the company of the kinds of men upon whom he had built his tough-on-crime career — African American and Hispanic men who were mostly serving sentences for drug offences. He was confronted by the realization of what he had done the first time he lined up for a meal at the federal prison camp in Duluth, Minnesota, in 1996: "It was just a sea of black faces. I said to myself, 'Oh, my God, I helped create this'" (Westcott 2002: 73).

Preate's transformation from law-and-order prosecutor to restorative justice advocate came through his subsequent experiences helping fellow prisoners file formal petitions challenging the lengths of their sentences and their release dates. In the process, he was compelled to question the very system to which he had dedicated his life: "Frankly, I was shocked by the number who had not received effective counsel.... Our whole system is based on advocacy, and it was clear many of these prisoners had not had competent advocates" (Westcott 2002: 74). In hearing their stories, he also came to appreciate the other prisoners differently. "What I was finding was there are a lot of good people in prison who made mistakes. Contrary to public perception that they are a menacing evil, the vast majority are not" (74).

Most prosecutors and politicians will never have the benefit of Ernie Preate's immersion experience on their political aspirations and actions. Rather, almost all of them will continue to be supported for the "get tough" stances favoured by special interest groups such as the California Correctional Peace Officers Association and U.S. National Rifle Association (NRA). The example of the NRA is particularly potent. The NRA's purpose is to defend the constitutional rights of private citizens to own and carry guns of varying degrees of force, including automatic weapons. The U.S. National Criminal Justice Commission conjectured that the NRA, with 3.4 million members and an annual budget approaching $150 million, has more clout over U.S. crime policy than any other private organization (Donziger 1996). In 1994, the NRA successfully urged Congress to increase allocation for new prison construction from $14 billion to $21 billion, and to eliminate crime prevention programs. It also bankrolled the first "three strikes and you're out" initiative, in Washington State. Later, it helped fund a similar, successful ballot initiative in California, and financed a successful campaign to convince the Texas legislature to spend $1 billion on new prisons. The NRA and others who prey on public fear of strangers divert attention away from gun control legislation and toward tougher law enforcement and prison expansion (Wright 1998).

The mass media, too, play a key role in generating and sustaining the public's fear of random crime. In democracies, a focus on crime appeals to all classes, particularly where economic inequality is pronounced (Chevigny 2003). Politicians, in turn, manipulate crime stories to elevate their image as defenders of public safety, promising *ad infinitum* to "get tough on crime." A striking example occurred during the 1988 U.S. presidential campaign, when George Bush Sr. was running as the Republican candidate against Democrat

Michael Dukakis. While Dukakis was the governor of Massachusetts, a state prisoner named William ("Willie") Horton was released on parole. Soon after, he was convicted of killing a man and charged with the sexual assault of a woman. Such serious incidents by prisoners on furlough or parole are not common, but they foment fear and public calls for law and order. Bush's campaign included a frequently run TV spot about prison furloughs and "revolving door" criminal justice, suggesting that Dukakis was easy on violent criminals and was releasing dangerous people (Jamieson 1993). The pundits agreed that these ads turned the election back to Bush's favour.

The fear-creating political campaign that targeted Horton was strongly criticized for the distortion of the facts of his case. Horton was later interviewed in the periodical *The Nation*:

> The fact is, my name is not "Willie." It's part of the myth of the case. The name irks me. It was created to play on racial stereotypes: big, ugly, dumb, violent, black — Willie. I resent that. They created a fictional character — who seemed believable, but who did not exist. They stripped me of my identity, distorted the facts, and robbed me of my constitutional rights. (Elliot 1993)

Critics also focused on the way the inaccurate ads "reinforced the mistaken assumption that violent crime is disproportionately committed by blacks, disproportionately committed by black perpetrators against white victims, and disproportionately the activity of black males against white females" (Jamieson 1993: 9). On the contrary, African-Americans and low-income people are most often *victims* of violence, men more often victims than women, and most crimes are intra-racial. The misuse of the Horton case for political gain also legitimated racism by fuelling a "black-male-savage commonsense theory of crime" (Galliher 1991: 246), echoing Stanley Cohen's (1972) treatise on folk devils and moral panics.

From the 1930s to the late 1960s, crime was rarely, if ever, raised as a major problem in U.S. public opinion polls (Chambliss 1999). The turn at the end of the 1960s toward a heightened public sensitivity to crime followed a decade of strategic calculation by conservatives, who had been relegated to the margins of political power. A law-and-order rhetoric that bolstered the Republicans' 1968 presidential campaign was "built on racist stereotypes of violent, criminal black men out of control and out of reach of the law" (16), setting the status quo for the Horton myth twenty years later. Republican Richard Nixon attacked President Johnson's "permissive" focus on the social conditions in which crime emerged, proffering an assertive alternative in the vigorous enforcement of law itself. From the sowing of these seeds, a tough-on-crime agenda has grown from the margins of criminal justice thought to the status of conventional, "commonsense wisdom."

In an interview with the *New York Times* a few years ago, former U.S. President Jimmy Carter spoke of a time when the politics-and-imprisonment nexus was considerably different than that which is currently in vogue. "He said that as a young Governor of Georgia, he and contemporaries like Reubin Askew in Florida and Dale Bumpers in Arkansas had 'an intense competition' over who had the *smallest* prison population. 'Now it's totally opposite,' Mr. Carter said. 'Now the governors brag about how many prisons they've built and how many people they can keep in jail and for how long'" (Mauer 1999: 56). Carter's comments underscore the phenomenon that incarceration constitutes a kind of political currency, where imprisonment rates are used as indicators of the success of iron hand governance instead of the failure of government to meet the needs of its people.

The Prison-Industrial Complex

Political and special group interests are not the only ones being served by a "lock 'em up and throw away the key" stance on criminal justice policy. The role of a free market economy and notions of superior management and service efficiencies, which gained momentum towards the end of the last century, also contributed to prison expansion in the U.S. At a time when the crime rate was decreasing (Hallett 2002), a broad range of manufacturers, distributors and service providers brought commercial interests to bear on the situation, supplying hardware, goods and services (Parenti 2000). Architectural and construction firms, Wall Street investment banks that handle prison bond issues and invest in private prisons, plumbing supply companies, companies that sell everything from bullet-resistant security cameras to padded cells to "body-orifice security scanners" to a wide array of razor wire and other forms of "securityware" (Lynch 2002) — all have a vested interest in prison expansion. Not only do companies make money selling this correctional paraphernalia to builders and operators of prisons, they also save payroll costs by employing cheap prison labour to manufacture it (Schlosser 1998). As Joel Dyer states, "the motive behind the unprecedented growth in the U.S. prison population is the $150 billion being expended annually on criminal justice, much of which eventually winds up in the bank accounts of the shareholders of some of America's best known and most respected corporations" (2002: 2).

Consider the following passage from *Barron's* magazine, promoted on its website as "America's premier financial weekly, the most sophisticated consumer magazine of its type":

No one is telling jokes about Corrections Corporation of America (CCA) today. Says one money manager: "What I want to know is how much of the stock can I get." Why the sudden change? Simple.

CCA Prison Realty Trust has several things going for it. Chief among those is a very compelling story.

The private prison industry is growing at an incredible clip, more than 30 percent per year. Furthermore, no one expects that growth to slow. Most analysts estimate the number of adult prisoners in this country at roughly 1.5 million. (That total is expected to increase by 7 percent–10 percent per year.) However, only about 80,000 of those prisoners are in privately run facilities.

What's driving the move to privatize prisons? Budget downsizing. Federal, state and local governments want to reduce expenditures, without compromising on issues important to voters. The public wants to lock up those who commit crimes, but when the choice is between a new road, school, football stadium or prison, voters generally prefer one of the first three. Politicians see prison privatization as a good way to eat their cake and have it too. Says one portfolio manager who runs a real-estate fund: "Everyone loves to talk about win-win situations. This really is one." (Vinocur 1997: 31)

In this scenario, of course, the winners are the politicians and the business investors. A 1994 article in the *Wall Street Journal* asserted that the private corrections industry used the war against crime as a lucrative business market in the same way the defence industry used the threat of communism during the Cold War. This article referred to the "iron triangle" between government bureaucracy, private industry and politics. This triangle creates an interlocking of financial and political interests, which pushes for the expansion of the criminal justice system (Schlosser 1998) and which has become known as the prison-industrial complex.[9]

The unspoken losers in this scenario are the prisoners and their families, and in the long run the integrity of civil society itself. The war against crime that began at the end of the 1960s became specifically a war on drugs, which continued a reliance on racism in a capture of even more fodder for the correctional industry. The war on drugs began with President Nixon in the 1970s (Parenti 2000), but President Ronald Reagan took it to new heights in the 1980s, resulting in a surge in prison populations. In 1975 the incarceration rate was about 110 per 100,000 in the U.S. This rate doubled in the 1980s and doubled again in the 1990s, to almost 500 per 100,000, and stands at well over 700 today. Drug-related convictions and related longer prison sentences were largely responsible for this steep upward curve. A dealer of marijuana might be sentenced to life in prison with no possibility of parole, as compared with someone committing armed robbery and serving five years, or committing rape and serving twelve years (Schlosser 1994).

In the U.S., over half of all prisoners are African-American, and the numbers of Latinos and Chicanos are also very high. The historical re-emergence of "a racially distinct *commerce* in imprisoned human beings" (Hallett 2002: 371, emphasis in original) — a link between slavery and criminalization — is evidenced by a new understanding of prisoners as commodities. Black men are five times more likely than white men to be arrested for a drug offence, although the rate of use is equal. William Chambliss (1999), past president of the American Society of Criminology, referred to the war on drugs as "America's Ethnic Cleansing." Convictions for possession of crack cocaine, a relatively inexpensive street drug for which blacks are targeted, result in much longer sentences than those received by whites who are convicted of possession of the more expensive powder, cocaine. In 1999, one in three African-American men in the U.S. were either in prison or jail, or on parole or probation (Mauer 1999). Blacks in Canada, as well as First Nations people, are similarly over-represented in prison (Tarnovich 2004).

In an article in the *Guardian Weekly* (Campbell 2000), it was noted that the cost of building jails in the U.S. averaged $7 billion dollars annually, the cost for running prisons was $35 billion a year, and "the prison industry employs more than 523,000 people, making it the country's biggest employer after General Motors." Given the economic activity generated by punishment agencies, it was predictable that capital would be invested in private prisons. At the end of 2002, 93,771 prisoners were held in U.S. prisons that were operating for profit (Harrison and Beck 2003). In Canada in 2001, the province of Ontario opened the country's first (and currently only) "super-prison," a 1,184-bed institution that was run as a provincial prison under contract to the U.S.-based Management and Training Corporation (Ontario Ministry of Community Safety and Correctional Services 2001). Located in Penetanguishene, Ontario, the Central North Correctional Centre has already experienced controversy over prisoner health services, working conditions for officers and a prisoner death.

By the end of the 1980s, as the scope of the drug war expanded in the U.S., prisons became dangerously overcrowded, with almost two-thirds under court orders to reduce overcrowding. This dire situation was transformed into a business opportunity, with private prison corporations stepping in to finance, build and manage prisons, as well as to provide services to prisoners and use them as labourers (Hallett 2002). The pragmatic efficacy of privately versus publicly run prisons is a growing interest in criminology (see, for examples, Austin and Coventry 1999; Harding 1999; Freiberg 1999; Mobley and Geis 2001; Hallett and Lee 2001; Camp and Gaes 2001). The critique of prison privatization yields a broad view of the implications of inviting dominant corporate interests into state punishment systems. This is particularly clear in the realm of politics, where the taint of corporate interest underscores state criminal justice policy.

Judith Greene, a criminal justice policy analyst, illustrates the implications of a corporate profit-prison nexus:

> The added spur of private prisons as economic development in the context of our "tough on crime" political atmosphere has had a corrosive effect on criminal justice policy making. Through political campaign contributions and deployment of the best lobbyists money can buy, the industry has spared no expense to promote the idea that prison privatization is the easy solution to the problem of overcrowded, dilapidated public prisons. In state after state the availability of private prison beds — especially those built on "spec" — has short-circuited important public policy debates about the appropriate balance between prevention and punishment, rehabilitation and incapacitation.
>
> Many early critics of prison privatization predicted that industry executives would lobby for tougher sentencing laws, directly influencing the decisions about who goes to prison and for how long. Indeed, CCA [Corrections Corporation of America] has wielded influence on these issues through a key leadership role within the American Legislative Exchange Council's criminal justice task force — a powerful body that brings state legislators together with corporate executives to draft and promote a conservative "get tough" crime-control agenda, as well as to promote the privatization of prisons. (2002: 112)

Given that crime rates were low and "the American economy was at its strongest ever… with the lowest rates of unemployment and inflation in a generation and more people living in their own homes than ever before" (Hallett 2002: 371), arguments that rapid social change and discontent prompted prison expansion seem insufficient to explain the popular support for this particular criminal justice policy (Useem, Liedka and Piehl 2003). The win-win conflation of private corporate interests with a crime-control political rhetoric does not necessarily amount to greater community safety; as many have argued, it might even compromise safety as a result of the effects of incarceration on prisoners and their families. Further, more public money for prisons means less for health care, education and social services, all of which are important tools in harm prevention.

Conclusion

It is steaming in this tiny cell. The walls drip, the floor perspires, and another bead of sweat rolls down my tattoos. Even they itch, rebelling against the heat and prison ink.

19

What to do? Go outside and hang out in the elbow-to-elbow, dust-caked, dog-kennel of a yard, listen to another man's drab lies of thug-life grandeur? Or drip sweat on a typewriter while tapping out my own lies. Make no mistake, it is all a lie — the system, who we are, why we are in here.

What is not a lie, this slow burn of incarceration, eating away a man's life an hour, a day, a year at a time?...

Maybe it wouldn't matter so much — the sweating walls, the deprivation, the hypocrisy, the spirit-squelching confinement — if I thought there was a reason. (James Blau, "Heat" 2001)[10]

Recently retired from the bench of the Territorial Court of Yukon in Canada, Barry Stuart has long criticized the professionally exclusive nature of formal criminal justice processes. Motivated by a sense of futility with the existing regime, he collaborated with native communities in Yukon in shifting court practices to accommodate community circle processes. While still a practising judge, Stuart noted: "Despite a widespread, long standing appreciation that we cannot remove crime from communities solely by removing criminals, and that the State can never effectively replace the contributions to well-being made by families and communities, we persist in desperately trying to do so. This is our 'March of Folly'" (1998: 90).

When Jimmy Carter and the other state governors boasted about low rates of commissions to prisons, it was because this was a barometer of how well their states were doing. Low prison rates indicated that state citizens largely had their needs met, that the level of civility among citizens was relatively high — essentially, that the political regimes of the day were doing their job. Somehow, the mission of governments to make it possible for citizens to meet their needs has shifted to a default position of punishing those who cannot become contributing members of their communities in a political context of diminishing government efficacy.

In the late nineteenth century, the emeritus sociologist Emile Durkheim commented on this social dimension of punishment, which is the focus of the next chapter. Embedded in his discussion of the mechanical solidarity of societies, Durkheim noted (1933 [1893]: 108):

[Punishment] does not serve, or else only serves quite secondarily, in correcting the culpable or in intimidating possible followers. From this point of view, its efficacy is justly doubtful and, in any case, mediocre. Its true function is to maintain social cohesion intact, while maintaining all its vitality in the common conscience.

Michael Tonry's response to his own question, "Why are U.S. incarceration rates so high?" summarizes this phenomenon succinctly: "America's unprecedented and unmatched taste for imprisonment and harsh criminal justice policies has little to do with them — the offenders who get dealt with one way or another — and everything to do with us" (1999: 435).

Notes

1. *Oz* is a weekly series (written by Tom Fontana) on the Home Box Office (HBO) cable station that features the life of prisoners, prison personnel and others in the fictionalized Oswald State Correctional Facility. See <www.hbo.com/oz/>.
2. Canadian Conservative Member of Parliament Randy White and tabloid journalist Michael Harris are examples of critics who have built careers on criticizing the "leniency" of Canada's prison system.
3. This discussion is based on the numbers provided in Table 1.1 ("Sentences Handed Down at the Criminal Assizes of Upper Canada, 1792–1835," in Oliver (1998: 14–15).
4. See Appendix A in Gosselin 1982 for a full listing of Canadian federal penitentiaries in historical order.
5. As a graduate student, Craig Haney was a research assistant to Dr. Philip Zimbardo in the now well-known "Stanford Prison Experiment" conducted at Stanford University in California in 1971.
6. Winston Churchill is often quoted on his July 20, 1910, statement in the British House of Commons that, "The mood and temper of the public with regard to the treatment of crime and criminals is one of the most unfailing tests of the civilization of any country." Taken from the Sub-Committee on the Penitentiary System in Canada *Report to Parliament* (1977).
7. States included in this sample were California, Georgia, Missouri, Nevada, Ohio, Pennsylvania, Texas and Washington. They were selected by the study's author "based on existing relationships between the Institute on Crime, Justice and Corrections [the author's research home at George Washington University] and their correctional administrators; the diversity in their demographics, crime, arrest, and incarceration rates; and their sentencing and release practices" (Austin 2001: 315).
8. Prominent examples of this are Melossi and Pavarini's *The Prison and the Factory* (1981) and Rusche and Kirchheimer's *Punishment and Social Structure* (1968).
9. See Pranis (2003: 158) for an example of campus activism that defeated a multinational's prison profiteering, motivated by "the need to oppose a 'prison-industrial complex' which functions much like the military-industrial complex."
10. See also Blau 2003 and 2007.

2

"If Punishment Worked,
I'd Be *Saint* Andrew"

· A Child of Seven Years

Mario Auger

Spend a few minutes with me. I will lead you on the path of my childhood. My parents divorced when I was seven. With my mother and brother, we moved to a poor neighbourhood. From the very beginning, I had difficulty in school. My mother was tired of life. I was all alone with my failures. I grew up thinking that I could not succeed in school. No one took my hand to lead me towards classes that could have helped me pass my examinations. I made new friends in this neighbourhood. In the evenings, we would go hang out in the streets, so I took my exams in the streets at night and I got good grades. We started a small gang. They did not want me because I was the youngest and the least tough. With time, I proved myself and hardened. At the age of seven, I was already walking on the path that led me behind these bars.

In my young heart, I only wanted to have my father close to me, have some support for my schooling, participate in activities with kids my own age. I learned to live in this world of lies, hatred, and crime. My new friends all lived in families where poverty was an everyday reality. Their idols were old criminals from the neighbourhood; with time, they became my idols too.

In school I only knew failure. I was looking; I was trying to find myself in this environment. I could not understand the consequences of my failures on my future. In my young heart the first seed of sadness had been sown with the first failure of school tests. At the age of eleven, I was already part of this other world of crime: first thefts in convenience stores, first cigarettes. I was a young boy who only wanted to play, discover life that was opening up in front of me. I needed to feel valued, to find an identity, an "anchoring point." Left to my own in the street, I learned to live by its rules. Day after day, I learned the reality of life. I, too, had my first dreams, but they made way for the reality of my road…. Today I am going to tell you a well-hidden secret: It hurts to be in jail, far from those I love, and to think about the sorrows that I caused them.

I want to tell you this: Tomorrow when you are on your way to work, look at this young boy of seven who is waiting for the school bus. Ask yourself what this boy is going through; what path will he follow through life? This boy, these boys will take one path or another without understanding the importance it will have on their lives.

My questions remains; I let you answer it for me. If I had passed my examinations, what would have been my path, my anchoring point? A child, who became an inmate: Mario Auger.
At the time of writing this book, Mario Auger was incarcerated in Leclerc Institution in Québec.

❧ ❧ ❧

Strawberry Alice: You just kicked the shit out of an innocent man.
Little Bill Daggett: Innocent? Innocent of what?
— from Clint Eastwood's film, *Unforgiven*, 1992

A few years ago, I had a conversation with a prisoner serving a life sentence in a Canadian federal institution. Andrew had been incarcerated for over three decades, many years of which he had been locked up in solitary confinement conditions, buried alive in some of Canada's most austere prisons. I had been wrestling with concepts begging reconsideration in my work in restorative justice, and our conversation became coloured by concerns with the practice of punishment in Western systems of social control. Frustrated with the reflexive acceptance and reification of punishment in different arenas of democratic life, I pondered its inefficacy for meaningful change and rhetorically asked Andrew if, in his experience, punishment "worked." He laughed, and, against the backdrop of our conversation venue and the recent recounting of his long prison history, responded, "If punishment worked, I'd be *Saint* Andrew."

Punishment has been given a sacred status in our societies. It is the unquestioned element of an authoritative response to behaviours or actions that disrupt the flow of life in a variety of contexts — home, school, workplace, sports and criminal justice. Its efficacy as a tool of corrective response to wrongdoing is presumed; to question its purpose is almost heretical. In criminal justice, punishment is the bedrock of the system. Yet for long-timers like Andrew, the pains of imprisonment are prolonged so far beyond the original offence for which the sentence was imposed that the crime and its punishment are virtually unrelated. Prison officials remind us that their chief responsibility is to manage prison sentences set by the court, so they do not see this disconnect as significant. Andrew's keepers are becoming younger; many of them were not even born when he committed his offences. He has become redefined, not as an individual with a life whose actions affected the lives of certain others, but as a punishable actor, a correctional commodity, an inmate without a warrant expiry date.

Restorative justice is often characterized as a "soft" response to crime or wrongdoing. This belief relegates the expression of restorative justice to low-end, minor transgressions; consequently in criminal justice, it is seen as mostly appropriate for young, first-time, non-violent offenders. As the argument of this book unfolds, you will be invited to reconsider this limiting notion, which is not supported by the growing body of research on restorative justice applications. For our immediate purposes, however, the characterization of restorative justice as a soft response to crime is among the contents of a box that requires further unpacking. At the bottom of this box is punishment, the inevitable conclusion we are supposed to come to, which is perhaps predictable given the legacy of criminal justice over the past two hundred years. But on closer examination, we see that restorative justice does not fit in this box at all; nor can it be found on the arc of the pendulum swing of punishment from tough to lenient and back again. Why not? Where does it fit? To determine this, we must revisit punishment, both as concept and practice, and consider what it implies and why that is problematic when looked at through the lens of restorative justice.

Reconsidering Punishment

So integral is punishment to the presumed behavioural and social order of things that very little has been written to challenge its place, even within discussions of restorative justice. Martin Wright has been, perhaps, the boldest of restorative justice advocates in his questioning of punishment. He asserts: "All punishment, in the normal sense of the word, is intended to cause pain and fear, and in some cases incapacitation" (2003: 5). The inflictor of punishment deliberately intends to apply pain, which factors significantly into the evaluation of punishment. To deliberately hurt others, whatever the presumed rationale for doing so, is an action that reflects on the inflictor. The old parental adage — "This hurts me a lot more than it hurts you" — resonates; the act of punishing in some way debases the punisher. As Nietzsche noted, "Mistrust all in whom the impulse to punish is strong" (1969 [1885]: 124).

Often punishment is explained away as a mere consequence of an action, akin to a natural law like gravity. Sometimes a more generic meaning of punishment is offered; Kathleen Daly, for example, argues that punishment is "anything that is unpleasant or a burden of some sort" and eschews the idea that the punisher's intention is determinative (1999: 4, fn. 4). The essential notion here rests on the principle that human beings can be motivated to act in certain ways based on their desire to pursue pleasure and avoid pain. Following this logic, pain is unpleasant and avoiding it requires some awareness of actions through which one brings pain upon oneself. Such consequential thinking encourages individuals to behave more responsibly, in order to lessen their impact on the wider social world. This is the conventional rationale for punishment.

One problem with this rationale is that it encourages people to be motivated in their actions by self-interest. The question of motivation in actions is a critical point of introspection when considering punishment. Alfie Kohn explains (1999: 172–73):

> If an auditorium were filled with bank robbers, wife batterers, and assorted other felons, we would likely find that virtually all of them were punished as children. Whether the punishments were called "consequences" is irrelevant: what matters is that these people were trained to focus not on what they were doing and whether it was right, but on what would happen to them if someone more powerful didn't like what they did. Thus, if it is argued that punishments and rewards are appropriate for children because adults act in response to these inducements, our answer is yes, some do. But are they the sort of adults we want our children to become?

The concept of punishment suggests that why we do things (or not) is unimportant. But that concept sidesteps our hope that, in the absence of authority figures to punish or reward behaviour, individuals will still act in ways that are good, or at least unharmful, for others and the environment. Behavioural psychology might suggest that we can get the same effect by training people like monkeys, through repeated feedback of contingent rewards and punishments, to be self-disciplined. Combined with the panopticon[1] effect, behaving correctly would become a conditioned reflex rather than as a result of reflective introspection.

Let us assume for the moment that this kind of operant conditioning might pose lesser ethical dilemmas than the harmful behaviour it is meant to curtail. In an upcoming discussion on the presumed educative components of punishment, we review some of the loftier ideas about punishment that might mitigate our uncertainty about its means and underpinning values. For now, we focus on the efficacy of punishment in shaping the psyches of individuals. Summarizing a body of psychological research on this subject, Huesmann and Podolski caution that even "careful" punishment of children can increase anti-social behaviours and that there is "little reason to believe that any kind of punishment by itself has much of a chance to change an offender's behaviour or to deter future offences unless it is viewed by the offender as an almost certain consequence of the behaviour" (2003: 79). Certainty that one will be punished is based on an equal certainty that one will be detected, arrested and convicted. Achieving this certainty is apparently a desirable goal to legions of police officers and court officials who opine the under-resourcing and ideological restrictions of their respective sectors of the criminal justice system. But taken to its logical conclusion, the creation of such an intensely observed and policed society seems both unviable and undesirable in a democracy. And beyond that, the large-scale diversion of public resources from education, health and social services to law enforcement would severely compromise any efforts to address social problems at their roots, before they grow into criminal justice issues.

As quoted at the end of Chapter 1, Durkheim observed that: "[punishment's] true function is to maintain social cohesion intact, while maintaining all its vitality in the common conscience." He dismissed the idea that punishment can effectively change the behaviour of law-breakers or bring healing to victims. Instead, he invited us to consider the *symbolic* utility of punishment for the larger body politic. The pervasive popular belief is that punishment is utilitarian — a proper response to wrongdoing because it educates the wrongdoer and corrects the behaviour. When restorative justice is used in a limited criminal justice context, it is more concerned with problem-solving within each conflict than it is with sending "strong messages" to wider society about appropriate choices. Indeed, moral education itself is seen as being most effective from the ground up, not the top down.

For the purposes of exploring restorative justice, the question of what motivates behaviour and the problem of whether punishment encourages compliance to norms is captured in Martin Wright's observation: "The idea that 'virtue is its own reward' is mirrored by the idea that 'wrongdoing is its own punishment'" (2003: 19). In restorative justice, the focus is on the *intrinsic* value and meaning of actions; we will do or not do certain things because of the internal meaning of these actions to ourselves and to others. The intrinsic reward of virtue is that one can interact in the world with a clear conscience. The efficacy of punishment in changing behaviour or contributing towards greater social safety seems to pivot on the issue of intrinsic or extrinsic motivation. Intrinsic motivation encourages moral decision-making based on values, whereas extrinsic motivation fosters decision-making based on punishments and rewards.

Punishment and Moral Education

From the time children are born, they are raised within a teaching framework that is largely based on punishments and rewards. This is often used to explain the inevitability of punishment in parenting practices, school disciplinary policies and the criminal justice system. Because we are inclined to consider punishment *within* a paradigm that is punishment-based, reconsidering the notion of punishment itself seems ludicrous. Abandoning punishment, in this context, amounts to doing nothing in response to wrongdoing.

Of course, the idea of doing nothing in circumstances of conflict or wrongdoing is not palatable to most people, and so the pull of punishment remains. As we will see in Chapter 4, restorative justice is a different paradigm requiring different responses to harm. In other words, *not punishing is not equal to doing nothing.* It is often said of restorative justice that what is required in response to harm within a restorative justice paradigm is much more demanding of individuals and communities than is the reflexive resort to punishment. For our purposes in this chapter, however, the task is to examine what the theory and research tell us about the efficacy of punishment in preventing harm (deterrence) and responding to it (rehabilitation).

We begin the discussion by asking, "What are the intended goals of punishment?" and then, "What are some of the unintended consequences of punishment?" Failing to ask these questions increases the difficulty of evaluating public policy. How are we to measure, quantitatively and qualitatively, the efficacy of punishment if we do not tie its practice to well conceived goals? And how well equipped are we to receive feedback on results that we did not foresee, so that we are accountable for our own actions? Section 718 of the *Criminal Code of Canada* details the principles of sentencing, which most closely approximates our current attention to the goals of our practices; this requires us to equate sentencing with punishment. Section 718 outlines six purposes (goals) of sentencing:

(*a*) to denounce unlawful conduct;
(*b*) to deter the offender and other persons from committing offences;
(*c*) to separate offenders from society, where necessary;
(*d*) to assist in rehabilitating offenders;
(*e*) to provide reparations for harm done to victims or to the community; and
(*f*) to promote a sense of responsibility in offenders, and acknowledgment of the harm done to victims and to the community.

For our purposes, we focus on subsections (d) and (f), regarding the rehabilitation and responsibility aspects of sentencing, which essentially state a desire to prevent further harms after an initial harm has been done.

An immersion in the theoretical and research literature on moral education and child development reveals interesting insights into the ways by which we learn how to conduct ourselves in the social world. Since all of our life trajectories begin with childhood, these areas of academic work offer us some information as we consider whether punishment is or can be an agent of change.

In the late 1800s, the German philosopher Immanuel Kant challenged the role of punishment in the realm of education. In a chapter titled "Moral Culture," he outlined the problem of punishment in moral development (2003 [1899]: 84, emphasis in original):

If you punish a child for being naughty, and reward him for being good, he will do right merely for the sake of the reward; and when he goes out into the world and finds that goodness is not always rewarded, nor wickedness always punished, he will grow into a man who only thinks about how he may get on in the world, and does right or wrong according as he finds either of advantage to himself.

"*Maxims*" ought to originate in the human being as such. In moral training we should seek early to infuse into children ideas as to what is right and wrong. If we wish to establish morality, we must abolish punishment.

This passage challenges us to consider the consequences of punishment without the comfort of its assured role in social systems. Kant's delineation between morality and punishment essentially notes that punishment cannot produce the kind of morality we uphold in democratic systems. This suggests that our punitive approaches might actually impede the cultivation of social morality in a country's citizens — yet we still believe that punishment works. Returning to Alfie Kohn and his auditorium of felons, "In response to the assertion 'Rewards [or punishments] work,' we need to ask, first, Work to do what? And second, At what cost?" (1999: 160).

To begin answering these questions, it is helpful to examine the existing research on moral education and apply it to the context of punishment. A few examples from a much larger body of research are presented in the following sections. Areas of interest in this arena include autonomy, intrinsic and extrinsic motivations, modelling and reasoning, among others of course. To capture these ideas, we need to keep in mind a wide range of punishments, from our own experiences as children and youth at home and school, work and recreation, and apply them to our thinking about criminal justice processes.

Autonomy

New parents often struggle with their roles as caregivers and teachers to their young children, and there are many books on the market from which to choose a parenting "strategy." Some will not read any childcare literature at all and rely instead on what they learned in their own families, based on their own memories of what worked and what didn't. Regardless, they will be required to parent in a world that expects parents to control their young. When children inevitably act in anti-social ways, it is tempting to move into an authoritarian role and assume ownership of them.

Normal healthy child development presumes a resistance to parental authority. Child development researchers Leon Kucynski and Grayna Kochanska noted:

The assumption that a certain level of resistance to parental authority is a positive sign of children's developing autonomy and asser-

29

tiveness is a long-standing developmental perspective. The motive to defend one's autonomy and independence from external control has been attributed to phenomena such as toddler negativism (Spitz 1957, Wenar 1982), counter-control (Mahoney 1974), and reactance (Brehm 1981) throughout childhood and adulthood. (1990: 398)

The need to be one's own person and to have individual agency is apparently a normal state of human existence. Throughout our lives, whether we are preschoolers or prisoners, the will to be autonomous percolates within us. Extending this need for individual autonomy from the home to the school, other factors come into play. The combined expectations for classroom behaviour and academic performance create a similar dilemma for conventional disciplinary standards, as noted by Edward Deci and his colleagues:

Previous research has shown that when teachers are oriented toward controling rather than supporting autonomy in their students, the students display lowered intrinsic motivation and self-esteem. The present study explored conditions that lead teachers to be more controlling versus more autonomy oriented with students. Impressing upon teachers that they are responsible for their students' performing up to standards leads them to be more controlling than teachers who were told that there were no performance standards for their students' learning. Teachers in the former condition talked more, were more critical of the students, gave more commands, and allowed less choice and autonomy. (1982: 852)

The evidence in this study suggests that the more authoritarian the teacher is in the classroom, the less the students demonstrate the attributes of independent learners. Education in this case is not an exercise motivated by intrinsic desires to learn more about the world. Instead, learning and teaching become chores, where the teacher's controlling methods suppress students' autonomy and thereby compromise their performance results.

More recent research in the areas of autonomy in learning and moral education has taken the variable of cultural differences into consideration. This is particularly important in nations such as Canada and the U.S. where multiculturalism affords richly diverse individual and social traditions. How is autonomy seen in this context? Valery Chirkov and colleagues conclude:

This study shows that, across diverse cultures, the issue of autonomy can be similarly understood and that, across diverse practices, autonomy is associated with well-being. We suggest that it is precisely because humans in different cultures must learn and adopt different practices and values that the issue of autonomy, or the degree of internalization, has import. Although some theorists have cast autonomy as an attribute of individualistic behaviors or an issue relevant to wellness only within Western societies, we believe that autonomy versus heteronomy in the regulation of behavior is a basic concern for all humanity. (2003: 108)

Autonomy, then, is a human need cross-culturally and is a necessary component for learning readiness and sustainability both in the family and at school. In the specific context of moral education and punishment, it can be argued that individuals who are raised in conditions in which their personal autonomy is assumed tend to be more open to change than those whose autonomy has not been respected. So how does punishment affect this state of affairs?

In considering the implications of punishment to moral education, Polly Ashton Smith reviewed the work of William Godwin, a moral philosopher from the eighteenth century, and noted (1998: 91–92):

> The fundamental focus of the moral education theory of punishment is the significance of moral autonomy for the maintenance of social cooperation and order… For Godwin, moral knowledge is of paramount significance for the development of independent individuals who advance the common good. Anything that impedes moral knowledge should therefore not be promoted or tolerated. Coercion does precisely that:
>
>> Let us consider the effect that coercion produces upon the mind of him against whom it is employed. It cannot begin with convincing; it is no argument. It begins with producing the sensation of pain, and the sentiment of distaste. It begins with violently alienating the mind from the truth with which we wish it to be impressed. It includes in it a tacit confession of imbecility. If he who employs coercion against me could mould me to the purposes of his argument, no doubt he would. He pretends to punish me because his argument is strong; but he really punishes me because his argument is weak. (Godwin 1976 [1793]: 641–42)

It is difficult to imagine a criminal justice system in which punishment was freely embraced by its recipient rather than being a coercive imposition. Further, is the problem just that the argument itself is weak, or is it also the way the argument unfolds that affects its veracity and thus ends in a resort to coercive punishment? Overall, there seems to be some agreement that people learn best if they are in conditions in which their personal autonomy is respected. Essentially, this means that people should not be treated as means to ends, but as ends in themselves. In other words, punishment, as a way of coercing law-breakers, may not be an effective way to facilitate moral education after all.

Intrinsic and Extrinsic Motivation

Ideally, democratic societies work best if citizens act from intrinsic rather than extrinsic motivation. Whether through punishments or rewards, extrinsic motivation offers limited value. Its roots in contemporary theories of punishment are found in Skinner's operant conditioning, in which it is assumed that when a "reinforcement" (reward) follows a behaviour, it is likely that the behaviour will be repeated (Kohn 1999: 5). Skinnerian behaviourists believe that almost everything we do is the result of reinforcement, whether positive (rewards) or negative (punishments). And on the surface of things, this would seem to be true.

However, research shows that rewards and punishments only work with rather banal behaviours over short periods of time in conditions in which there are constant reinforcements. This may be possible in a prison, but not so easily — or desirably — in an open society. We also know that if people enjoy and pursue doing something without reward, once given a reward for the same activity they will no longer do it for the simple enjoyment of it. Consider the observations of researchers who conducted a meta-analysis of 128 studies on the effects of extrinsic rewards on intrinsic motivation:

> Careful consideration of reward effects reported in 128 experiments leads to the conclusion that tangible rewards tend to have a substantially negative effect on intrinsic motivation…. Even when tangible rewards are offered as indicators of good performance, they typically decrease intrinsic motivation for interesting activities. (Deci et al. 1999: 658–59)

In other words, rewards kill interest (Kohn 1999: 71). Furthermore, sustaining appropriate behaviour entails creating a bottomless "goodie bag" from which to dispense rewards. This not only seems inefficient but treats individuals as objects to be manipulated, which compromises their autonomy.

Intrinsic motivation means that people will act in certain ways without the reinforcements of punishments and rewards. In Chapter 7 we consider the idea of *values*, which is the motivational centre from which we hope to animate moral behaviour. In the family, schools, workplace and criminal justice system, appropriate conduct is sustained for much longer — and at less cost — if the autonomous individual is intrinsically motivated rather than requiring the extrinsic motivation central to operant conditioning. But the research raises another, perhaps more important issue.

Four decades ago, a couple of researchers (Hoffman and Saltzstein 1967: 54) argued that the result of reinforcement conditioning was that it served to make the subject aware of how their actions affected *themselves* rather than others:

> As much animal and human learning has now shown, what is learned will depend on the stimuli to which the organism is compelled to attend. Disciplinary techniques explicitly or implicitly provide such a focus. Both love withdrawal and power assertion direct the child to the consequences of his behavior for the actor, that is, for the child himself, and to the external agent producing these consequences. Induction, on the other hand, is more apt to focus the child's attention on the consequences of his actions for others, the parent, or some third party. This factor should be especially important in determining the content of the child's standards. That is, if transgressions are followed by induction, the child will learn that the important part of transgression consists of the harm done to others.

This passage encourages us to see the limitations of behaviourism as manifested in the "me-ness" of motivation — the fact that the individual's incentive is always centred on the reinforcements of pleasure (rewards) or pain (punishment) to *themselves*, rather than a deeper need or will to act in ways that do not harm *others* as a measure of their individual character. The sustainability of intrinsic motivation is clearly more desirable for two reasons: first, it portends that people will act pro-socially and responsibly without the need for reinforcements, and second, it relieves the state and other overseers from the burden of an endless need to furnish punishments and rewards.

The dark side of punishment as an extrinsic motivator is that it not only does not work to achieve its goal, it actually exacerbates anti-social behaviour. As Viktor Brenner and Robert Fox note in their research on parental discipline styles,

> parental discipline emerged as the strongest predictor of reported behavior problems in 1 to 5-year old children... Parents who use frequent punishment have more behavior problems with their children, whereas using less discipline is related to having fewer behavior problems. (1998: 254)

If punishment does not work to correct the behaviour in question, the popular response is not an evaluation of the efficacy of punishment *per se*, but an increase in its application or intensity. Herein are the unintended effects of punishment.

This brings us to the question, "How *do* we best teach morality?" Again, in considering this, we must think of everyone, from children in families and schools, to adults in the workplace and those being processed through a formal criminal justice system. If punishment does not get us there, what does? In this final section, we consider educational strategies of reasoning and modelling in response to this question.

Reasoning and Modelling

The subtitle to Kohn's parenting book (2005) — *Moving from Rewards and Punishments to Love and Reason* — nicely summarizes the status quo and the alternatives we partially explore in this section. (We consider the "love" component of the alternative in Chapter 7.) Reasoning with children affords parents the opportunity to let their children know what is important for social life and why, while also engaging children's minds to promote independent thought in processing moral questions (195). Reasoning also models a non-violent approach to traditional uses of power.

A study by Walker and Taylor in 1991 of family interactions and the development of moral reasoning demonstrates the importance of modelling in moral education:

> The parental discussion style that predicted the greatest moral development in children entailed a high level of representational and supportive interactions. The representational category includes behaviors such as eliciting the child's opinion, asking clarifying questions, paraphrasing, and checking for understanding—reminiscent of the Socratic style of questioning. The children of parents who relied on an operational and informative discussion style developed relatively little. This operational style is one in which the child is directly challenged; counter considerations and critiques of the child's position are presented. In the context of a discussion of the child's moral problem, such high-level cognitive conflict may be perceived as hostile criticism and thus arouse defensiveness. Similarly, an informative style is one in which parents are providing their opinions. In this context, it might be seen as something of a "lecturing" style and therefore less effective. (280–81)

The parental actions listed in this study obviously require two conditions: first, that the parent be physically and emotionally present for the child, and second, that the parent take the time to work through the reasoning process in a respectful way. This is not always the case in contemporary society, where both parents have to work to pay the family bills, families might be supported by a single adult, and family time together is limited and the stresses are great. It reminds us that resorting to punishment in response to anti-social conduct occurs in a wider context in which adults' capacities to reason and model helpful conflict resolution skills in their families may be taxed and compromised by other demands.

A later study by Carla Herrera and Judy Dunn considered the related issue of the influence of early experiences with family conflict in shaping children's ways of handling disputes with friends, engaging both concepts of both reasoning and modelling:

> We found particularly strong associations between the early use of argument by the mother and sibling and the child's later successful resolution of conflicts with a close friend. Some have argued that resolutions are salient and potentially revealing aspects of conflicts that may have a unique set of determinants from the strategies used during disputes (Hay 1984; Shantz 1987). The present study supports these arguments. It is also noteworthy that the measures most strongly associated with the child's successful resolution of conflicts were those representing the early use of other-oriented argument by the mother and sibling. (1997: 877–78)

These study examples (peer-reviewed academic journals contain many related studies demonstrating similar phenomena) offer support for the idea that what we do is what we get. Since we are reconsidering whether punishment has valuable educative purposes for the individual who is sentenced, we also need to be attuned to what the research tells us about what *does* work towards the same goal. This demonstrates our commitment to solving problems rather than avoiding them.

Another reason to pay attention to childhood moral education and what children learn in the home environment are the implications of this for democratic society as a whole. John Braithwaite, an early restorative justice theorist, notes:

> It is in families that most of us learn most of what equips us to be effective democratic citizens in community organizations.... Children are not born democratic. They must learn to be democratic citizens — to listen, to deliberate, support others when their rights are abused, speak out against injustice (Barber 1991). For most of us these are gifts of deliberative competence induced by participation in healthy family decision-making. (2004: 201)

Contrast this observation to the moral teachings of punishment (in the family or otherwise) noted by Kohn: "*All* punishment... teaches that when you are bigger or stronger than someone else, you can use that advantage to force the person to do what you want" (1999: 167, emphasis in original).

What begins in the family (private) extends into our wider social lives (public) and holds enormous implications for the health of a democratic society as it operates in daily-life interactions of its citizens. Democracy must not merely be an abstract idea or a justification for war; it must be a *lived experience* for its citizens. Currently we favour using punishment to deter or suppress anti-social conduct in an open society, over the use of reasoning and modelling to prevent, guide and respond to anti-social conduct. "Bigger and stronger" may be an attractive resort to a frustrated but loving parent, but do we really believe that the way to create a healthy society rests on a "bigger and stronger" philosophy of education?

To sum up this overview of punishment and moral education, it is helpful to remember the significance of autonomy, intrinsic and extrinsic motivation, and reasoning and modelling as efficacious methods of encouraging behavioural changes in and toward peaceable democratic societies. Researchers Joan Grusec and Jaqueline Goodnow sum up relevant research in the area of parenting which supports the importance of these areas:

> Children must accurately perceive the message parents intend to convey, and they must be willing to accept the message, that is, allow it to guide their behavior. Acceptance involves three components: The child must perceive the message as appropriate, the child must be motivated to comply with the message, and the child must feel the message has not been imposed but rather has been self-generated. (1994: 17)

Reasoning and modelling work in encouraging the child's perception that the message is appropriate. The child is intrinsically motivated to comply with the message, and given that their autonomy has been protected, they feel that the message has come from within rather than from others. The question now, is how to take these lessons from the realm of family life and apply them to social institutions that were created to serve the people in democratic states.

Punishment in the Criminal Justice System

The emphasis on parenting and early childhood experiences may seem misplaced in the context of the criminal justice system, which, in Canada, can legally intervene in a person's life from the age of twelve years and on. But a problem with punishment as a response to harm or wrongdoing is that it fails to address the underlying reasons or motivations for behaviours; it only attempts to suppress harmful behaviours through external reinforcements. In this chapter we look to the research for insight into how to build the alternative, to create more peaceable societies. Essentially, the question is, "What are the goals of punishment?" In this chapter, we are considering the educative goal of punishment for the individual rather than for the masses. Although it is an unpopular assertion, it is well known empirically that investing in the first five years of a person's life pays high social dividends in the long run. This means that ensuring a good start in life — proper nutrition, consistent and mature care, loving attachments and healthy neurological stimulation — can not only save later heartache but also the financial costs of mental and physical health care, social welfare and criminal justice measures.

There is no evidence that punishment effectively deters crime or teaches moral values to apprehended law-breakers. One obvious reason to assert this is that it is not realistically possible to measure deterrence, given the myriad variables and logistical problems of finding out how or why every citizen in a society acts or does not act. Nor could we find exact measurements of recidivism, unless it were possible to obtain truthful responses from every ex-law-breaker about the activities they undertook after serving their sentences. The accuracy of both measurements would depend on individuals responding truthfully when asked to recall unlawful actions, the recounting of which could result in punishment — and we know that the first casualty of punishment is truth.

Therefore, assessing the educative value of punishment for individuals within the criminal justice system is always going to be a difficult proposition. But since all adults were at one time children, it is probably safe to argue that the research into child psychology and moral education resonates in the realm of adult behaviour. This is hardly a radical proposition. Anyone examining the files of violent or persistent law-breakers will recognize behavioural patterns that hearken back to childhood — patterns that are also reflected in the criteria of popular risk assessment tools. As noted by the authors of a Canadian violence prediction scheme, "Prior history is, as the reader will know, taken strongly into consideration when establishing an actuarial score" (Webster et al. 1994: 49). The starting point of this "prior history" is early childhood experience, and salient points include (but are not limited to) family history, adjustment to legal adulthood, schooling and medical history.

Although criminal justice actuarial instruments recognize the critical significance of childhood experiences in shaping an adult's present or future conduct, this understanding is limited. We need a wider lens to capture a picture large enough to take a person's whole life into account. Logically, if we know that we can predict that violent adult behaviour is a likely outcome of unhealthy childhood experiences, it would make crime prevention sense to marshal our attention and resources to address the needs of all children. But children do not vote, and responses to child abuse and neglect typically amount to more institutionalization through both family and criminal justice courts and social welfare agencies.

Even those who believe in the value of institutional punishment acknowl-

37

edge that its utility has some natural limits. In fact, genuine remorse may be the most severe punishment, causing the suffering of the person whose actions caused harm, particularly if it is not possible to repair the damage or the victim is not forgiving. A study of restorative justice inspired by Ojibway elders grappled with the question of whether punishment is a necessary or even plausible feature of a justice system. Denise Breton and Stephan Lehman (2001: 5) raise the perennial question of how one can calculate the precise measure of punishment to satisfy the state's requirement for retribution:

> On the one hand we want to make punishment humane, but on the other hand, the [penal] model claims that we establish justice by inflicting pain, especially in the form of loss — loss of money, resources and possessions, loss of freedom, of identity and individuality, even loss of life. How much pain is called for? If hurt creates justice, wouldn't it follow that the more brutal our methods of punishing, the more justice we'd have?

Breton and Lehman pointed out the ways that a retributive society becomes a defensive culture, with everyone quick to declare, "It's not my fault!" instead of working together to regain balance. By contrast, in the Ojibway community, when there is a conflict,

> they bring together not only the victims and offenders but also the extended communities of each along with the elders and law enforcement people. Everyone is involved. The principals tell their stories, as do their families and friends. Expressing feelings is essential to the healing dynamics, from remorse and apology on the offender's side to pain and possibly forgiveness on the victim's.
>
> [J]udgement and punishment... belong to the Creator. They are not ours.... A return to balance can best be accomplished through a process of accountability that includes support from the community through teaching and healing. The use of judgments and punishments actually works against the healing process. An already unbalanced person is moved further out of balance. (49–50)

Rupert Ross, a former crown attorney in northern Ontario, notes his experience of the cultural differences between Western and Aboriginal societies on the subject of punishment:

> I frequently watch Aboriginal people shake their heads in disbelief at how often Western countries fall back on imposed "Codes of Minimum Behaviour" backed up by the threat of punishment. The belief seems to be that unless the spirit of the individual is changed, such codes will only anger them by forcing them to do what they

don't want to do in the first place. Then, once angered, they will try to beat the codes any way they can. Further, they will never go *beyond* the bare, legislated minimums. Most importantly, they are likely to take their anger out on precisely the people whom the codes were meant to protect, using ways that have not yet been legislated. Reliance on codes is therefore seen as never-ending, self-strangling, counterproductive and a great waste of time. (1996: 90–91)

Nils Christie, a pioneering Scandinavian legal scholar, has advanced our understanding of the ways that rituals of punishment weaken communities. From abundant research into the political, personal, economic and social effects of prisons, he concludes:

I cannot imagine a position where I should strive for an increase of man-inflicted pain on earth. Nor can I see any good reason to believe that the recent level of pain affliction is just the right or natural one. And since the matter is important, and I feel compelled to make a choice, I see no other defensible position than to strive for pain-reduction (1982: 11)

By definition, punishment is the intentional infliction of pain, but its effects are intended to extend from the law-breaker to those who may be deterred from crime by the law-breaker's suffering. Theoretically, then, the threat of punishment coerces compliance with the law, rather than the law invoking voluntary compliance based on shared values. In fact, as we saw earlier, not only is there is little empirical evidence of the deterrence value of punishment, but it seems that most people obey most laws most of the time for reasons other than fear of punishment. Another purported benefit of punishment is that it teaches responsibility and accountability, but in fact resentment and hostility are more common reactions.

Why, then, is punishment taken for granted? A dominant theory is that punishment of law-breakers is an essential ritual designed to compensate not only the direct victims of harm but also all those who uphold the law. The belief is that in committing a crime for personal gain, the law-breaker achieves a benefit not available to law-abiding citizens and must therefore suffer a consequence to re-set the balance of the social order. It is generally thought that anyone who breaks the law must "pay the consequences," even though in reality only about 3 percent of individuals charged with crime end up in prison. The social ethos demands that if some individuals benefit at the expense of others they must be punished to "even things out," out of respect for the principle of equality of rights and responsibilities (de Haan 1990: 114–17). This is referred to as the "unfair advantage" theory, or the "benefits-and-burdens" theory (Von Hirsch 1994: 114–18). Willem de Haan refuted this perspective, asserting that punishment is illogical in a just social order because "it involves additional suffering rather than... compensating [the victim] for loss, suffering and pain." A penal abolitionist, de Haan enjoins moral and political philosophies in a rational rejection of punishment, concluding that "punishment is incompatible with justice" (de Haan. 1990: 128). His words echoed those of a Cree elder in Alberta, who remarked to a colonizer, "You have a *legal* system; we're just not sure it's a *justice* system" (Breton and Lehman 2001: 50).

Proportionality — making the punishment fit the crime — is another seldom-realized intention of punishment. People with privilege are often granted more lenient sentences than those who lack privilege. And it is very difficult to establish levels of blame, given the many variables and mitigating factors among individuals and the details of the offences they commit. Legislation determines the limits of punishment, but judges have discretion and parole boards sometimes confine a prisoner indefinitely. Therefore, one person may receive a much harsher sentence than another for committing the same crime. Also, the same punishment for the same crime could be extremely painful to one person and insignificant to another. Michael Tonry observes:

> If punishment is principally about blaming, surely it is relevant whether the offender was mentally impaired, socially disadvantaged, a reluctant participant, or moved by humane motives. Surely it is morally relevant, whatever the path to conviction, what the offender did, with what *mens rea* [intention], and under what circumstances. Surely it is morally relevant whether a particular punishment will be more intensely experienced by one person than by another.
>
> Punishment schemes that attach high value to proportionality necessarily ignore the differing material conditions of life, including poverty, social disadvantage, and bias, in which human personalities and characters take form....
>
> The problem of "just deserts in an unjust world" is a fundamental problem for a strong proportionality constraint. Whether retributive theories are rationalized in terms of benefits and burdens, or equilibrium, or blaming, or condemnation, or penance, they must presume equal opportunities for all to participate in society. (1994: 151–52)

It becomes clear that, if we are to have criminal justice, we must also have social justice. Currently, people are punished not only for what they have done but also for where they are positioned in the social hierarchy. The quest for equal justice is a multi-dimensional and ongoing process, which commonly does not engage the interests of many of those who are themselves exempt from poverty and discrimination.

Conclusion

I say advisedly that the situation in the U.S. reminds me of some of the comments of the Danish sociologist Svend Ranulf when he looked into Germany in the middle, late '30s. He was not looking for Naziism in terms of genocide or where they were headed in terms of war; he was looking only and specifically at criminal justice policy. And, he said, everywhere he looked he saw a disinterested need to punish on the part of people. Punish, punish, punish. And then it was a matter of finding who to punish. And he related it to the disempowerment of the middle class in the Weimer Republic and to the frustration of the shopkeepers and people at that level, and it made them very ripe for the kinds of things that subsequently happened. And, I think, there's something of that dynamic going on in the U.S. now. (Jerry Miller, in Cayley 1996: 10)

Critical analyses of criminal justice phenomena report on the destructive elements of adversarial systems that selectively criminalize and incarcerate. Herman Bianchi, another Scandinavian critical scholar, has suggested that the very idea of punishment must be dispensed with if human societies are to evolve an actual system of justice:

The very thought that one grown up human being should ever have a right, or duty, to punish another grown up human being is a gross moral indecency, and... cannot stand up to any ethical test. The punitive response should be replaced by a call for responsibility and for repair, and punishment should be replaced by reconciliation. Punishment is destructive... because it is violent: reconciliation serves society, and is a lesson in humanity. (1994: 341–42)

Erik Erikson, a psychologist interested in the development of identity and child psychoanalysis, further challenged our presumptions about our "right" to punish in his later writings about Gandhi:

Gandhi reminds us that, since we can not possibly know the absolute truth, we are "therefore not competent to punish" — a most essential reminder, since man when tempted to violence always parades as another's policeman, convincing himself that whatever he is doing to another, that other "has it coming to him." Whoever acts on righteousness, however, implicates himself in a mixture of pride and guilt which undermines his position psychologically and ethically. (1969: 412–13)

It is worth further mention that Erikson's work looked at the influence of culture on personality and noted that the messages we transmit as a society have impacts on individual psychosocial development. State punishment practices model that inflicting harm — even for "correctional" purposes — is an acceptable manner of addressing conflict. Ultimately, we are left with the questions: "Is this the best we can do? What are our goals and interests, and in what ways does punishment help or hinder these?"

Note

1. In *Discipline and Punish* (1979) Foucault notes the metaphorical and practical utility of the prison architectural design of the panopticon for the ordering and control of people. Described by Cousins and Hussain (1984: 190), "The Panopticon consisted of a circular building to house prisoners in individual cells at the periphery, with an inspection tower at the centre. Each cell was to have two windows, one facing the outside and the other facing the inspection tower, which itself was dotted with windows rendering each cell fully visible from it. Windows in the tower were to be covered with Venetian blinds in order to make the inspector invisible to the prisoners." The idea is for the people confined in the cells to behave as if they are being watched continuously, in a power structure where behaviour is influenced by punishments and rewards. It is expected that externally imposed discipline will be replaced by self discipline. The idea of the panopticon was first articulated by Jeremy Bentham (1789).

3

Justice as a Human Problem

Justice

Per Jespersen

One day Suzan was on her way to the king's castle, which was situated by a great lake. Here rush and reed grew and many birds were singing. Outside the castle Suzan could see the guards, but they would not let her in.

But Suzan had seen that the king was standing near to a window in the castle. So she asked the guards to look up there, when they saw the king nod his head. Then they let her in anyway. Suzan had never been here before. But the king knew her from her school. She had once given him a bouquet of flowers at a celebration. A king remembers such events. And Suzan is good at remembering, too; she wants to ask the king about something very important.

Inside the gateway there was a butler; he showed her the way to the throne room. He bowed for her, as if she were a queen from a foreign country. Then he walked with her through a lot of shining halls to the door of the throne room. As the door opened, he disappeared so quietly, that you could not hear him leave. In the nearness of a king on his throne you really have to be quiet! That was why Suzan tiptoed towards the throne.

How wonderful it was! Made from gold and with emeralds and rubies at its sides, and with ivory on its legs. "I am glad you came," the king said nodding to a man, who was standing by the window, writing. His nod meant that the man had to write down every spoken word. "What is your name?"

"Suzan." "Of course. You gave me flowers at your school, didn't you?" "Sure," Suzan said. "Do you really remember?" "That sort of thing I do remember. But I think you want to tell me something."

"Sure. You are the one in charge in this country, aren't you?" "So they say." "Are there problems you cannot solve?"

The scribe stopped for a moment. He did not know whether to write Suzan's words down. But the king nodded again, so he continued his writing. But frowning. "Sure. Then I ask my advisers. I do not have many of them. The cleverest of them is now standing by the window. He is able to write and to recall and to figure out different things."

"I want to ask you, why all the old forests of our country are being felled?" "How do you know that?" "I've seen it, and my mum told me. Why do you not leave the forests alone?"

"I will tell you." He got up as if he were going to hold a speech. Then he shook

43

his head and asked the scribe, "Scribe, fetch the thick book in the cupboard!" The scribe fetched the protocols and started to turn over the leaves.

"I don't understand why you cannot recall why you decided to fell the forests," Suzan said.

"Neither do I. But wait a minute and you'll see!" The scribed fumbled with the protocols and finally found the page he looked for. "Your Majesty — houses are to be built for all citizens in the country, especially for those without a house."

"What has that to do with the forests?" the king asked. The scribe cleared his throat for moment. "Perhaps because the houses are expected to be situated on the place where the forests have been." "Yes, that's it! We have to fell the forests to build all those houses," the king proclaimed.

"How did you find out?" Suzan said. "How do people really find out the value of things? What has the greatest value, houses or forests?" The scribe fumbled again, but he could not find the answer in the protocols. So the king said: "I cannot answer your question. Politics is not easy."

But Suzan said: "What if you tore down all the houses and planted trees instead?" The king scratched his hair. "I never thought of that! What do you say, scribe?" But he could not answer when it was not in the protocols.

"I want to tell you a story," Suzan said. "Great," the king said. "I love stories, especially the true ones." Especially the true ones, the scribe wrote.

And then Suzan began her story: "Once upon a time there was a squire who discovered that one of his grooms stole his corn and sold it in town. He had him caught and he was led into the barn where he was questioned. The groom kept saying that he had not stolen anything. The squire was stubborn, saying, 'I'll come again in an hour, and then you must admit your crime.' Then he rode his horse to the rye-field, which was being cut. With satisfaction he saw the hundreds of women cutting the field. Then one of the women came up to him. She fell down on her knees, weeping, 'Good squire, please spare my son! He is not guilty!' 'How do you know that I have him in the barn?' 'They all say so. Good squire — he has not stolen. Please spare his life. I cannot do without his work and money. Please show mercy!' The squire looked down upon her, thinking deeply. Then he said, 'You are a good woman. Listen, if you can cut this very field of rye in one day without help from anyone, I shall spare your son's life. But you have to finish your work before sunset tomorrow. If you have not finished, your son shall hang.' The woman knelt at his feet, saying, 'Good squire, thank you so much!' By sunrise the next morning she started her work, while all the other workers stood watching her. The squire was there, too. And he thought to himself: 'She will never reach it. Her son cannot be saved.' As the first beams of the rising sun reached the rye, she bent down and started the cutting. She worked and worked and her back was in deep pain. And yet she continued without a pause to save her son. The day was hot and her face was burnt by the sun and her back was in pain. At sunset she really had managed to cut the whole field. Happily she fell to the ground, whispering: 'My son is saved. He will be spared!' 'Yes, he is saved," the squire said.' Then the woman's body shivered and she was dead."

The king got up. "That was not fair," he said, "It was not fair!" "No it was not," Suzan said. "But it is not fair to fell the forests either." "That's something else," the king said. Something else, the scribe wrote in the protocol.

"Justice is justice," Suzan said. "If you do not water all the flowers in your garden and cut all the roses and all the perennials before noon this very day, I shall make the forests grow around your castle, so that you cannot look out and you will have to wander in darkness for the rest of your lifetime!"

"Look in the protocols, scribe," the king shouted. "What do they say about justice? Tell me!" The scribe was in his sweat. "There is not a single word about justice in the protocols."

"You cannot find wisdom in books," Suzan said. "Wisdom is in our very minds."

"I give up," the king said. Then he went out of the door. Suzan went home a little later. She could see the king watering all his flowers, and she thought: "So, Justice is alive, anyway." She knew that no more forests would ever be felled in that land. (*Courtesy of SK-Publishers, Randerup, Denmark. Retrieved at <http://home12.inet.tele.dk/fil/justice.htm>*)

❧ ❧ ❧

This story was written to introduce children to the concept of justice as something different than what is found or delivered in law. The scribe notes there is "not a single word about justice in the protocols," almost as if he had read the *Criminal Code of Canada* (CCC). This is not exactly true — the word is contained in the title of Part IV, "Offences against the Administration of Law and Justice," although "justice" is not included in the Part's definitions (s. 118). Curiously, it is not listed in the CCC's index either. We do find a definition of justice, finally, offered in s. 2 of the CCC, and here we are told that it means "a justice of the peace or a provincial court judge, and includes two or more justices where two or more justices are, by law, required to act or, by law, act or have jurisdiction." It would seem that the law's use of the term "justice" is insufficient for the needs of the general public. In the above story, justice is discussed as a "big concept," one that often underpins private and public discourses. This is important, because a tension exists in what justice means to us as individuals living in a democratic society under the rule of law. We seek justice in our daily lives, in our personal relationships, in our workplaces and on the sports field. How do these understandings of justice compare to the justice sought in criminal courts?

The story highlights an issue salient to a "big concept" discussion of justice: *relational power differences*. What elements of justice are found in laws that set penalties of death for the property crime of corn stealing, or for that matter, any other crime? What elements of justice can we find in the squire's act of mercy in setting an impossible task for the mother trying to save her son's life? The questions lead us to necessary reflections on power differences in expressions of justice and the fragility of notions such as equality and freedom. Setting clear behavioural expectations with clearly articulated consequences (such as in criminal codes) may be fairer than the arbitrary whims of feudal despots, but what power differences remain? The story is important not only for children but adults as well.

And then there are the questions of value, posed by Suzan in the story: "How do people really find out the value of things? What has the greatest value, houses or forests?" Perhaps there was a time when this could be decided to the satisfaction of everyone, but it seems more likely that discussions of value have been continuous. But who is invited to participate in these discussions? Is it just the court personnel? Is it anyone who is called to witness in criminal courts? Or do conversations about how to reconcile competing values in pursuit of justice take place at peoples' kitchen tables or on public buses? Nils Christie made many observations about the weaknesses of a formal, institutionalized and professionalized justice system and considered the losses, one of which speaks to this point directly:

> The big loser is us — to the extent that society is us. This loss is first and foremost a loss in *opportunities for norm clarification*. It is a loss of pedagogical possibilities. It is a loss of opportunities for a continuous discussion of what represents the law of the land. How wrong was the thief, how right was the victim? Lawyers are, as we saw, trained into agreement on what is relevant in a case. But that means a trained incapacity in letting the parties decide what *they* think is relevant. It means that it is difficult to stage what we might call a political debate in the court. When the victim is small and the offender big — in size or power — how blameworthy then is the crime? And what about the opposite case, the small thief and the big house-owner? If the offender is well educated, ought he then to suffer more, or maybe less, for his sins? Or if he is black, or if he is young, or if the other party is an insurance company, or if his wife has just left him, or if his factory will break down if he has to go to jail, or if his daughter will lose her fiancé, or if he was drunk, or if he was sad, or if he was mad? There is no end to it. And maybe there ought to be none…. Maybe decisions on relevance and on the weight of what is found relevant ought to be taken away from legal scholars, the chief ideologists of crime control systems, and brought back for free decisions in the court-rooms. (1977: 8, emphasis in original)

These provocative statements hit on some of the limitations of the new special needs courts created to address weaknesses in the current system; in Canada, these take the form of community courts, drug courts, mental health courts and Gladue courts (Aboriginal). Even in such venues, the problems are still handled by professionals, with regular citizens relegated as usual to the sidelines.

Our beginning story was authored by Danish educator Per Jespersen, whose work over the past two decades has focused on philosophy for children (also known as P4C). Children are a key focus in Chapter 2, in the discussion of the efficacy of punishment in moral education, and children also offer a lens through which to consider the other concepts reconsidered in this book. Restorative justice is, among other things, a problem-solving approach to conflict and wrongdoing and so invites us to bring all possibilities to the circle. Adulthood is on a continuum of life that begins for us all when we are children, and past experiences contain important information that can help to better identify and address the problems underlying current actions. An attention to childhood opens different possibilities for change; harm prevention must, by definition, be rooted in beliefs and practices that produce a kind of society in which harms are few.

It seems that the idea of justice — what it is, how we find it and how we express it — is imbued with a variety of meanings. In this chapter we explore some dimensions of justice generally, in order to lay the groundwork for a discussion of restorative justice specifically.

What Is Justice?

J. Edgar Hoover, the former long-time director of the Federal Bureau of Investigation in the U.S., once said, "Justice is incidental to law and order." His cynicism was shared by Robert Lindler:

> When one pauses to give the matter some thought, it is rather surprising and somewhat naïve of man to look for and expect justice. Certainly it has not been his habit to receive this quality in all his weary history. Regarded from the large viewpoint of the species, justice is the thing that has been rarest in its toilsome biography….
>
> Such is the bald history of the evolution of the system perpetuated to our day for the implementation of the quality called justice, that quality which the history of man gives him no cause to expect, but for which he continually yearns. (1946: 370, 372)

Generally, vengeful justice is understood as payback, a need for revenge. Webster's Dictionary makes a distinction between vengeance and revenge: "Revenge is dictated by passion; vengeance by justice." Revenge is "a malicious or spiteful infliction of pain or injury, contrary to the laws of justice." By contrast, to avenge a harm is to inflict a measured degree of pain to right a wrong and is intended as closure. However, whether we call it revenge or vengeance, evening the score by any means invariably sustains conflict, and acts of violence beget more violence.

State-authorized responses to illegal wrongdoing are predicated on notions of justice that are not always questioned in meaningful ways. What do we mean by "justice"? What do different "stakeholders" (victim, harm-doer, community) want or need from a "justice" process? What does it mean to them? Sometimes referred to as the "Just Us" system, the North American system works particularly well for privileged elites and particularly poorly for those members of society who have the fewest resources. Perspectives on justice are influenced by one's social location, as illustrated in Figure 3.1.

Daphne Dukelow and Betsy Nuse's legal dictionary (1991) defines justice as "the principle of giving each person her or his due," which originated in Aristotelian philosophy 2,400 years ago (384–322 B.C.E.). Aristotle saw justice as a domain idea in political philosophy and considered the execution of justice the main purpose of the state. He made a distinction between *distributive* and *commutative* justice. Distributive justice concerns the distribution of goods among a class and treating equals equally. Commutative justice concerns the treatment of the individual in particular transactions; justice involves giving people what they have a right to receive. Critics argue that a philosophy of giving everyone their due is backward-looking, individualistic and unrealistic. How can society fulfill, satisfy and secure for everyone their

Figure 3.1

Source: The idea for this image came from Dr. Karlene Faith, Professor Emerita in the School of Criminology at Simon Fraser University.

diverse desires and expected just deserts — that is, what each person perceives as their deserved entitlements?

The authors of the (now defunct) Law Commission of Canada's[1] "Restorative Justice: A Conceptual Framework" suggest that "justice is a response to the powerful intuition that 'something must be done,' that something (someone) has disturbed the way things ought to be and something must be done to right the wrong, to make things right" (Llewellyn and Howse 1999). This impulse to respond has been powerfully illustrated in the U.S. by initiatives in response to the terrible events of September 11, 2001, which they call "Operation Infinite Justice." Another perspective on justice was offered by retired Manitoba Associate Chief Justice Hamilton, whose attempts to formulate an idea of an Aboriginal court compelled him to consider the very question itself. He finally concluded: "Justice… is a concept and it is a reality. In its conceptual form, justice is fairness, the treating of everyone equally and meeting everyone's needs. In its application within a justice system, the emphasis changes to a balancing of competing needs and competing claims; it changes from merely being just, to doing justice" (2001: 191).

Justice in Historical Thought

An early philosophical definition of justice emerges in its Latin tag, *suum cuique tribuere*, which roughly translates as "to allocate to each their own." This notion of justice looks to the past and is individualistic; it also poses problems. For example, how are we to assess for everyone their own diverse and expected entitlements? Following Aristotle's view of the execution of justice as the main purpose of the state, today, this takes the form of law enforcement, court processes and punishments. Marge Simpson, of *The Simpsons* cartoon fame, captured the twenty-first-century version of state justice: "You know, the courts may not be working any more, but as long as everyone is videotaping everyone else, justice will be done."

Thomas Hobbes (1588–1679), an English philosopher famous for a version of the social contract predicated on the need to prevent "a war of all against all," saw justice as a political, coercive force that ensured that everyone kept to their social contract with one another — except the sovereign, who could assault at his pleasure. John Locke (1632–1704), an English Enlightenment philosopher who believed that land should belong to those who work it, argued that "justice consists in respecting the natural rights of each individual." His contemporary, Jean-Jacques Rousseau (1712–1778), believed in justice as a form of natural goodness, that it is natural for human beings to do what is best for themselves with the least possible harm to others. Immanuel Kant (1724–1804) took the more conventional view that justice is morality and consists of acting from social duty rather than self-interest. Such a society would produce free, equal, reasonable citizens who are purposeful and further society's aims.

Writing in the late eighteenth century, William Godwin (1756–1836) considered political justice in a treatise titled *Enquiry Concerning Political Justice and Its Influence on Morals and Happiness*. As with his understanding of punishment, Godwin reduced broad conceptions of justice to their application on an interpersonal rather than a communal abstract field (1976 [1793]):

> By justice I understand that impartial treatment of every man in matters that relate to his happiness, which is measured solely by a consideration of the properties of the receiver, and the capacity of him that bestows. Its principle therefore is, according to a well known phrase, to be "no respecter of persons."
>
> Considerable light will probably be thrown upon our investigation if, quitting for the present the political view, we examine justice merely as it exists among individuals. Justice is a rule of conduct originating in the connection of one percipient being with another. A comprehensive maxim which has been laid down upon the subject is "that we should love our neighbour as ourselves." But this maxim, though possessing considerable merit as a popular principle, is not modeled with the strictness of philosophical accuracy.

Simply stated, justice must be lived every day, between individuals, if it is to be realized in a society as a whole. Invoking the "golden rule," Godwin recognized that justice in philosophy is not always reflected in practice.

Contemporary approaches sometimes go back to these earlier writings. One example is Denise Breton and Stephan Lehman's *The Mystic Heart of Justice*, valuable for its Socratic/Platonic approach. In outlining their interpretation of justice, the authors note:

> In dialogue after dialogue, Socrates and Plato shift the focus in the opposite direction: from outer to inner concerns, from appearances to essences, from visible forms to invisible ideas and values. The dialogues aim to deepen our connection to what's within — to know ourselves — assuming that the inner reveals who we are and therefore stands as our true authority and guide. Justice must serve this core relation we have to ourselves, if it's to function as something worthy and good, which Socrates and Plato assume it is. (2001: 35–36)

The inference to justice in relationships paints a different picture than our popular images of justice as an entity to "be brought to" or "delivered." In the latter interpretation, justice is seen as a commodity or a destination place; we go to courts to "get justice" and justice is the purview and product of institutions. In the Socratic/Platonic approach, alternatively, justice is seen as relational and necessary to our individual well-being; it appears to be based on values rather than laws.

A further modern contribution to our understanding of justice is found in Herman Bianchi's *Justice as Sanctuary*. In this book, he revisits the evolution of modern legal systems in an examination of Roman law and biblical translations of concepts that are domain to current understandings of justice. Bianchi offers a provisional definition of justice as "a principle to assess rules of law and their just operation and eventually to assess whether their promised effect has been realized" (1994: 5). This definition is forward-looking as it evaluates the fruits of the justice intervention; it is not only a response to what happened but to the integrity of the effects. In other words, Bianchi's writing challenges us to look not only at the *intentions* of justice interventions but also at the results.

Bianchi challenges conventional interpretations of the evolution of legal justice, noting that centuries ago this system functioned without an emphasis on punitive crime control, preferring to focus on compensation. He argues that this changed between 1200 and 1750 with the Roman Catholic Inquisition, which established the "first crime," of heresy (through the "phenomenon" of "witchcraft"), and the concomitant punitive repression of what we now call "criminality." In his view this 550-year shift was significant:

> The Holy Roman Church, a self-appointed keeper and guardian of Roman traditions during the Middle Ages, wanted for political reasons to make the religious life and dogmatic opinions of the faithful an object of inquisitory examination. The idea that one could be an object of examination had until then been alien to free people. (1994: 16)

The inquisitory examination was eventually adopted by secular authorities and is still evident in systems around the world, criminal justice and otherwise. Socrates' idea that "The unexamined life isn't worth living" was spoken out of the realization of his own humanity. The examination was self-generated and for the benefit of the individual, who might ask, "What's the point of my existence and where is it taking me?" Via the emergent practices of the Christian Church, this is now the purview of external institutions and professionals, whose inquisitorial examinations aim to further "justice" rather than self-reflection.

Rejecting the typical image of justice as scales, Bianchi offers the Hebrew *tsedaka* instead — a model of justice as a continuous reaching for peace and reconciliation. So rather than "bringing people to justice" we should endeavour to bring *tsedaka* to the people. *Tsedaka* is a communitarian concept;

it infers the bringing together of people, particularly the parties in conflict, and trying to find *tsedaka* (justice) in their relationship. It is an experience of justice that, according to Bianchi, has become lost in translations of the Bible over several centuries, particularly in the sixteenth- and seventeenth-century Protestant countries like England, the Netherlands and Scandinavia through the King James version. He suggests that, additionally, these translations confused understandings of justice, for example, in the use of the word "retribution," which does not exist in Hebrew and is used in place of the Hebrew word *hishlim*, which has to do with shalom, or peace.

According to Bianchi, there are three criteria of *tsedaka* justice. First, it must include some practical way to achieve absolution or release from guilt. Our retributive system tends to stigmatize offenders permanently in powerful rituals to certify deviance, but none to decertify it. Second, it must include the confirmation of truth, since truth is relational and found through the process of dialogue. To Bianchi, tests of truth are sincerity and reliability and not just facts; he challenges the legal idea that something is either true or not true, countering that many things can be half-true, or a little bit true, or true on one occasion and not on another. The third criteria of *tsedaka* justice is that there must be substantiation — when no one has been lied to, when victims have been fully heard and offenders have been offered the possibility of redress and release. Justice in this sense is known by its results not by its intentions and forms; one can only know afterwards that reconciliation came to the people. The definition and aim of *tsedaka* justice is peace.

Justice and Punishment: G.H. Mead

Most writing about criminal justice proceeds on the basis that justice is a self-explanatory idea and punishment a necessary evil. Commonsense notions of justice include reference to punishment as if it were an axiomatic part of the constitution of justice. As in the chapters to come, a deeper exploration of restorative justice renders this thinking problematic, so that we might ask the question, "Can there be justice without punishment?"

Almost a century ago George Herbert Mead, the prominent philosopher and social psychologist from the University of Chicago, pondered the relationship between justice and punishment in an article titled "The Psychology of Punitive Justice" (1918). Mead's article is particularly interesting for the purposes of this chapter, not only because of its focus on the psychological underpinnings of legal justice but for its expression of alternatives that are remarkably similar to restorative justice practices.

Mead wrote specifically about legal justice: "It is the assumption of [criminal court] procedure that conviction and punishment are the accomplishment of justice and also that it is for the good of society, that is, that it is both just and expedient" (1918: 582). This description was a launching point for his discussion on the social psychology of punitive attitudes. The notion of law as justice is based on symbolism: "We do not respect law in the abstract but the values which the laws of the community conserve... A threatened attack upon these values places us in an attitude of defense, and as this defense is largely entrusted to the operation of the laws of the land we gain a respect for the laws which is in proportion to the goods which they defend" (584–85). While Durkheim did not explore the psychological implications of punishment to members of a society, he noted, much as Mead did, that punishment was functional to the social cohesion of citizens who largely upheld the laws, rather than to victims or offenders themselves. Punishment invoked by the state is thus seen as assuaging the hostile impulses of its citizens; it provides a response to the thought that "something must be done" and is equated with justice.

However, a problem exists in deciding what is a proportionate punishment for a specific crime, a decision that appears to affect perceptions of the quality of legal justice. Susan Jacoby argues: "[Retributive institutions] remove the practical, not the psychological, burden of revenge from individuals. If they fail — or are seen to fail — in the fulfillment of their practical function, they are likely to increase rather than decrease the psychic burden of vengeance" (1983: 12). Thus, if the public feels that punishments are too lenient, there will be a diminished experience of justice and a corresponding desire for revenge. This situation is exacerbated by a prolific mass media that exaggerates and amplifies representations of crime (Surette 1992) and by politicians who use isolated horrific crimes to cultivate public support for law-and-order campaigns and repressive legislation (Gaucher and Elliott 2001).

Mead's analysis of the function of legal justice and the psychology of punitive justice yields two related, yet problematic, observations:

> Hostility toward the lawbreaker inevitably brings with it the attitudes of retribution, repression, and exclusion. These provide no principles for the eradication of crime, for returning the delinquent to normal social relations, nor for stating the transgressed rights and institutions in terms of their positive social functions.
>
> On the other side of the ledger stands the fact that the attitude of hostility toward the lawbreaker has the unique advantage of uniting all members of community in the emotional solidarity of aggression.... Furthermore, the attitude reveals common, universal values which underlie like a bedrock the divergent structures of individual ends that are mutually closed and hostile to each other. Seemingly without the criminal the cohesiveness of society would disappear and the universal goods of the community would crumble into mutually repellent individual particles. (1918: 590–91)

53

The claim here is that punitive responses to justice offer either 1) a transference of hostility onto an individual but no harm prevention, no healthy reintegration and no wider teaching of values or opportunities for clarification for the community at large or 2) a bonding experience, of sorts, among most community members in a solidarity of the rejection of the criminal, which is to use a person (criminal) as a means to an end (cohesion of society).

Mead warns that a generally persistent attitude of hostility is damaging for the health of individuals and the community:

> Where simple social aggression or defense with the purpose of eliminating or encysting an enemy is the purpose of the community, organization through the common attitude of hostility is normal and effective. But as long as the social organization is dominated by the attitude of hostility the individuals or groups who are the objectives of this organization will remain enemies. *It is quite impossible psychologically to hate the sin and love the sinner.* We are very much given to cheating ourselves in this regard.... [The] two attitudes, that of control of crime by the hostile procedure of the law and that of control through comprehension of social and psychological conditions, cannot be combined. *To understand is to forgive and the social procedure seems to deny the very responsibility which the law affirms,* and on the other hand the pursuit by criminal justice inevitably awakens the hostile attitude in the offender and renders the attitude of mutual comprehension practically impossible. (1918: 592, emphasis added)

In this passage, Mead's scenario alludes very much to the "prison paradox" — the contradictory and conflicting mandates of punishment and rehabilitation. A society "dominated by the attitude of hostility" may produce legal justice, but this justice does not come with real peace. This raises an important question: Can there be justice without peace?

Later in the article, Mead raises an issue for which it is not clear that restorative justice has yet offered an adequate response. Given the psychological effects of broadly based hostilities for social solidarity, what are the implications for our sentiments of justice if we respond to harm without resorting to punishment? As Mead notes, "If then we undertake to deal with the causes of crime in a fundamental way, and as dispassionately as we are dealing with the causes of disease, and if we wish to substitute negotiation and international adjudication for war in settling disputes between nations, it is of some importance to consider what sort of emotional solidarity we can secure to replace that which the traditional procedures have supplied" (1918: 594). When we are united against the "criminal" or wrongdoer, we experience an emotional solidarity with the others in society — one possible explanation for the impetus of groups of children to outcast individual peers, an act otherwise known as bullying.

Finally, Mead describes a juvenile court that includes many of the elements of today's restorative justice practices. This is where "we meet the undertaking to reach and understand the causes of social and individual breakdown, to mend if possible the defective situation and reinstate the individual at fault" (1918: 594). This understanding of, and approach to, justice, in Mead's view, provides an alternative to punitive justice:

> In centering interest upon reinstatement the sense of forward-looking moral responsibility is not only weakened but is strengthened, for the court undertakes to determine what the child must do and be to take up normal social relations again. Where responsibility rests upon others this can be brought out in much greater detail and with greater effect since it is not defined under abstract legal categories and the aim in determining responsibility is not to place punishment but to obtain future results. Out of this arises a much fuller presentation of the facts that are essential for dealing with the problem than can possibly appear in a criminal court procedure that aims to establish simply responsibility for a legally defined offense with the purpose of inflicting punishment. Of far greater importance is the appearance of the values of family relations, of schools, of training of all sorts, of opportunities to work, and of all the other factors that go to make up that which is worth while in the life of a child or an adult.... They are the ends that should determine conduct. It is impossible to discover their real import unless they can all be brought into relationship with each other. (595)

If nothing else, Mead's argument indicates that there is nothing wholly new or radical about restorative justice that in practice, through conventional democratic institutions such as schools or criminal justice agencies, often appears to be a problem-solving approach to crimes or harms. As the following chapters show, restorative approaches to justice tend to concentrate more on values than on laws or rules and to focus on healing harms rather than on punishing wrongdoers.

Justice in Psychology and Religion

Mary Clark, in "Skinner vs. the Prophets" (2005), contrasts perspectives on justice from two belief systems from the respective domains of psychology and religion. She argues that there are consequences to a culture's beliefs about human nature for its perceptions of justice. This affords another analytical tool in discerning the genesis or factors contributing to our understanding of justice and highlights the significance of culture and its myriad expressions in this analysis.

B.F. Skinner was a twentieth-century radical behaviourist who believed that behaviour was determined and not free, and that this could be demonstrated in experimental analysis of behaviour. Concepts such as operant conditioning and schedules of reinforcement come from Skinner's work. The implications of his approach are that human beings are determined to behave in certain ways and can be trained to behave differently — as decided by another person in control. By the mid-twentieth century, the radical behaviourist school was challenged by a new, emerging school of psychology known as cognitive science — a multidisciplinary study of mind and behaviour. The other perspective Clark examines includes the wisdom of the world's major religions, such as Buddhism, Christianity and Islam. An example of common religious understanding is the golden rule — "do unto others as you would have them do unto you" is the Christian version of this understanding, which is similarly expressed in other religious beliefs (Buddhism: "Hurt not others with that which pains yourself"; Judaism: "What is hateful to you, do not to your fellow men. That is the entire Law; all the rest is commentary.")

The base understandings of human nature differ between the perspectives of behavioural psychology and religious teachings. In explaining the difference between the perspectives, Clark refers to George Lakoff's writing on moral politics (2002) and how political debates are shaped in the U.S. (2004). Lakoff uses a parenting metaphor in his discussion, with one perspective being that of the strict father (Skinnerian psychology) and the other of the nurturing parent (the religious prophets). This metaphor carries the implications of the two perspectives to our understanding of how best to respond to harm-doing and conflict, and further into the wider arena of politics and governance.

For the strict father, a set of assumptions about people and the world anchors the foundation of the following rationality:

> The world is a dangerous place, and it always will be, because there is evil out there in the world. The world is also difficult because it is competitive. There will always be winners and losers. There is an absolute right and an absolute wrong. Children are born bad, in the sense that they just want to do what feels good, not what is right. Therefore, they have to be made good. (Lakoff 2004: 7)

In this framework, the strong, strict father has enormous responsibilities in a difficult world to protect and support his family and teach his children right from wrong. The father is the moral authority and his children must be obedient. Obedience is taught through punishment, which inculcates the self-discipline necessary for restraint from committing wrong acts but is also valuable for expediting self-interest in the bigger world. Prosperity and self-reliance are the goals for the individual; the strict father model links morality with prosperity.

Played out in the governance realm, specifically in the contexts of social programs and criminal justice, the strict father model tends to result in sparse resources for welfare, preschools, counselling, education, job creation and so on, and relatively limitless resources for police, courts and prisons. Lakoff also applies his metaphor, which equates well-being with wealth, to Adam Smith's "law of nature":

> If everyone pursues her own self-interest, then by the invisible hand, by nature, the self-interest of all will be maximized. That is, it is moral to pursue your self-interest, and there is a name for those people who do not do it. The name is do-gooder. A do-gooder is someone who is trying to help someone else rather than herself and is getting in the way of those who are pursuing their self-interest. Do-gooders screw up the system. (2004: 8)

In this model, a good, moral person is disciplined enough to be obedient and has learned and does what is right, which is to prosper and become self-reliant. If a person has failed in this, the strict father or government will not help.

Lakoff summarizes the prophet's perspective, that of nurturing parents:

> Both parents are equally responsible for raising the children. The assumption is that children are born good and can be made better. The world can be a better place, and our job is to work on that. The parents' job is to nurture their children and to raise their children to be nurturers of others.... [Nurturance] means two things: empathy and responsibility. (2004: 12)

Nurturing parents assume that in order to take proper care of children, parents also need to take care of themselves. Parenting is difficult, and parents have to work hard at it to become strong and competent. Empathy for their children means that parents try to provide protection from the dangers of the world; they also want their children to have happy, fulfilled lives, and therefore it is important for them to be happy and fulfilled in order to model this. For social governance, this is translated into policies that assist citizens to acquire the skills and opportunities necessary to become healthy contributing members of society even if they have not benefited from supportive parents or wider society as children and youth.

Other nurturing values hold implications for wider social governance. *Freedom* is significant because it is necessary for individuals to be free to seek fulfillment. In order to have freedom, there must be opportunity and prosperity. Nurturing parents want their children to be treated with fairness. Empathetic connection with children requires honest, open two-way communication. The health of communities affects how children grow up, so community building and community service are valued, as is cooperation (Lakoff 2004: 13). All of this requires trust. Governments using the prophet vision of justice tend to emphasize robust social programs to compensate for unequal access to opportunities and prosperity. Criminal justice systems are predicated on some imperative of fairness in the contest between the individual and the state, and focus more on rehabilitative than punitive strategies.

These metaphors — behavioural psychology with the strict father, and the prophets with the nurturing parent — provide a useful framework for understanding peoples' different interpretations of justice, which begin with disparate views of human nature. Criminal justice debates, then, might be better served if we were to begin with a re-assessment of the basic assumptions we hold about human beings. The strict father approach reflects the retributive version of justice; the nurturing parent suggests a restorative justice approach.

Aboriginal Perspectives of Justice

In pondering our understanding of justice, it is useful to consider different cultural perspectives. The example of Aboriginal philosophy is helpful to this discussion in two ways. First, Aboriginal thought on justice is framed in a different paradigm and therefore opens a space for us to question some of our own basic assumptions. Second, since Aboriginal people in Canada figure prominently in our criminal justice landscape, it is worthwhile to consider how the clash of justice paradigms influences the lot of Aboriginal people within state criminal justice.

A collaborative session with elders, spiritual leaders and professionals of several First Nations communities in North America produced an explanation of justice as a gift of the North, one of the four directions of the medicine wheel, "an ancient and powerful symbol of the Universe" (Bopp et al. 1985: 32). On this topic, it was noted:

> The final lesson of the North is the lesson of balance, for wisdom teaches how all things fit together. And balance, when applied to the interconnectedness of all human beings, becomes justice. Justice is the greatest gift of the North. With its aid, the traveler can see all things as they really are. Without it, there can be no peace or security in the affairs of the world. (71)

In this explanation the concept of justice refers to balance and interconnection. In practice, "The primary meaning of 'justice' in an Aboriginal society would be that of restoring peace and equilibrium to the community through reconciling the accused with his or her own conscience and with the individual or family that is wronged" (Sinclair 1994: 178).

Rupert Ross offers a story of a conference workshop in which participants were asked to take the role of a community justice committee making recommendations to a court about a particular case (1994: 241–42). On being presented with a lengthy jail term as an option for the offender, Aboriginal members of the workshop group were unanimously opposed:

> An Inuit man, through his translator, said that this was exactly the problem when the court came into his community. He complained that the Crown and the judge always called people "bad." He said you can't do that if you want someone to be good. An Aboriginal lady complained that just because the community hadn't been able to alter the abuser's behaviour so far didn't mean that the healing approach was no good. She talked about how the western system had kept on using jail for hundreds of years even though it didn't work.... Another asked how jail could be any protection, given that when the offender comes out he still needs healing, only now the task is made harder because of where he's been, what he's learned and how angry he has become. "To give protection in your way," said another, "you'd have to keep him there forever."
>
> I have heard such perspectives expressed in a growing number of Aboriginal communities across the country. They seem to be speaking about a picture of justice that is very different from the one I've been trained in. Indeed, many who speak from within this perspective don't even seem to begin their analysis of justice where we do.

As we learn in the next chapter, many of the differences between Aboriginal and Western paradigms of justice pertain to the kinds of questions that are deemed relevant.

This brief outline of Aboriginal meanings of justice is sufficient to demonstrate that a clash of paradigms is immanent when Aboriginal justice meets Western justice. Aboriginal overrepresentation in the criminal justice system cannot be addressed meaningfully by merely tinkering with the system's mechanisms. As Patricia Monture-Angus notes (1999: 33): "The essential and often overlooked step in creating a renewed relationship between Aboriginal Peoples and Canadians is an examination of the meaning of the concepts we are building our relationship with."

Conclusion

While the concept of justice entails a variety of ideas a universal definition of it remains elusive. Gordon Bazemore, a prominent American academic in the area of restorative justice, summarizes the problem of the punishment-justice nexus:

> Public discourse appeared to shift to rhetoric that assumed that punishment was the equivalent of justice. On the one hand, if asked to define "justice," most Americans use words such as fairness, similar or equal treatment, lack of discrimination, due process, and equal opportunity. Yet, when asked what is meant when we hear that someone has been "brought to justice," we inevitably think first of punishment—often severe punishment. Unfortunately, much flows downward from this overarching logic of justice as the equivalent of deserved retribution to provide support for what much of the world must now recognize as an American addiction to punishment. (2007: 652)

Bazemore's uncomfortable conclusion seems to be that justice equals prison, at least in the minds of most Americans. The implications of this logic seem rather obvious, in view of the material covered in Chapter 1.

But justice can be conceived in myriad ways. Another long-time contributor to the restorative justice and peacemaking literature, Hal Pepinsky, offered this understanding of justice:

> Correct me if you hear differently but when I hear people talking about doing justice, I infer that they are bent on achieving a pre-ordained outcome, as in just deserts or social equality. The more passionate the commitment to that result, the more violent the passion is to me, by definition. I am perfectly willing to use the term justice in another way: as a synonym for karma — the recognition that in fact all social actions have consequences. I share the view that over generations, human beings and indeed the universe are all connected. In this scheme of things I also postulate that, on the whole, violence begets violence and peacemaking begets peace. In my view of things, justice, like shit, just happens, even if it takes some generations for what goes around to come around. As I perceive it, doing justice or remedying injustice amounts to playing God and, at its most successful, becomes political revolution in which one ruling class supersedes another. I see the task of peacemaking as one of trying to democratize our social relations, which entails allowing ourselves to be surprised by the consequences. (in Sullivan 2003: 70)

Pepinsky's view of justice helps to set the stage for the unveiling of restorative justice. He borrows from Navajo wisdom in conceptualizing the processes of justice: "Show up. Pay attention. Tell the truth. Don't be attached to outcomes."

Serious thinkers are concerned with the question of justice because the imbalances that produce injustice are the perennial, pressing issues in every society that aspires to be democratic. Even with a charter of human rights and freedoms — a global model of protecting individual and group rights — one cannot have justice without political, economic and social equity. One can, however, locate glimpses of justice or anomalous moments when justice is vividly expressed. Sometimes this happens in a courtroom. More often, justice is revealed in the interrelationships that are forged or healed through processes of creating or restoring balance. As observed by Patricia Monture-Okanee, "What I have come to understand is that justice is not a legal problem. It is a human problem" (1994: 231).

Note

1. The Law Commission of Canada was shut down in late 2006 by the newly instated federal Conservatives.

4

Restorative Justice
A Vision of the Good

A Story of Restorative Justice
Wendy Keats

Elizabeth had been extremely traumatized by the armed robbery during her shift at the convenience store. The crime scene had been absolute chaos. The masked robbers had screamed death threats as they held her captive with a knife to her throat. She had wet herself from sheer terror.

Even months after the robbers had been caught, life did not return to normal. Word had got out about her fear-induced loss of bladder control, and customers and co-workers teased her mercilessly afterwards. Not only did she have to cope with fear and shame, but past traumas in her life returned to haunt her. She became ill with bulimia and lost 85 pounds. Insomnia kept her awake night after night. Family and friends quickly became impatient with her. "Look, you didn't get hurt. Let it go. What's your problem?"

Elizabeth herself couldn't understand the unrelenting torture. Why did she suffer nightmares every time she closed her eyes for a few moments? Why couldn't she resume her life? As her health deteriorated, her marriage broke down and her relationship with her children changed dramatically.

Meanwhile, Charles, the 21-year-old offender, was serving five years for the offence in a federal institution. He had been raised in a violent environment by a family deeply involved with drug and alcohol abuse. His string of surrogate fathers were mostly ex-offenders and addicts themselves. He and his sisters were victims of continuous abuse and poverty.

He had committed minor offences as a juvenile, but this was his first serious crime. To him, the offence was the result of an extremely bad acid trip. Completely out of his mind on booze and drugs, Charles had no idea of the trauma caused by his actions. Charles first learned of Elizabeth's situation when he became aware of her insistence that the court allow her to submit a victim impact statement. She had not been invited by the courts to submit a statement as she was not identified as the victim. The convenience store was.

As Elizabeth fought for her right to somehow be included in the process, her anger and frustration grew. She was terrified that Charles and his accomplice would come back to get her as they threatened they would. She was isolated from her family and friends by this time. She was frightened, emotionally haggard, and physically sick.

Finally after two years and many counseling sessions, Elizabeth realized that she had to find a way to "let it go." She realized that, in order to do that, she had to try to find the answers to the questions that haunted her. So when Charles' parole hearing came up, she traveled by bus for four hours to the institution... alone and suffering from pneumonia. During the hearing, Charles turned around and tried to say something to her, but victims and offenders are not allowed to speak to each other during these hearings, and he was cut off.

Back on the bus, she kept wondering, "What did he want to say to me?"

At this point, she contacted the National Parole Board with a request for a face-to-face meeting and they referred her case to MOVE. I was the assigned mediator. When I first met Elizabeth, I asked her why she wanted to meet her offender. "I cannot live like this anymore," she said. "I have to get the answers to my questions. I have to find out whether he is coming back to get me or my family. I have to tell him how I feel. I have to look him in the face and tell him how he has changed my life."

All valid reasons for mediation. And so I went to see the offender.

Charles was amazed by Elizabeth's fear. "Doesn't she know I wouldna' never hurt her? Don't they give them convenience store clerks some training that tells them to just hand over the money and nobody will get hurt?" he asked incredulously. "Doesn't she know that every robber says, 'don't call the cops or I'll come back an' git ya?' That's just the way it's done. Gee, I'm really sorry about this... I had no idea."

Without hesitation he agreed to meet with Elizabeth to try to do whatever he could to make up for what he had previously thought of as just a bad night... too drunk — too stoned... and one for which he felt he was the only one paying a heavy price. By this time, Charles had been in prison for two years and it was no picnic. He slept with a knife under his pillow because there were so many stabbings going on around him. Like Elizabeth, he lived in daily fear.

The mediation was arranged to take place in a room within the prison itself. Neither of them slept the night before... each racked with doubts and fears. By the time the two of them came together, face to face across a 30-inch wide table, they were both peaked with emotion.

However, the controlled process of mediation soon took its effect and the story telling stage began. Elizabeth said everything she had been thinking for the past two years. Charles listened intently, and when it was his turn, he answered most of her questions as his own story unfolded. As the dialogue continued, they started to chuckle about a detail. This broke the tension and they really started to talk: face-to-face and heart-to-heart. They had shared a violent experience, albeit from entirely different perspectives. A relationship had been formed that night that, until now, had been left unresolved.

Elizabeth got the answers to all of the questions that had haunted her that day. She learned that Charles had never intended to come back and harm her, and that he was genuinely sorry for what he had done. They struck an agreement about how they would greet each other on the street when he is released from prison and returns to their home town. As they finished, they stood up and shook hands. "You know," Elizabeth said, "we will never be friends, you and I — we come from different worlds — but I want you to know that I wish you the best of luck and when I think of you I will hope that you are doing okay. I forgive you."

Leaving the prison, I asked her how she felt. "It's over. It's closed. It's done." Five months later, she tells me that she has not had even a single nightmare since. "I don't feel like the same person anymore. There is no more fear. It's just gone."

I have learned from Charles' case manager that he is doing well. Staff feel it was a maturing experience for him and that there is a much better chance of his responding to rehabilitative treatment and taking life more seriously. No guarantees. He's twenty-three years old. My own guess is that he will never forget this experience, and that it will have a profound effect on future decisions. After mediation, Elizabeth requested that a letter be sent to the National Parole Board. She no longer wants to be used as a reason to keep Charles incarcerated. "If they want to keep him in prison, that's their business, but I don't want it done because of me. For me, this matter is over. I am healed." *(Told by Wendy Keats of MOVE, a New Brunswick initiative in restorative justice, in Breton and Lehman 2001: 57–60)*

❧ ❧ ❧

Elizabeth's story might be surprising to many because of the extraordinary measures she took to overcome the effects of her traumatic victimization. Not everyone would choose her course of action, and it is not the purpose of restorative justice to impose encounters between parties to a conflict even if it is presumed to be in their best interests. But the story opens the possibilities of restorative justice for crimes of violence, despite a broadly held view that the value of restorative justice is largely limited to relatively minor, non-violent crimes committed by young people. On the contrary, research demonstrates that restorative justice has its greatest impact in violent cases.

Howard Zehr has made foundational contributions to this field, namely through the publication of his seminal book, *Changing Lenses*, in which he offers an analytical reconstruction of the notion of crime and justice through a "restorative lens":

> Crime is a violation of people and relationships. It creates obligations to make things right. Justice involves the victims, the offender, and the community in a search for solutions which promote repair, reconciliation, and reassurance. (1990: 181)

This description stands in contrast to how we normally understand crime: as a violation of laws or rules, where culpability is determined and the guilty are punished. What is not commonly understood is that in the Canadian and U.S. criminal justice systems, all crimes are committed against the state. Victims, the people who have been actually violated by the crime, have their status usurped by the state, which relegates them to the role of witnesses.

This is the major reason why crime victims experience such frustration with the system and why accommodations such as victim impact statements are so unsatisfying.

The term "restorative justice" was first coined in 1977 by Albert Eglash in the specific context of restitution. In the same year, Nils Christie's article "Conflicts as Property" argued for a different way of looking at justice that laid out some of the fundamental issues of restorative justice, without using the term. Predating both academic articulations of the concept, however, was the first modern recorded practice of RJ, in Elmira, Ontario, in 1974 — an important reminder that, at least in Canada, RJ practice has always been ahead of RJ scholarship. In an interesting twist of events, one of the two young men in the Elmira case, Russ Kelly, only learned of its impact many years later, when a back injury forced him to retrain for a new career at the Conestoga College in Kitchener, Ontario. A guest speaker from the Community Initiatives of Waterloo Region in his community services class talked about the Elmira case, and Kelly recognized himself in the story. Now interested in restorative justice, Kelly returned home and typed the words into his computer's search engine and came up with 50,000 hits. He later became a volunteer with CJI in Waterloo (Kelly 2006)

In this chapter, we consider the meaning of "restorative justice" and review some of the key issues and debates. The difficult task of defining restorative justice begins the chapter, followed by a consideration of some ideas germane to theory and practice. From the beginning, articulations of restorative justice have been expressed within a criminal justice context; we discuss the limitations of this approach. Finally, a holistic perspective of RJ is introduced.

What Is Meant by "Restorative Justice"?

The term "restorative justice" has entered mainstream discourses to describe myriad philosophies, principles, theories, practices and programs. Emerging within the realm of criminal justice practices, RJ has spilled into the domains of schools, workplaces and organizations (see Roche 2001). As more people deploy what are framed as restorative practices, debates ensue as to what actually qualifies as RJ. McCold (2000), for example, took on the challenge of clarifying purist versus maximalist models of RJ, where the former is a voluntary cooperative approach and the latter comprises court-imposed sanctions. Concerns raised by purists raise the warning bell of co-optation.

A key factor contributing to co-optation lies in the different questions offered by each of the justice paradigms. Retributive justice asks: Was a crime committed or a rule broken? Who did it? What punishment do they deserve? Restorative justice asks: What is the harm and who was affected by it? What are their needs? Whose obligations are these? The answers to these two sets of questions take us down different paths of action.

Susan Sharpe, formerly of the Edmonton Victim Offender Mediation Society, referred to restorative justice as a philosophy. According to Sharpe, restorative justice is

> a justice that puts its energy into the future, not into what is past. It focuses on what needs to be healed, what needs to be repaid, what needs to be learned in the wake of a crime. It looks at what needs to be strengthened if such things are not to happen again.... [Therefore, justice should strive toward]
>
> 1. Inviting full participation and consensus.
> 2. Healing what has been broken.
> 3. Seeking full and direct accountability.
> 4. Reuniting what has been divided.
> 5. Strengthening the community, to prevent further harms.

The difficulty in defining restorative justice can be traced to the observation that "restorative justice has many roots that cannot be easily separated" (McLaughlin et al. 2003: 2). Dave Gustafson, of the Fraser Region Community Justice Initiatives Association in Langley, B.C., conceptualized restorative justice as "a healing river" — a flow of discourse that includes the contributions of a number of tributary streams. These contributions include neo-traditional dispute resolution approaches such as bargaining and negotiation (e.g., Fisher, Urry and Patton 1981); Aboriginal teachings and circle processes (e.g., Ross 1996); faith-based approaches such as dyadic mediation (e.g., Hadley 2001); victimology and therapeutic discourses (e.g., Herman 1997); peacemaking criminology (e.g., Pepinsky and Quinney 1991); and penal abolitionism (e.g., Mathiesen 1990).

The Law Commission of Canada, which strongly advocated a shift to restorative justice, offered the following definition:

> Restorative Justice refers to a process for resolving crime and conflicts that focuses on redressing the harm to the victims, on holding offenders accountable for their actions and on engaging the community in a conflict resolution process. (2003: 3)

Bazemore follows in a similar criminal justice vein: "Although it is often viewed mistakenly as a program or practice model, restorative justice is most accurately understood as a holistic framework for criminal justice reform, and even more broadly as an overarching approach to informal conflict resolution and healing" (2007: 656). Tony Marshall offers a commonly referenced definition of RJ: "a process whereby all the parties with a stake in a particular offence come together to resolve collectively how to deal with the aftermath of the offence and its implications for the future" (1999: 5). These definitions all allude to an idea that RJ is about criminal justice, owing in good measure to the inclusion of the word "justice" in the term. The discussion in Chapter 3 reminds us that justice is not the property of institutions alone. Since RJ is about resolving conflicts that contain in some way the notion of justice, it is difficult to extricate "justice" from our understanding, although this is precisely what is done by scholars who refer to it as "restorative practices."

For the purposes of our introduction to RJ, Howard Zehr offers the most open and yet focused definition of the concept: "It is a kind of coherent value system that gives us a vision of the good, how we want to be together... they are the values that seem to have some universality" (in Coben and Harley 2004: 268). Chapter 6 considers the notion of RJ values in greater depth; for now, our task is to outline some key concepts relevant to most understandings. These can be grouped into two categories: "Who is involved?" and "What is the focus?"

In the criminal justice system the "victim," the "offender," the community and the government each play a particular role. However, the spotlight is on the offender and the government, with the victim and community playing supportive roles if they are included at all. In RJ, the focus is different for each of the players; further, the fundamental components are often challenged by specific exceptions. The questions, "Who was harmed?" and "How are they affected?" position victims at the theoretical centre of the RJ response. Victims have the opportunity to tell their stories, to bring or acquire support for their own recovery from injury, to overcome fears generated by the harm and to wholly participate in the decision-making processes that produce reparative plans. Offenders participate similarly, by telling their stories, supported in the process by people of their choice, and engaging in the development of reparative agreements. The community is represented by those who support victims and offenders, by others who might have been affected (such as witnesses) and by volunteer facilitators trained to participate in community-based processes. Government is involved mainly in the areas of funding and making referrals, although in criminal justice encounters, the spectre of the government's retributive system looms in the background (for example, ready to take over if parties to the harm reject the restorative process or parties charged with harm-doing fail to honour agreements).

The foci of RJ interventions also differ from familiar practices. Rather than finding out "whodunnit" and determining appropriate punishments, RJ has at least three goals. The first of these is to consider, at all stages, the *needs of the participants*: those harmed, those who did the harm and the affected community. This includes, but is not limited to, the need for information, meaningful supports, opportunities for truthful dialogue and possibilities to act on personal and collective responsibilities. The second focus is on *healing harms*, which includes a broad interpretation involving not only the responsibilities of harm-doers to make genuine reparations, but also the community taking stock of conditions that facilitate the production of harms. And finally, a good RJ intervention is a process that *embodies and reflects the desired/identified core values of the community* — that is, it is a process that is itself safe, respectful, caring, inclusive and so on.

Restorative Justice Theory and Practice

One of the most prolific scholars in the arena of RJ theory and research, Gordon Bazemore, summarized RJ theory as follows:

> Three "big ideas" provide the basis for a normative theory of restorative justice. These core principles — *repair, stakeholder involvement*, and the *transformation of community* and *government roles* in the response to crime... — most clearly distinguish restorative justice from other orientations and define the core outcomes, processes, practices, and structural relationships that characterize restorative approaches. (2001: 206)

Bazemore's synthesis is useful for remembering core principles of RJ. The goal of the RJ process is to *repair*, as much as possible, the harm done as well as the damaged relationships that existed prior and post harm-doing. This is sometimes described as healing, but it is somewhat different; healing is a voluntary individual process of recovering from harm and not something that an RJ process can command. The story of Elizabeth at the beginning of the chapter exemplifies the idea and value of repair. But generally, repair is about fixing things, problem-solving, generating and implementing plans to change conditions for the well-being of all. Stakeholder involvement, as we have seen, renders the main parties central to the conflict, harm and crime in the process, rather than subordinating them to professional and institutional processes. In Elizabeth's story, she and Charles are the principal actors in the RJ process, with the mediator playing an important supportive role. In RJ, the community and government roles also change, as the collective conditions are examined for ways and means of ameliorating social conditions that are likely to foster harm.

Academics often attempt to explain RJ within narrow lenses. Theo Gavrielides, for example, questions whether RJ is a theory or an alternative criminal justice process (2005: 87), which would limit its practice to criminal justice and exclude its use in schools and other contexts. Using a three-level, concentric-circle model of justice theories, with punishment theories in the centre, justice theories in the middle and theories of political morality and ethics in the outer circle, Gavrielides argues that RJ falls into the middle ring. He suggests that RJ cannot fit into the outer ring of theories of political morality and ethics: "Can [RJ] teach us how to behave towards the centralised authority that co-ordinates the living of all entities in a community? Can it show us how to lead our lives? Does it distinguish a *telos* that we should pursue so that we make our lives meaningful and worthwhile? These simple questions can help us conclude that RJ, in its current form, does not aim to address this type of issues" (90). In this analysis, Gavrielides presumes a limited criminal justice scope for RJ rather than addressing it as a set of values for how to live together peacefully — as suggested by Howard Zehr. Likewise, Kathleen Daly (2002) hopes to tell the "real story" of RJ on the basis of her research experiences in one specific area of the world, the South Pacific. Canadian RJ practitioners, particularly those on the West Coast, might not recognize themselves in these academics' claims and conclusions. Since the promise for change is greatest when RJ focuses on values in being (what we are) and process (what we do and how), attempts to circumscribe it within limited realms of experience may be undesirable or, at the very least, premature.

Disagreement on a specific and comprehensive articulation of RJ yields its own problems. As Sandra Walklate notes, "there is a lack of clarity concerning what restorative justice actually means. It is in part this lack of clarity that also renders this policy open to manipulation" (2005: 167). She raises critical questions about the lack of rigour in questioning RJ, and again in the specific experience of the U.K., with reference to the South Pacific. RJ in these areas tends to be practised through official bodies such as government ministries and police agencies, unlike in British Columbia, where most RJ programs are community-based.

Critical questions, however, seem to flavour RJ dialogue in North America so that enquiries into power and safety at the level of practice are common. However, Bazemore cautions that such concerns may affect the ability of RJ to work within the current system:

> As a reality check, it is important to acknowledge that it is pretty much only restorative justice proponents who think about and debate issues such as coercion and the value of informal vs. formal process. Although we should embrace a vision in which there is no coercion or need for formal rules, if we don't want to feel like failures in all efforts to implement restorative justice, our standard of comparison, at least for now, should not be some otherworldly ideal, but the current coercive, retributive/crime control system. (2000: 472–73)

On a different note, questions about power and safety in RJ processes can also explore its symbolic and "mystical" characteristics, features that pull it out of the realm of the retributive system. Practitioners witnessing transformative moments in RJ processes may be more attuned to the subtle effects of power and safety. For example, Ida Hydle writes:

> As a student of Norwegian restorative justice I see not only the rituality of the encounter between parties and mediators or facilitators. In anthropology the study of ritual is closely linked to the study of magic. It is not often easy to separate the field of magic from ritual belief. As Seymore-Smith (1986: 175) says, "Magic is ritual which is motivated by a desire to obtain a specific effect, magic being seen as the attempt to manipulate... spiritual forces or agencies by ritualized means."... The late modern Norwegian experience of magic within the conflict resolution ritual seems to me, both as an outsider and as an insider (I have actually experienced it), to be the unexpected and unexplainable moment when disagreement about the act of malevolence is turned into agreement about acts of restoration, restitution, and perhaps reconstruction of dignity. I have experienced how this procedure of restoration continues among the parties as if self-contained once the mediators leave the room. In the criminal court, control of the ritual lies in the hands of the legal professionals, the specialist magicians.... For the parties in restorative justice, the roots of the magic may lie in their influence over control of the ritual as well as the fact that a prospective resolution is totally in their own hands—with the possibility of forgiveness as an act of the future. (2006: 263–64)

The salient factor, of course, is the willingness to consider conflict and its resolution as the property of its owners, rather than of criminal justice professionals. Using the current system as a standard of comparison confines RJ to the examination of elements familiar to the conventional system, while examining the elements of RJ that differentiate it from this system — as in the "magic" of the moment when conflict is transformed — opens our understanding of conflict to dimensions that we may not have considered before.

Just Another Criminal Justice Program?

The discussion to this point leads us to a common concern about interpreting RJ as a program rather than a larger vision. Generally, the notion of RJ as program is endemic to practices that are directed by, or imbedded in, the current criminal justice system. Government-led, or top-down, RJ programs will be limited by the desire for them to be consonant with existing retributive practices; that is, RJ processes will be allowed to exist only insofar as they do not challenge the core elements of the retributive system. This relegates RJ to an "add-on" status and, given its less formal processes, usually means that mostly low-end conflicts are sent to RJ, opening it to criticisms of widening the net of criminal justice.

One effect of a limited, RJ-as-program approach is the need to subject it to existing standards. A problem with RJ, according to some, is its failure to provide a crime control blueprint that can successfully challenge the status quo (locking up offenders) (Levrant et al. 1999: 22–23). Theoretical rigour and evidence of the efficacy of RJ are important prerequisites for overall system change in "the policy world in which criminal justice organizations exist" (Lemley 2001: 61). Proponents of RJ programs working within the existing system are thus constrained by the expectations of the system, whether or not these expectations resonate with the larger vision of RJ. This view of RJ also precludes restorative practices in schools and other social institutions, formal or informal.

A strength of RJ is its capacity to expand the lens of enquiry into conflict such that it includes a wider range of issues than is afforded by the retributive questions: "Was a crime committed or a rule violated? Who did it? What do they deserve?" The current political trend of simplifying unwanted behaviours and actions by criminalizing them means that the deeper meanings of social problems remain unexplored. Kent Roach explains:

> The criminalization of politics occurs when social, economic, cultural, and political problems are addressed primarily through criminal justice reforms…. Restorative and aboriginal justice are less conducive to the criminalization of politics than retributive justice because they provide a means to relate offending to larger issues…. The holistic approach of restorative and aboriginal justice resists the urge to simplify complex behaviour. The potential of restorative justice to relate crime to these larger issues is one of its greatest strengths. (2000: 274)

The idea that conflicts can be mined for evidence of bigger problems lends itself to a discussion of RJ as harm prevention, which is the focus of Chapter 10. The implications of Roach's comments, however, go beyond the criminal justice perspective reflected by the palaver participants. The criminalization of social problems has the opposite effect of RJ: the retributive system places the primary responsibility for issues like mental health, poverty, education and so on into the realm of criminal justice, which is not set up structurally or conceptually to address these issues. Everything is reduced to individual "bad" people making "bad" choices, without meaningful consideration of larger social forces.

The idea of RJ as a program has the effect of compromising the healing of three of the main stakeholders in the conflict — commonly referred to as victims, offenders and the community. The fourth stakeholder — the government — is the source of this compromise, since it is generally the need to comply with government processes that makes it difficult to prioritize the needs of the main party stakeholders. Martin Wright (2002: 664–65) offers several suggestions for a more victim-sensitive justice in the United Kingdom that would require greater government flexibility. Acknowledging that criminal procedure is not always the best way of handling acts that might be labelled crime, he argues that there be an option to address these acts through civil mediation. He also suggests that offences committed by strangers to the victim be divided into categories of seriousness as determined by the effect on the victim rather than by law. Further, system personnel would have to be trained in victim awareness and RJ principles. And finally, the system would have to include more community involvement. Concerns are commonly raised about how victims fare when RJ is used as a criminal justice program; but perhaps the concern should be about how victims fare in the retributive system, where they are used as a means to an end (to successfully convict the accused) rather than being seen as ends in themselves (within a process that includes meaningful assistance to victims before, throughout and following the RJ encounter).

Moving our focus from victims of harm to the individuals who have committed the harm, RJ programs attached to the criminal justice system tend to follow that system's expectations for law-breakers. Usually this means reparation that has some concrete connection to the circumstances of the offence. Less attention, if any, is paid to the implications of harm-doing to future actions by the perpetrator. Considering recidivism, Gwen Robinson and Joanna Shapland note:

> Instead of thinking about restorative justice as a new-style intervention — something which is "done to" offenders — we might be better advised to re-frame restorative justice as an opportunity to facilitate a desire, or consolidate a decision, to desist. Desistance, by definition, implies crime reduction. Those agencies which have crime reduction as their primary aim might find it helpful to start to think in terms of restorative justice as a key tool (providing, of course, that they can offer a proper service to victims as well). We have suggested that, to the extent that such encounters are voluntarily entered into by offenders, there is a high likelihood that at least some will take the opportunity to participate as a means of consolidating or reinforcing a decision to desist. For such offenders, the opportunity to express or discharge feelings of shame/guilt/

remorse is likely to be more significant than exposure to "shaming" by others. Further, access to opportunities to develop social and/or human capital may be crucial to the maintenance of momentum on the road to desistance. Looked at another way, we might argue that for such offenders, the restorative justice encounter may serve to maximize their motivation or "responsivity" to engage with other sources of "rehabilitative" help. But, by the same token, and to reiterate a point made above, the absence of such opportunities may be equally decisive: an intention to desist may be undone in the face of a lack of social support and/or other (appropriate) "rehabilitative" resources. (2008: 352–53)

The implication is that failing to use RJ as anything other than an add-on represents a lost opportunity — an opportunity to support people who have committed harm by taking them through a long-term process that goes beyond the specific act in question and instead focuses on their future actions. RJ as a program is usually limited by the need to "close the file," an imperative of the formal system.

Community-based programs use volunteers to facilitate RJ encounters and are governed by volunteer community boards. Other community volunteers may participate as mentors to individuals (usually offenders) following an RJ encounter. However, when RJ operates as an add-on program — that is, when it is used as a "softer" alternative to the range of punitive responses undertaken by legal institutions — it tends to undervalue the input of community members who do not have a direct personal stake in the conflict, on the basis that they are not professionals with institutional accountability. Braithwaite argues that one underestimated potential of RJ processes is that they offer a meaningful space for individual democratic participation in the matters of one's own community:

One reason restorative justice is popular is that it hands a little piece of power back to the ordinary people. We have become such mass democracies that face-to-face meetings on important questions of governance only include the elite. Not only are New England town meetings a democratic form that is hard to translate to a mass society, but also most citizens do not want to participate in community meetings. Most citizens do want to attend restorative justice conferences, however, when asked by a victim or offender to come along to support them. There is something humbling and ennobling about being asked to help someone in trouble; people tend to be honored to be chosen as a supporter. The personal touch makes it a little opportunity to salvage some democratic participation, and the evidence indicates that most people relish being able to participate…. The procedural justice findings, moreover, show this feature of "process control" by ordinary citizens engenders a sense of fairness. (2007: 689–90)

Facilitating communal participation in the process of conflict resolution offers individuals something further, both in revisiting community values and developing personal skills that enhance peaceful civil conduct. And the more peaceful the social conduct of individuals, the less there is a need for, and the expense of, formal institutional intervention in their lives. This is democracy as lived experience rather than as mere ideology.

Finally, we consider the role of government in the limitations of RJ as a criminal justice program. One critique of RJ within institutions is that professionals, rather than community volunteers, facilitate and safeguard the resolution process. Indeed, the spectre of liability in a risk-focused society might well, for these reasons alone, exclude the efforts of civilians. Christie's characterization of "professional conflict thieves" evokes images of lawyers, probation officers, clinical therapists and so on. In this context, ordinary citizens, neighbours and friends are not "qualified" to help others in the processing of conflict. However, Susan Olson and Dzur Albert argue that there is a role for professionals in RJ that still affords meaningful inclusion while protecting legal requirements: "As democratic *professionals*, those involved in restorative justice are responsible for ensuring that the core legal value of fairness to offenders is not sacrificed. As *democratic* professionals, they are responsible for nurturing citizen participation in the process" (2004: 172).

A Holistic, Expansive View of Restorative Justice

Zehr's description of RJ as "a kind of coherent value system that gives us a vision of the good" offers an excellent starting point for an expansive exploration of RJ. Rigorous attention to RJ principles and processes alone is not sufficient to guarantee healthy treatment of, and outcomes for, participants. We delve into the implications of this more fully in Chapter 6. For now, we consider what an expansive view of RJ might be and what it might mean for our understanding of harm and how to respond to it.

In a debate on the confusion between community justice and restorative justice, M. Kay Harris argues that the key to honouring both perspectives "lies in developing greater consensus around the *core values and goals* underlying these evolving orientations and then *holding all proposed practices up against those standards*" (2004: 119, emphasis added). The argument is simple: RJ is based on core values and must be evaluated on the basis of these values. If an RJ program or organization is based on the values of respect, honesty and caring, for example, the measure of how well we are doing will be based on whether the people served by the process report that they were treated with respect, honesty and caring. In the words of Gandhi, "We must *be* the change we wish to see in the world."

Chapter 5 looks at what happens when the RJ paradigm meets the legal paradigm. This is where the holistic vision of RJ based on values comes face-to-face with the rules-and-rights vision of the legal system. Braithwaite suggests a legal approach to RJ values based on existing international covenants and declarations, such as the following, which include respect for fundamental human rights (2000a: 438–39):

- The Universal Declaration of Human Rights;
- The International Covenant on Economic, Social, and Cultural Rights;
- The International Covenant on Civil and Political Rights and Its Second Optional Protocol;
- The United Nations Declaration on the Elimination of Violence Against Women; and
- The Declaration of Basic Principles of Justice for Victims of Crime and Abuse of Power.

Human rights values are central to RJ practices, but it is best if the values are lived rather than being rules to enforce; as A.J. Muste said, there is no way to peace, peace *is* the way (1942). Declan Roche notes that values and process are central to understanding and "doing" restorative justice (2001: 351). We sometimes refer to the kernel of this idea as *values-based processes* — that the processes we use to handle conflict model the core values we share in the community.

Highlighting process as something that is bound more to values than rules (as in the rules of evidence and procedure familiar in legal systems) is a significant feature of a holistic vision of RJ. Speaking specifically of circle processes, Carolyn Boyes-Watson notes, "It is the quality of the process which remains paramount to defining restorative justice and to preserving what is most promising about restorative justice as a source of institutional change. It is the process which enables the issue of responsibility to be understood as simultaneously individual and collective" (2000: 449). The argument here is that a goal of RJ is to *animate* values in a broader group than just the immediate stakeholders. Individual responsibility is the focus of criminal justice; RJ processes, which are more inclusive of supporters and the community at large, afford the potential for examining responsibility and other values in a broader context. This speaks to the idea of RJ beyond the silo of criminal justice, as noted by Barbara Gray and Pat Lauderdale:

> The success of restorative justice depends on a society's traditional preventative structures and practices working together to create

justice and prevent injustice. Focusing only upon restorative aspects of justice without incorporating existing preventative mechanisms creates injustice. It breaks the web of justice and leaves individuals and the community without the necessary cultural foundational structures to heal and prevent crime. (2006: 33)

This reminder of the important component of social justice to RJ holds promise for the notion of RJ as community development.

A broader view of restorative justice invites us to consider discussions in criminology on the problematic limitations of the concept of crime itself. Crime is a legal construction; there is nothing intrinsically unique to all acts that we call crimes. As such, crime has no ontological reality.[1] Even killing, which would seem to be a universal crime, is not always a crime (for example, state-sanctioned wars, law enforcement use of force or self-defence). When we say crime has no ontological reality, we are saying that there is nothing integral to every criminal act that crosses provincial, state or international boundaries and makes the act a crime, except for the legal designation as such. Legal categories of crime are not integral to the acts themselves, as laws constantly change and what could be a crime yesterday may not be tomorrow. "Crime," then, is a construct and not a thing unto itself.

That said, we all recognize that there are acts that call for our attention and intervention. Louk Hulsman (1986) refers to these as "problematic situations," and since there are many different kinds of problems that fall into the category of crimes, there are no standard responses that will be effective for all of them. Paddy Hillyard and Steve Tombs (2007) further argue that the vast majority of acts defined as crimes do not cause much personal hardship to victims (and many crimes are victimless), while many acts that cause serious harm are not even considered crimes. They suggest an alternative designation of "social harms," which would encompass physical, financial/economic, cultural and emotional/psychological harms. The conceptual shift from "crime" to "harm" also opens up the possibility of a greater variety of responses than those at the disposal of formal criminal justice systems. Simon Pemberton bluntly asserts: "There seems little point to be continually tinkering around the edges of a failing system, rather the challenge appears to be to promote alternative and more productive responses to a wider range of harms, and arguably more serious harms, than the criminal justice system currently deals with" (2007: 31). He suggests that a social harms perspective should be detached from the criminal justice system and more progressively located in the discipline of social policy. Social harms may be defined as cases in which people are harmed by the non-fulfillment of their needs, specifically needs that are essential for human well-being rather than mere wants or desires (37).

This crime-to-harm debate in criminology is clearly relevant to the arena of restorative justice. Indeed, it neatly encapsulates the first of the three pillars of RJ described by Zehr: harms and needs (2002).[2] It also speaks to the idea of an expansive holistic vision of RJ, one that is not contained within a criminal justice framework but encompasses a larger terrain of social life. If we speak about harms and needs, we can talk about conflicts with family and friends, in community groups, in schools, in corporate-community relations and so on. Harris explains the importance of a healing imperative within RJ, as a response to harm:

> Many of us who embrace a restorative justice orientation see that as representing a commitment to healing, and our understanding of healing does not end with direct efforts to assuage pain and repair injury resulting from a specific crime or conflict. Rather, we envision action to promote the overall health and well-being of those involved, conditions which have physical, emotional, mental, and spiritual dimensions. In this view, restorative justice means a demonstrated commitment to mutual care, with a corollary emphasis on relationships and a recognition that healthy individuals do not exist in isolation. Hence, restorative justice requires attention to the network of relationships and circumstances in which individuals are embedded. (2004: 120)

The suggestion that the healing of harms is inextricably linked to relationships is a central theme in RJ generally, not just the expansive view. But within the expanded RJ vision, we are free to explore the myriad relationships of participants, as sources of both harm and healing, outside the strict parameters of a criminal justice conflict.

Conclusion

The story of Elizabeth and Charles reflects a number of themes covered in this chapter and is told in the context of criminal justice. But the mediated encounter between the two was not a necessary function of the criminal justice system; indeed, most violent crimes never result in RJ dialogues between victims of harms and those who have harmed them. The story reveals the impact of social harm, both on the person who was robbed and the one who stole. It outlines the limitations of criminal justice for addressing the needs of the parties preceding and following the robbery and offers a narrative of possibility for addressing these needs.

A good way for understanding the difference between criminal justice and restorative justice lies in the questions implicit in each paradigm. Zehr summarizes these questions (2002: 21):

Criminal Justice	*Restorative Justice*
What laws have been broken?	Who has been hurt?
Who did it?	What are their needs?
What do they deserve?	Whose obligations are these?

One advantage of RJ is that the questions asked centre the victim in the conflict equation while also considering the needs of the harm-doer. It responds to the protocol referred to by Dennis Maloney in his thought experiment, introduced at the beginning of the book. The criminal justice questions do not include a meaningful reference to the victim, while the RJ questions do. The RJ focus also has the advantage of forcing us to consider both individual and social problems and how we might best respond to these. And the final question speaks to the looming desire to discern accountabilities of both individuals and communities, as we take responsibility for what we have or have not done in the context of harm.

Notes

1. Ontology is a branch of philosophy that studies existence or "being."
2. The other two pillars are obligations and engagement.

5

Restorative Justice and
the Retributive Legal Context

Opening the Heart Within Systems

(Following are excerpts from a transcribed interview with an anonymous director of a secure Department of Youth Services detention facility in Massachusetts.)

My concept of restorative justice and circles was almost nonexistent. I'm on the conservative end of the department. I think in terms of schedules, rules. Things are usually black and white as far as policies go, more of a military nature. By the second day of the training, I could not see the Circle working in detention at all.

When we were doing the guidelines for the Circle, confidentiality came up. Well, I said I have no solution, because I will not agree to that, and therefore it's never gonna work in detention.... It just can't. Treatment, maybe, but never detention. Then we had a break, thank god, because I had a migraine headache by then. I was just so miserable.... I can't even tell you. I thought this is awful. I'll be very honest with you, I didn't want to go back for the last two days. If it were up to me, I would have left.

So I'm standing on the corner with Harold [Gatensby] having a cigarette with my coffee, and in my sarcastic tone, I said, "Oh, this is going great," and he said, "Yes, it is going great." And he was serious! I said, "How could you say that?" And he said, just let the process work. You'll see, a solution will come." Thank god I didn't go home the first or second day, because I would have said, "waste of time."

We came to an understanding really that you can agree to disagree. But what was really important was for me to tell them something. There were people in that Circle who were anti-system and that bothered me. Like they have no idea who I am. I consider myself to be — or was at one time — anti-system too, especially growing up. My purpose for coming into the department was because I didn't like some of the things going on in the community, and I figured I would go in and change some of those things. I believed that was possible to some degree. So I challenged people at that Circle, "You people who are anti-system, if you don't like the system, why don't you join it and change it?" I mean I really do believe that.

By the third day, I thought, well, maybe this Circle is good, maybe if we have a small number of kids, just the good kids. But then I learned that you gotta be inclusive of everyone in Circle, so I'm like, "Oh my god, it's not gonna work, there's just no way." Then by the final night I thought, "Okay, I'll take the risk, because I'm tired of seeing the same kids over and over and over again. They go home, they come back, and it's just a revolving door."

I got excited because there were a few kids in the Circle training who were really hardened, like those I see at DYS [Department of Youth Services] too. At the beginning of the four days, I thought to myself, "They're gonna get nothing out of this and neither am I." But little by little, I saw them pushing themselves to engage. I think they felt safe in the Circle and that said something to me, because that's one of the problems we have in detention: you don't have enough time for kids to feel safe. The Circle seemed to expedite the way they feel connection and are willing to talk. So that was one of the things that impressed me, observing these kids. No one was pushing them saying you must talk, but the whole concept of Circles is very welcoming to them. They feel comfortable to just say things. I thought that was extremely impressive. (in Carolyn Boyes-Watson 2008: 176–79)

✺ ✺ ✺

This story tells of an encounter, at a personal level, of the criminal justice system with one restorative justice process — the circle. The circle holds much symbolic weight for a number of reasons. In a circle there is no hierarchical structure, no sage on the stage, no beginning and no end. Circles are conducive to dialogue because their structure accommodates individual expression, one by one in turn, around and around until the issue is worked out or opposing groups understand each other better. Further, circles are grounded in core RJ values; these values are the terms by which the dialogue occurs. That is, the dialogue is governed by keepers who remind participants of the need to use respect, honesty, fairness and so on, in each one's expression of their own thoughts and needs. Circles help to build relationships and deepen understanding of each other's perspectives on issues that affect us all. They remind us of the important ideal of integrity: that we will endeavour to act on our values at all times, even when having difficult conversations, while at the same time understanding that as fallible humans we will also make mistakes along the way.

Contrast this ideal and process with the criminal justice system in which the youth detention administrator in this story worked. Criminal justice itself is hierarchical, and within it, prisons are the most hierarchical of all, both within the staff and prisoner ranks. The participants come in one door and go out another in a system that is wholly responsive to limits — of space (the prison is a total institution) and time (timetabled routines, sentences of time). There is little need for dialogue, only decisions, which are made by the one in charge. The interactions are governed by rules and policies, and individual conduct is measured by obedience and compliance. No wonder the administrator in the story had trouble seeing the possibility of circle processes in a juvenile detention centre, at least at first. Yet four days later, something had changed. What was the difference?

The administrator is a person occupying a role in a system. It was the person, rather than the role, of the administrator who obviously cared for the kids she worked with; what was important to her was not the kids' compliance with rules but their willingness to open up and talk. The value of circles was in the opening of communication and the affirmation of safety. The administrator person was emotionally engaged with the process, not merely operating with technocratic efficiency. An apt metaphor is the "ghost in the machine," Gilbert Ryle's (1949) critical description of Descartes' mind-body dualism; the administrator is the ghost inside the prison machine. There is a disconnection between the ghost and the machine, which Ryle posed as a criticism of the simplistic dichotomy of Descartes' model. There remains a question of how the person can effect change within the system, how the person and the system mutually interact.

In our introduction to key RJ concepts in Chapter 4, we use Hillyard and Tombs' invitation to reframe the problem as that of harm rather than crime. This shift in terms opens possibilities of engagement within a wider scope and focuses on the things that seem to matter most to us — a civil society based on shared values such as respect, inclusion, fairness, kindness and both physical and emotional safety. If individuals attempted to live their lives in accordance to these values, they would experience fewer harmful events in the long run than they would in a society with a singular focus on post-harm criminal prosecution and punishment. I earlier argued (Elliott 2002: 462):

> Crime prevention — reducing the number and magnitude of harms and numbers of damaged people — is surely more desirable than the fleeting satisfaction of retaliation garnered in punitive retribution. In modern western societies, punishment is not just a word — it is a sentence, literally. As a primary response to crime, locking people up in the vain expectation that this will somehow create safer communities detracts from the real work that must be done.

A focus on harm also reframes our response to one of healing over punishment. Often this is the restorative justice deal-breaker — that some acts (fortunately very few) are so brutal and shocking that not only do they require punishment but demand terms of incarceration as well. The use of incarceration for restraint is a different issue than punishment. Prisons, until the past two hundred years, were only used as tools of restraint — to keep people until travelling assizes arrived to try them, or the state hangman arrived to execute them, or until their families paid off their debts. The prison sentence, or the idea of "doing time" for punishment, is a relatively recent innovation.

In this chapter we consider the questions this story poses: how does restorative justice work within formal institutions such as those in the criminal justice system, or schools? Can RJ work within such systems while maintaining its own integrity of values and process? How does the RJ paradigm fit with the rule of law under which democracies operate? We answer these questions by considering some of the areas of interest and concern as they appear in the literature and in the field.

Law and Punishment

Western democracies operate on the basis of the rule of law, an abstract power. Explained by Thomas Paine during the American Revolution in 1776: "For as in absolute governments the king is law, so in free countries the law ought to be king; and there ought to be no other." In a system based on the abstract notion of the rule of law, no one is above the law — not the king and not the elected representative at the top of the government structure. Laws are created or repealed by elected assemblies in democracies and enforced by the administrative bureaux of the government. Police agencies make arrests and collect evidence, the courts process charges in ways that are meant to respect the various laws and legal procedures, corrections agencies carry out sentences in custody or in the community. The exercise of law is intended to be objective, and its practice is monitored for compliance to fair process expectations.

We can understand different dimensions of a phenomenon if we consider its symbols. The symbols for law are remarkably consistent with the characterization just presented. Benjamin Sells explains: "Law is full of overt symbolism. Two of these symbols have been especially enduring: the scales and the sword. The scales are usually taken to represent an approach to justice based on impartial balancing and weighing of evidence. The sword suggests that force and the threat of force are essential attributes for justice" (1996: 39). The woman holding the scales is blindfolded, intimating lack of bias. However, this expectation is difficult for a human being to deliver:

> In both law and science, objectivity's preferred approach is analytic and its preferred analytic tools are abstraction and rationality. Abstraction and rationality are the intellectual work-horses of "objectivity." They are the means by which objectivity works, and, as means, are instructive as to the ends objectivity seeks. Abstraction means "to draw away from," while "rationality" connotes "computation, sum, or number."... What does objectivity feel like from within? What are its psychological dimensions? (41)

The rigidity of automated control reflected in this description denies in large measure the flexibility and fluidity of human interactions and the related individual capacities we exercise in our daily lives. In this highly regulated world, the less an objective official relates to the individual at hand, the better. There are consequences to these expectations in human relationships and values generally. It is the dilemma of the demands of objectivity on the subjective human and the effects of this that are significant.

The second symbol in Sells' description is the sword. The connotation here is force and its related themes of coercion, violence and punishment. In Chapter 2 we consider the research on how to teach morality and cultivate conditions amenable to expression of civil behaviours. We suggest that moral education is better expedited through a respect for the individual's autonomy, encouragement of intrinsic motivations and teaching through reasoning and modelling than by threats of force, extrinsic punitive motivators and operant conditioning. Here again, we are confronted by the spectre of punishment, which is another meaning of the sword. Explaining the relationship between law and punishment, Michel Foucault (1987: 33–35) writes:

> If it were self-evident and in the heart, law the would no longer be the law, but the sweet interiority of consciousness. If, on the other hand, it were present in a text, if it were possible to decipher it between the lines of a book, if it were in a register that could be consulted, then it would have the solidity of external things: it would be possible to follow or disobey it. Where then would its power reside, by what force or prestige would it command respect? In fact, the presence of the law is its concealment.
>
> And of transgression. How could one know the law and truly experience [the law], how could one force it to come into view, to exercise its powers clearly, to speak, without provoking it, without pursuing it into its recesses, without resolutely going ever farther into the outside into which it is always receding? How can one see its invisibility unless it has been turned into its opposite, punishment, which, after all, is only the law overstepped, irritated, beside itself?

Foucault's description of law underscores the significance of punishment to legal systems. The sword looms in the background; punishments are the teeth that give the law its bite. Law and punishment are two sides of a coin.

Many attempts have been made over a couple of centuries to deconstruct, rationalize, explain and justify punishment. That it should provoke such attention speaks to our unease with punishment. The core of this unease relates to Wright's sense that "all punishment, in the normal sense of the word, is intended to cause pain and fear, and in some cases, incapacitation" (2003: 5). De Haan expands on this notion of punishment as the deliberate infliction of pain: "Crucial to punishment is that a person be degraded and, literally or symbolically, expelled from his or her community... punishment intends inflicting pain, suffering or loss" (1990: 112). No matter what one thinks of punishment, these descriptions of punishment fairly describe its intents and outcomes. And it seems clear that, at its core, punishment in practice (as opposed to theory) may be about the intentional infliction of harm by agents authorized to do so — be they the state, the school principal or the parent. Punishment connotes justifiable infliction of pain, within the context of a society under the rule of law.

Utilitarian arguments for punishment might consider this justification for the calculated infliction of pain as merely a necessary evil means to a virtuous end — general and specific deterrence. But research evidence from a large study on general deterrence by Kleck and colleagues (2005) contradicted this belief. The researchers conducted telephone interviews with a representative sample of 1,500 people in fifty-four large American urban counties, asking questions used to measure individuals' perceptions of punishment levels with actual punishment levels from official statistics. They found no relationship between peoples' perceptions of the average certainty, severity or swiftness of punishment in their county and the actual sentences of those convicted of crimes. This finding held, in the even weaker correlations in a sample of self-reported arrestees between perceived and actual punishment levels. People are not inclined or able to understand and remember punishment ranges for offences, even when they are criminally active, and thus are not susceptible to the presumed deterrent influences of longer prison sentences. Possible reasons for this are that they do not expect to be caught (based on a belief that the crime plan is foolproof); they want to be caught (prison seems to be a better alternative than homelessness or an unsafe home); they don't have the mental capacity to make reasonable judgments about cause and effect (for example, in the case of people with mental disorders or fetal alcohol spectrum disorder [FASD]); or the pull of a substance addiction in the moment is stronger than the concern for consequences later.

The collective will to punish, of course, precedes the criminal law's ability to do so. Notwithstanding the research evidence that demonstrates the inefficiency of punishment to change offending behaviour either as a deterrent or after the fact, some Western societies are prolific punishers. To understand why this is so, we begin with the idea of the social contract. Offering a cogent explanation of this idea, Jeffrey Reiman wrote:

> The social contract asks us to think of our laws as if they are the product of a voluntary and reasonable agreement among all citizens. Though different authors describe this exercise in different ways, it has a general form. We start by imagining a condition in which no

one has political or legal authority, commonly called "the state of nature." In this condition, people are to consider and finally agree to some set of political and economic institutions…. The social contract is not a historical theory; it is a *mental experiment*. And it is a mental experiment designed to yield a normative conclusion. The state of nature is a mental construct, an imaginary place, and the agreement in it is an imaginary agreement. It does not ask whether you do or did agree to the rules that govern your state's institutions, rather it is a way of asking whether it would be reasonable for you to do so. If it would be, then that is a strong argument that the laws and institutions of your state are just — or just enough — and its authority legitimate enough for citizens to be obligated to obey. (2007: 4–5)

This description of the "deal" we operate under in democratic societies is a good launching point for another view of the relationship between law and punishment, one that includes the element of emotion. J.M. Barbalet describes the conventional account of the relationship between crime, human emotions and law, "whereas crime might express emotion, emotion is extinguished in the operations of law" (2002: 279). He then offers an alternative, in the work of a relatively unknown sociologist:

The Danish sociologist, Svend Ranulf, offered an appreciation of the relationship between emotions and criminal law that is very different…. The question Ranulf addressed was: what social conditions are required for the advent of criminal law? He characterized criminal law as a "disinterested tendency to inflict punishment" (1964 [1938]: 2) and argued that such a tendency arises in societies in which there is a developed lower middle class. (280)

The emotions generated by the controlled strains of a lower middle-class — those who "buy in" to the social contract but are at the lesser end of the material wealth scale — manifest as moral indignation directed toward citizens who would break this contract for individual purposes, those who do not "buy in." These emotions often fuel a get-tough belief about criminal law-making, at least in the political realm. The "disinterested tendency to inflict punishment" is another interesting legal expectation — that the application of law be objective and cleansed of any emotion. In a punishment-by-proxy social arrangement, the person punishing has no real relationship with the one being punished. It is similar to the prospect of a teenager having their parents pay someone else to stay in their house to make sure they don't leave when they're grounded, instead of doing it themselves. Ranulf saw the emotion as the catalyst for the necessity of state punishment and the punishment administered by "disinterested" agencies. But agencies are animated by human actors. We are reminded of Sells' questions: What does objectivity feel like from within? What are its psychological dimensions?

The particularly keen impulse to punish in the United States has residual effects in Canada, with some focus at the beginning of the 2008 federal election on new tough crime-control policy offerings before the stock market disaster of early October of that year. Whitman looked back in American history to 1833 and the work of de Tocqueville and de Beaumont, who studied America's then admired prisons and presented their findings to their native French society. U.S. moral leadership in the world had its roots in the way it handled criminal punishment in the early nineteenth century. The society de Tocqueville and de Beaumont studied was a nascent democracy, built from the seeds of new world visions of equality and freedom. These values were extended into the developing criminal justice system, which was in stark contrast to the shaming and violent punishments of the old world. The rational use of law was accompanied by a measured use of punishment. James Whitman points out that a different contemporary European approach to punishment has usurped the American claim to moral leadership:

> European punishment is relatively mild largely because the Europeans have embraced norms of dignity in punishment. This means that they have rejected many practices still used in the United States, such as the use of degrading prison uniforms and barred doors on prison cells. But it means more than that: it means that European law works systematically to guarantee that criminal offenders will be treated as human beings, entitled to a certain high minimum of respectful treatment. This insistence that offenders are human beings contributes mightily to the making of a punishment system that resists the inevitable human urge to punish harshly — to show contempt when we punish. (2007: 264–65)

Thomas Trenczek, on the other hand, offers a contemporary vision of criminal law that is judicious about its use of punishment, both in form and intensity:

> A penal law that is built upon the principles of autonomy and freedom has to allow and to lighten the voluntary assumption of responsibility and cannot block up a socially constructive path. The fulfillment of the facts of the (criminal) case is a necessary but not a sufficient condition for a sanction. The necessity of a penal sanction does not follow from a behavior which meets the facts of the case but from the impossibility of the enforcement of priority alternatives. (2002: 31)

In other words, we should consider punishment when there is no possibility of anything else. We can extend this further by arguing that, in making decisions about punishment, we need to consider the needs of everyone affected — those who inflicted the harm, those who suffered it and the people around them. This vision of law opens the prospects for restorative justice.

Restorative Justice and the Law

Let us begin with a couple of core restorative justice assumptions at the forefront. Zehr's (2002) three pillars of RJ — harms and needs, obligations and engagement — are not well expressed in the criminal justice system. Instead, the focus of criminal law is on crimes and punishment of offenders, symbolic debts to society and separation of the parties in conflict. At first glance, it seems unlikely that RJ could find a hospitable resting point within the existing legal system. The three main questions asked by each paradigm also mean that the foci are on two different expectations. Uncomfortable questions are raised. For example, if restorative justice is about healing harm, and punishment (a necessary corollary of law) is the deliberate infliction of harm, aren't we faced with an important contradiction? If RJ is about values-based processes, how are we to reconcile this expectation with the hierarchical, exclusive and rule-bound processes of the legal system? Using the specific context of sentencing circles, Dan Markel adds other issues to the discussion:

> Because restorative justice sentencing circles operate voluntarily and in an environment largely devoid of standards to ensure that similar crimes are punished similarly, restorative justice, with all its attendant reliance on the role of luck — and the outsourcing of punishment authority away from the state and into the unaccountable hands of "community" figures — effectively abandons the pursuit of the goal of equal justice under law. Restorative justice, then, risks leaving two rule of law "casualties" in its wake: equality under law as well as certainty of sanctions. (2007: 1409)

The expectations of RJ can also be quite limited if held tightly within the existing legal framework. The expression of remorse by convicted people in courts, for example, is fraught with potential misplays exacerbated by the public context of court. The accused might be limited by ability or time, or the victims might not be in attendance to hear the apology. In spite of any altruistic intention, the efforts to apologize might be interpreted as attempts to manipulate the situation for a lighter sentence. Conversely, apologies made in an RJ context offer better opportunities for convicted people to offer their own expressions of remorse in the presence of those most affected by their actions (Szmania and Mangis 2005: 356–58).

The limitations of the criminal justice system to motivate and support changes in the harm-doer's social conduct are located in the punishment model. As we saw in Chapter 2, the research shows that these changes are supported by means other than, and conceptually different from, punitive measures. Tom Tyler (2006) argues that, of the two approaches to dealing with rule/law breaking — the punishment-focused, sanction-based model and the RJ model — the latter, with its greater focus on connecting with people who have harmed others and activating internal values, holds greater promise in cultivating moral development.

Concerns have also been raised about the potential conflicts RJ poses to the rule of law itself. In a meta-analysis of many RJ programs, veteran RJ researchers Lawrence Sherman and Heather Strang argue that this is a matter of interpretation:

> On the evidence so far, RJ does not conflict with the rule of law. Nor does it necessarily conflict with the basic framework of common law. What it does offer is an alternative to conventional interpretations of that framework as they have developed in the industrial world. As a public safety strategy for the post-industrial era, RJ may offer better results within the same basic principles. By providing more opportunities for questions and answers, face-to-face or otherwise, it may actually make law far more accessible to the people. The evidence of satisfaction with RJ suggests that it may reinforce the rule of law. There is no evidence that wider use of RJ would undermine the rule of law. (2007: 45)

Andrew Ashworth, initially much more sceptical of RJ from a legal perspective, conceded in earlier academic RJ discussions that state-run criminal justice has, from the outset, offered "diminishing recognition of any entitlements of the victim. Indeed, attention to the interests of the victims of crime seems to have reached its nadir in the middle part of this century" (1993: 277). An unfortunate and unfair cost of the modern adversarial system is that all contests are between the accused and the state, which in Canada is represented by the queen (the "R", or "Regina," in "*R. v Smith*"). Given this structural reality, it is no wonder that victims feel orphaned by the very system they believe exists to protect them. This reality cannot be fixed by any conventional recourse to limiting offender rights or increasing punishment of convicted individuals. These responses are still focused on the offender rather than victim.

In spite of these trepidations, RJ has managed to be incorporated into systems of law in several jurisdictions. The first example is New Zealand, which legislated RJ processes into its *Children, Young Persons and Their Families Act* (1989), shifting the framework and processes for dealing with child abuse and neglect and criminal offending to a family group conferencing model of decision-making (Maxwell and Hayes 2006). This incorporated extended family members and system professionals into a collaborative process aimed to better address core problems. All but one Australian jurisdiction (Victoria) has had statutory frameworks for restorative justice since 1994. Outcomes of these practices have been evaluated in most jurisdictions, demonstrating clearly the possibility of incorporating RJ processes at the pre-sentence stage of both adult and juvenile systems (Maxwell and Hayes 2006: 148).

The Canadian experience with RJ and the legal system is represented in examples, the *Youth Criminal Justice Act* (YCJA, 2003) and the *Gladue* (1999) decision. The YCJA incorporates aspects of restorative justice ideals and processes in the form of "extrajudicial measures," to be used by police and crown attorneys in lieu of the youth justice court system. Police officers had already begun to use these measures, particularly those which have been called "informal cautioning" in New Zealand and Australia. Also included in these measures were "extrajudicial sanctions," known as "alternative measures" under the predecessor *Young Offenders Act*. Of particular resonance with restorative justice processes is the YCJA's provision under s. 19 of a "conference," defined as a group of persons convened to provide advice in accordance with this section of the legislation.[1]

One Canadian province — Nova Scotia — has taken a systematic and encompassing approach to mandating the use of RJ measures within its youth criminal justice system since 2001. Bruce Archibald and Jennifer Llewellyn (2006) note the interests of criminal justice players in the founding of the Nova Scotia Restorative Justice program. The sweep of this approach was enabled by the interconnection of criminal justice players in the province who were educated in RJ philosophy and processes and motivated to take it to the forefront of the youth justice agenda. The authors point out some of the challenges experienced in efforts to institutionalize comprehensive restorative justice in Nova Scotia. Key for our concerns about the compatibility of RJ and legal system practices is their critical comment: "A significant question for the future development of the program is whether there will be the governmental flexibility to allow for and encourage the sort of cooperation and integration required to support a holistic, relational conception of justice. Or rather, will there be continued compartmentalization and adherence to departmental and programmatic silos leading to turf wars over budget allocations?" (340). "Silo thinking" is a common complaint among RJ practitioners across the country, where efforts to holistically address the aftermaths of harm are stymied by artificial institutional limits. It makes crime prevention efforts involving various government partners a nightmare of conflicting or disinterested mandates, and movement schedules that are reminiscent of geological time clocks. But this also offers us a few clues about some of the changes that might need to be made to government institutions as they struggle to meet the needs of citizens they exist to serve.

As intimated previously, the optics of RJ are also suspected of being at odds with the legal system's goal of sentencing uniformity. The image of myriad community-based RJ programs processing conflicts with attention only to the needs and wishes of process participants rather than sentencing norms is unwelcome to formal, objective systems. On this issue, Michael O'Hear notes:

> I have argued that the term "uniformity" means quite different things to different people. It turns out that the notion of similar treatment for the similarly situated (and different treatment for the differently situated) is not nearly as simple as it sounds. The uniformity ideal merely begs the question: What exactly makes two offenders similar in ways that matter to us? Uniformity is an empty concept without some underlying theory about the purposes and priorities of the criminal justice system. (2005: 307)

Of course, the system doesn't provide this theory, although experienced criminal justice practitioners well understand O'Hear's point. Working with people attunes us to their individual subjectivities, to the differences in peoples' life experiences and how these play into the harm in question. The problem may be not that RJ doesn't attenuate well to the demands of the criminal justice system but rather that the criminal justice system doesn't attend well to the needs of people.

Finally, there is the question of public acceptance of RJ in the context of public awareness and understanding of the current criminal justice system. Common responses are that RJ measures are soft or lenient in comparison with punitive legal sentences. This suggests that the role of emotions remains a critical factor in public perceptions of criminal justice, as suggested by Svend Ranulf and also by Mead and Durkheim (noted in Chapters 2 and 3). To this end, Gromet and Darley (2006) conducted a study testing peoples' perceptions of the acceptability of RJ procedures. In this study, respondents were asked to assign cases to RJ or retributive justice. When cases were returned to them for judgments about sentences, they made considerable reductions in sentence for cases where conference facilitators and victims were satisfied with outcomes; when this satisfaction was missing, respondents gave the offenders standard sentences for the crime. This suggests that public perception can shift when given more information.

Restorative Justice and System Professionals

It is not an understatement to suggest that the professionalization of criminal justice has resulted in a shift in the kind of relationships that exist between people who have an interest in a conflict. Benjamin Sells is a former lawyer who later became a psychotherapist. These experiences afford him a unique insight into the effects of law practice on the individual human lawyer. The following excerpt from his book on the personal effects of practising law well demonstrates the historical paradox of the current professional credo of impartiality and professional distance in criminal justice:

It is mid-morning in old Athens and a precursor of the modern lawyer has risen to speak on behalf of a litigant. He begins his oration with a personal testament to the litigant's good character, honesty, and forthrightness. Having laid this foundation, the citizen advocate then affirms his personal belief in the rightness of the litigant's cause. He takes his seat and another citizen rises to repeat the litany — I know the litigant to be honest, his cause just, and I cast my lot with his.

In those early days (roughly the second half of the fifth and first half of the fourth century B.C.E.), it was assumed such orators were expressing their personal belief in both the litigant and his cause. Usually these advocates were chosen precisely because of some close personal connection with the litigant.... In a very real sense, they were at once advocates and character witnesses, and it was therefore essential that they be willing to profess their belief in the litigant on the basis of personal knowledge and truth.

It was unthinkable for an orator to argue on behalf of a litigant without this personal conviction. In fact, payment for advocacy was seen as a form of bribery that disgraced both the litigant and advocate.... Only later, in the latter half of the fourth century B.C.E., did professional, paid representation become a common practice. The early predisposition against paid advocacy was based on a belief that it gave the rich an advantage over the poor, and that advocacy on behalf of someone you believed in was part of a citizen's duty. Under this view, paid representation degraded civic responsibility.

We obviously have come a long way. The modern lawyer not only isn't seen as sharing his or her client's views and beliefs, such a correlation of belief is now seen as irrelevant. Not only are lawyers not expected to be character witnesses for their clients, they aren't allowed to be even if they want to. Their job is to advocate the client's position, whatever the lawyer might personally think about it. I remember well my surprise in law school when I learned that a trial lawyer isn't allowed to express his or her personal belief in the rightness or honesty of the client or the client's position. I wasn't allowed to say, "I believe Mary is telling the truth" or "I know John to be an honorable man." Such comments, I was told, were inappropriate, objectionable, and could even lead to a mistrial. On the other hand, such prohibitions notwithstanding, it was permissible (and encouraged as good advocacy) to send these messages subliminally. Although I couldn't say outright that I believed in John or his cause, I could stand beside him in the courtroom, my hand on his shoulder, and call him by his first name in an orchestrated attempt to show I believed he was a good fellow, honest and true. (1996: 163–64)

Many questions can be raised about our current human costs in the arena of criminal justice system (CJS) professionals generally — not only lawyers. Sells writes of the contemporary expectation of a deliberate disconnection between lawyers and their clients. This objective impartiality may be good in theory, but on an interpersonal relational level they are not so easily proscribed by policies and rules. In the trenches, social workers, police officers and correctional officers argue for discretionary privileges in the grey area of criminal justice — the moment of encounter and interaction between the worker and the client. We are right to be concerned about individual abuses of power, especially by state agents, which is why transparency in governance is so important in a democracy. But we must also acknowledge that there is something else at stake for CJS workers in that "encounter" aspect of their jobs and encourage a meaningful dialogue on the this grey area.

A few years ago, a retired prison warden who was a guest speaker in my corrections class gave an example of this grey area. She recounted a hostage-taking that took place in her prison and the orders she was given by more senior personnel in a national headquarters located several provinces away. Knowing who the players were in the incident and understanding the social context in which it was happening, the warden's sense of how to handle the situation to result in the least amount of harm differed from the orders she received. Ultimately, she decided to obey her instincts over the orders and rules, and the situation was resolved with no one being physically hurt. Her remark to the class was something along the lines of: "I decided that I could live with my own conscience a lot easier for disobeying an order from headquarters, than I could for obeying the order and endangering the lives of the staff and prisoners." For this warden, it was the people that mattered the most. It was her subjective, not objective, actions that she relied on.

Given the kinds of tensions expressed by CJS professionals, it is little surprise that many of them are attracted to RJ practices within their institutions.. Probation services are a prime example. In Canada, some police departments also sponsor RJ programs; indeed, the RCMP for a while had a section dedicated to RJ training and programs. Institutional professionals are accustomed to working within heavily structured regulations and policies, while community-based practitioners are used to having more flexibility in modifying restorative practices to meet the needs of particular participants. Tensions are to be expected when the two groups try to work together, particularly when institutional personnel are typically imbued with more authority than community volunteers. Studying the deployment of RJ processes in a criminal justice context and the resulting tensions, James Dignan and his colleagues (2007) described them through an analytical lens of dramaturgy — the art or technique of dramatic composition or theatrical representation. Courtroom processes have long been recognized for their theatrical features. The authors explain how the dramaturgical analysis includes RJ:

> In using [theatrical imagery] we are not suggesting that participants in restorative justice are merely "acting" rôles, which do not reflect their own experiences and perceptions. The offences with which restorative justice deals are real events, causing very real effects and consequences for both victims and offenders. All participants will of course be presenting their own views — that is the essence of restorative justice — though there may be differences in the spontaneity and sincerity with which some of these views are conveyed, as there are in all social encounters. In using the theatrical metaphor, we are suggesting restorative justice may be likened to a reality-based documentary, not a fictional representation. In this, restorative justice is different from criminal justice. Most of the dominant players in criminal justice (judge, prosecutor, defence lawyer) perform *occupational* rôles and are necessarily detached from the events to which the cases in which they are professionally engaged relate. In restorative justice the rôles of the main participants usually relate directly to an event that happened in the course of their everyday lives and activities and in which they were personally involved. (2007: 6–7)

The underlying similarity between adversarial criminal justice and restorative justice, expressed through theatrical imagery, is the focus on storytelling. The tension between these two paradigms comes in *how* the storytelling occurs.

Concerns have also been raised about the potential of CJS tools and expectations to compromise the integrity of restorative practices. Lois Presser and Christopher Lowenkamp (1999), for example, argue for better offender screening in RJ to minimize traumatic impacts on victims. They admit that screening instruments might make RJ resemble formal system processes but might be necessary in communities where people do not know each other

(240). In practice, however, most community-based programs have screening mechanisms of their own, with similar criteria such as the accused must have pleaded guilty or taken responsibility for some significant aspect of the harm in order to be considered for a restorative process. The problem with institutional formality is that flexibility is more difficult; it is one thing to have screening instruments available for use when desired, and another thing to uphold an expectation that the instrument must be used in order to ensure uniformity.

Restorative processes have also permeated other domains of government agency; child protection and social work generally are two key areas. New Zealand's foray into this realm was materialized in family group conferences (FGC) with child and family services, as well as criminal justice. FGCs have been used with mixed results in Hawaii, illuminating some of the problems with the encounter between RJ and existing institutions:

> Shifting the role of the state away from controller of families in the child protective services system to one of regulatory partner with them is extraordinarily difficult. Hawaii's experience suggests that adoption of FGC in the mainstream of child welfare and implementation of its core values, principles, and practices require a reorientation of professional practice and bureaucratic functioning. (Adams and Chandler 2004: 113–14)

Changing a bureaucratic culture within institutions is a formidable task. Social workers working deep in the community in peoples' homes and in the streets have grappled with this problem for a while:

> Social work and social workers have long been concerned with finding ways to make bureaucracies, policies, and procedures responsive to the simultaneous promotion of the autonomy of individuals and the well-being of communities. Staking out this dual focus for the profession has meant that workers have considerable experience working along the fault lines between what formal organizations require through their policies and procedures, including the ways they organize the use of workers' time and allocated resources, and the needs of the people they work with. Social workers well know the dilemmas for families of trying to maintain control over the definition of their situation, especially when faced with multiple, categorical, and frequently conflicting avenues to get the help they need. (Burford and Adams 2004: 21)

The experience of social workers summarizes the tension between RJ and the system and probably also says a lot about the high burnout rate of social workers. Negotiating the relationship between the people in need and the institutions that are ostensibly there to serve them is stressful, not just because of the internal conflict experienced by Sells' lawyers but due to the social workers' inability to motivate service-providers to furnish meaningful and timely support to their clients. In summary, a quandary for professionals generally is the suspicion that the needs of the institutions they work within have become more important than the needs of the people they are meant to serve.

Restorative Justice, Law and Aboriginal People

Gladue is a Supreme Court of Canada decision made in the case of an Aboriginal woman that holds implications for everyone. This is the chief focus of this section but, at the risk of falling into pan-Indian generalities, we begin with thoughts about Aboriginal ways of perceiving the world. Some ideas are useful for understanding the difficulties experienced by Aboriginal people in the CJS.

We begin with Patricia Monture on the subject of law and what it means in one Aboriginal context:

> Whenever I am struggling to understand tradition (that is to say, who I am), I always try to reclaim the meaning of the words in my own language. In the Mohawk language when we say law, it does not really translate directly to the "Great Law of Peace" as many of us have been told. What it really means is "the way to live most nicely together." When I think about courts, when I think about police, when I think about people's experiences at law school, or maybe constitutional negotiation — to really bait you — are these the experiences of law that reflect living nicely together? The Mohawk standard is the standard I carry with me and compare my experiences against. Living nicely together is an onerous standard. (1994: 227)

Monture's message presents a positive model of law. Unlike the prohibitive nature of criminal laws — "Thou shalt not do *this*, or we will do *that* to you" — where we are told what *not* to do, Mohawk law seems to be telling us what we *should* do in a general sense. It is notable that Aboriginal cultures are not inclined to tell anyone what they should do specifically in any situation. Explained by the Mohawk psychiatrist, Clare Brant, "[The] principle of non-interference is all-pervasive throughout our entire culture. We are very loath to confront people. We are very loath to give advice to anyone if the person is not specifically asking for advice. To interfere or even comment on their behaviour is considered rude" (in Ross 1992: 13).

It is a timeworn understanding in Canada that Aboriginal peoples are

overrepresented in the criminal justice system. Beginning with such different starting points on the meaning of law itself, Aboriginal people do not
fare well in the system. This cultural conflict is becoming better understood,
and efforts are being made — with varying degrees of success — to accommodate Aboriginal people in a system that, in many ways, is structurally
and conceptually at odds with traditional ways. It is in this context that we
consider the Supreme Court of Canada decision in *Gladue* (1999).

Jamie Gladue was an off-reserve Aboriginal woman who, in an evening
celebrating her nineteenth birthday, stabbed her common-law husband to
death in a dispute over perceptions of marital infidelity and within a context
of ongoing relational violence. She pleaded guilty to manslaughter and was
sentenced to three years of imprisonment. Gladue appealed, and the British
Columbia Court of Appeal upheld the sentence. The matter was then moved
to the Supreme Court of Canada (SCC), on a question arising from the s.718
statement of the *Criminal Code of Canada* on the purposes and principles of
sentencing. For our purposes, it is s. 718.2 that is of relevance:

> 718.2 A court that imposes a sentence shall also take into consider-
> ation the following principles:
>
> (a) a sentence should be increased or reduced to account for any
>   relevant aggravating or mitigating circumstances relating to the
>   offence or the offender, and, without limiting the generality of
>   the foregoing...
> (b) a sentence should be similar to sentences imposed on similar of-
>   fenders for similar offences committed in similar circumstances;
> (c) where consecutive sentences are imposed, the combined sen-
>   tence should not be unduly long or harsh;
> (d) an offender should not be deprived of liberty, if less restrictive
>   sanctions may be appropriate in the circumstances; and
> (e) all available sanctions other than imprisonment that are reason-
>   able in the circumstances should be considered for all offenders,
>   with particular attention to the circumstances of aboriginal
>   offenders.

The question of whether the trial judge erred in not following the
specific sentencing principle outlined in s.718.2.(e) is addressed in the SCC
decision. The SCC argued that s.718.2(e), with its emphasis on the words
"with particular attention to the circumstances of aboriginal offenders,"
had a remedial purpose that should alter the analysis of judges sentencing
Aboriginal offenders (22–23).

This case also holds significant potential for non-Aboriginal people in
sentencing. As Kent Roach and Jonathan Rudin explain:

The court [in *Gladue*] recognized that s.718 contains not only traditional sentencing goals such as deterrence, denunciation, and
rehabilitation, but "new" restorative goals of repairing the harms
suffered by individual victims and by the community as a whole,
promoting a sense of responsibility and an acknowledgement of
the harm caused on the part of the offender, and attempting to
rehabilitate and heal the offender' [*Gladue* 1999]... [*Gladue*] will
be a leading case whenever any offender asks a court to consider a
sentence that has a restorative purpose. (2000: 362)

Two subsequent cases, *Wells* (2000) and *Proulx* (2000), further challenged the Supreme Court of Canada to refine its thinking on the use of
imprisonment for certain circumstances, notwithstanding s. 718.2(e). Here
the focus is on conditional sentences (s. 742.1) and when to use them, taking
into consideration s. 718.2(e). In both *Wells* and *Proulx*, the sentences were
less than two years, but both offences involved violence: sexual assault and
dangerous driving causing death. These SCC decisions, Roach noted, set up
"a dichotomy between the restorative and punitive purposes of sentencing...
In most cases, so-called restorative sanctions that respond to the needs of
offenders, victims, and the community but do not generally involve the use
of imprisonment will not be appropriate for the most serious offences" (2000:
259).

It is therefore not clear whether *Gladue* will ultimately address the overrepresentation of Aboriginal people in the criminal justice system. As Rudin
notes, the problems experienced by Aboriginal Legal Services of Toronto
in manifesting the benefits of *Gladue* for its clients resulted in the creation of
"Gladue Court" in that city. Further, Roach and Rudin warn: "If conditional
sentences are only used in less serious cases, Gladue may well contribute to
a process of net widening" (2000: 384).

Conclusion

There appear to be many challenges to the accommodation of RJ within
legal institutions, particularly if we are concerned to preserve the integrity
of RJ values in process. Nonetheless, criminal justice is the main terrain in
which the two paradigms currently interact. How well this works is yet un-
determined. Criminal courts are designed to prosecute crimes, not to heal
harms. Criminal justice professionals trained in an adversarial culture may
not be able to easily accommodate RJ philosophy and practices; there is no
concern that the criminal justice system might be co-opted by restorative
justice. In spite of this, however, examples of successful criminal justice and RJ
partnerships exist, where the integrity of RJ values and processes is respected.

The following excerpt from a newspaper article on the aftermath of major conflicts in Africa's Sierra Leone, however, outlines the tension between RJ and formal legal systems:

> The ICC [International Criminal Court] is working on cases in five African countries, and its proponents say high-profile trials will build true protection for human rights. Until now, countries such as Sierra Leone and Liberia have had "a culture of low expectations: The ones who are powerful will get away with whatever they want," says Corinne Dufka, a former investigator for Sierra Leone's special count who now monitors that country and Liberia for Human Rights Watch.
>
> "That has practical implications for democracy. People also expect impunity for corruption…. In Sierra Leone, the efficacy of the special court in helping to establish the rule of law, which is the bedrock for a peaceful society, is very hard to judge — and won't be judged by the indictment or acquittal of 10 people. It's much longer term."
>
> That may be true — but Ms. Dufka, while hugely respected for her knowledge of the conflict, is an American, and a remarkable number of those who support the court and other forms of international justice are also outsiders.
>
> In Africa, critics are more common: They accuse the ICC and other international-justice initiatives of derailing prospects for peace in some of the more intractable conflicts, deepening the gulf between states such as Sudan and the West, and being highly political and subject to a Western agenda. Perhaps more gravely, they say, the courts have done little or nothing at all for victims.
>
> "I'm not putting a price tag on justice, but whose justice is this?" asks John Caulker, who heads an organization called the Forum for Conscience in Freetown. "In whose interest do we have the ICC? I should not be saying this, as a human rights advocate, but when I put on my Sierra Leonean hat, I have to ask: Is this justice to please the international community or to meet the needs of ordinary Sierra Leoneans?"
>
> He runs reconciliation programs in which he meets thousands of people who suffered horribly but know they will never receive redress. "'Yes,' these people say, 'the court is trying those of greatest responsibility, but every day in the road, I have to live with the person who did all the things to me.'" (Nolen 2008)

This excerpt challenges the notion of rule of law as the great panacea for all social ailments. Again, we see the needs of victims subordinated to the mandate of capturing, prosecuting and punishing offenders.

Yet the rule of law is not so contradictory to RJ, if we take into consideration Daniel Van Ness's historical reminder:

> We are used to thinking of criminal law as the means through which government prohibits criminal behavior and punishes criminals. We take for granted the distinction between private and public wrongs, which separates the law of torts from criminal law, a distinction ingrained in our common law tradition. But there is another, older understanding of law that resists this duality, affirming that no matter how we administer the law, one of the primary goals of justice should be to restore the parties injured by crime. (1993: 252–53)

The will to restore people and communities to better health is the motivation that draws many people to the field of criminal justice. Remember the juvenile correctional administrator in the story at the beginning of this chapter: "I consider myself to be — or was at one time — anti-system too, especially growing up. My purpose for coming into the department was because I didn't like some of the things going on in the community, and I figured I would go in and change some of those things." Institutions are still run by people, and, wherever people connect, there is potential for restorative justice.

Note

1. Section 18 of the YCJA also permits for the convening of Youth Justice Committees, which are meant to encourage community involvement in youth justice. They differ from conferences as they have a broader mandate and may play a role in monitoring the implementation of the Act, advising governments on how to improve the system and provide public information about the workings of the youth justice system.

6

Values and Processes
"Being the Change"

Mr. Fisher
Irene Wood

When I was going to high school I had the good fortune to have Mr. Fisher for Grade 11 History. The class was "People and Politics." It was a history of the 20th century, the good and the bad. Mr. Fisher used to be a boxer, and he moved around his classroom like a boxer dances around his ring. I had heard stories about Mr. Fisher and his history class. I heard that during his description of Vimy Ridge he got up on his desk and rat-a-tat-tatted an imagined machine gun at the students in their desks. I heard that Mr. Fisher waved around a blue handkerchief. I was curious to say the least.

During our first week, Mr. Fisher taught us the basics of how he wanted assignments handed in for his class. We were to underline the date, title and our name with a red pen, and we were to use a ruler. Our writing was to be legible, or assignments would be handed back. I saw a few people get papers handed back on the basis of poor penmanship. Mr. Fisher did not fool around.

During our study of World War One, Mr. Fisher made the trenches imaginable for us. We were stunned, and horrified by what we learned. He explained the tragedies of a soldier's suffering with tears streaming down his face, his big blue handkerchief always at the ready. We were learning, and learning well.

There was a boy named Dennis who sat in front of me in Mr. Fisher's neatly ordered rows. Dennis was a trouble maker. Dennis often had his assignments handed back to him. Dennis was often late for class. In Mr. Fisher's world, lateness was not acceptable. One day, in the middle of term, Dennis came in late, and sat down after tossing his assignment onto Mr. Fisher's desk. Mr. Fisher had reached his boiling point. He stood up, pushed back his chair, grabbed Dennis' paper, ripped it in half and threw it into the garbage can. He rushed over to Dennis' desk, pointed his finger in his face and began a two minute tirade, berating Dennis for everything from his tardiness, to his messy hair. The whole class was uncomfortable. The longer the tirade continued, the quieter the room got. And Dennis never said a thing. He didn't even look up at Mr. Fisher.

Suddenly, he stopped, patted Dennis on the shoulder, and said "Thank you Dennis." Then Mr. Fisher turned his eyes on all of us. "I stood here for two minutes completely humiliating this boy in front of you all, and not one of you said anything. You all knew I was out of line, and had no right to be saying those things to Dennis, yet nobody tried to stop me. Why? Because I am a teacher, a figure of authority? Because you were afraid?" Not one of us could meet his gaze, so he continued, "Dennis was expecting this today, because I asked him to come in late, throw his homework on my desk and asked his permission to rant at him like a lunatic for a couple of minutes." All of us looked up at Mr. Fisher and Dennis mouths agape.

"Today," he said, "we begin our study of the Holocaust, and the Second World War, and how it all got started."

There are not many things that I remember about Grade 11. I don't remember how to do polynomial equations anymore, and I'm not sure how to conjugate the past participle of a female pronoun in French, but as long as I live, I will never forget that morning in Mr. Fisher's class. Yes, he was eccentric, and yes, he did get up on his desk and reenact gun battles from the First World War. But he also celebrated with us when Nelson Mandela was let out of prison, and wept as he read the article detailing Mandela's first hours of freedom. He used his blue handkerchief to blow his nose, mop his brow, and always to wipe his tears. Mr. Fisher taught us to be accountable, to be empathetic, and not to be afraid to stand up when we knew something wasn't right. In the four months that I had him as a teacher, I grew to love him like a father. I can only hope that more children have a Mr. Fisher in their lives. *(Aired on CBC Radio's* Vinyl Café: *November 27 and 28, 2004)*

✄ ✄ ✄

The adage that we learn by experience is not exactly true — we learn by *reflecting* on experience. Restorative justice processes create environments in which reflection on experiences of an event can help everyone affected to learn and grow. The teacher in this story staged a conflict that created discomfort for its witnesses, but he also afforded them the opportunity to reflect on this discomfort in related course curriculum. Why didn't the students speak out when they knew something wasn't right? What values were challenged and conflicted by the teacher's mock tirade? How do people learn morality, and what were the applications of this personal moral learning to the subject matter of the Holocaust?

The story of Mr. Fisher resonates with a few ideas we reflect on in this chapter. The student impacted by the event remembers its lessons many years after its occurrence, suggesting that she has reflected on its meaning often. The significance of empathy is noted, and empathy is an important value in restorative justice. The story's author also mentions "accountability," a popular buzzword in criminal justice parlance, particularly in reference to people charged or convicted of criminal offences. But in this case, the author seems to be referring to our individual and collective accountability to values rather than laws or rules. Sometimes, in a society based on the authorized power of some government officials over people generally, the rules or laws seem less compelling than a call to act on core values. Lawrence Kohlberg, whose work we consider later in this chapter, identifies this stage of moral development as "post-conventional" — a social orientation that, at its minimum, is based on thinking of the social contract and individual rights and, at its maximum, is based on principled conscience. The significance of values to a deeper understanding of restorative justice is found in the aim of RJ to create safe places for individual change — and therefore also collective change toward a more civil society, one in which less harm is created and both the individual and collective inclination is to reduce human suffering. RJ processes are accountable to core values, generating questions such as, "Was this process respectful of everyone involved? Did it include everyone who felt they needed to be there? Was the outcome fair for everyone involved?"

Restorative justice as peacemaking is activated through value-based responses to conflict. "Circle" values also speak to the ways we live in relationship with others. How we deal with conflict embodies the values we share with others in our various communities. Do we practise what we preach? How might we respond to conflict in ways that model the values of a peaceful society?

Ideas of restorative justice, values and processes fall into the theoretical realm of peacemaking criminology. Richard Quinney, one of the eminent grandparents of this criminological approach, offers the following explanation:

> Crime is suffering and… the ending of crime is possible only with the end of suffering. And the ending both of suffering and of crime, which is the establishing of justice, can only come out of peace…. To eliminate crime — to end the construction and perpetuation of an existence that makes crime possible — requires a transformation of our human being….
>
> A *criminology of peacemaking* [is] a criminology that seeks to end suffering and thereby eliminate crime. It is a criminology that is based necessarily on human transformation in the achievement of peace and justice. Human transformation takes place as we change our social, economic, and political structure. And the message is clear: Without peace within us and in our actions, there can be no peace in our results. (1991: 11–12)

With this view in mind, we explore the meaning of values and the significance of these to processes that strive towards peace.

Restorative justice is about a set of values on how we want to be together. Consistency requires RJ processes to embody and express these same core values. We begin by looking at core values and their significance for RJ. How a culture's values are taught — values education — is the next focus, followed by a review of educational psychology literature on moral education and development. Next, we discuss the specific values of care and justice in the context of Gilligan's and Kohlberg's ideas and how these relate to RJ. We then look at values education for citizenship, as we explore how RJ values might assist us in cultivating a more meaningful democracy. Finally, we reconsider the idea of values in process, which is fundamental to RJ as a whole.

Core Values

To this point, we have made reference to specific values such as empathy, peace and justice. These concepts are salient to the subject matter of this book, but, as we have seen thus far, they are not universally understood. Now we consider a number of values as they relate to peacemaking processes, which attend to a more forward-looking justice. The goal is to generate an imaginative response to values, where the "talk" is reflected in the "walk."

Before we embark on a discussion of specifics, however, we should establish a working definition of "values." As defined by Cynthia Brincat and Victoria Wike, the word "value"

refers to a claim about what is worthwhile, what is good. A value is a single word or phrase that identifies something as being desirable for human beings. Values are acted on and applied by theories and then rules. We have guidelines about what types of decisions are moral because we have identified certain things as being good, which these decisions seek to uphold. Values are those goods that our theories, rules, and decisions work to bring about in the world. (2000: 141)

Through this definition we can surmise that values underpin laws, which are the rules that circumscribe behaviour that offends social values. As Durkheim noted, "There exists a social solidarity which comes from a certain number of states of conscience which are common to all the members of the same society. This is what repressive law materially represents, at least in so far as it is essential" (1969 [1893]: 109). These states of conscience include core values.

Values may also be described as virtues, or positive qualities such as compassion, tolerance, forgiveness, love and so on.[1] The Dalai Lama cautions that virtues cannot be learned merely as acquired knowledge:

What we are talking about is gaining an experience of virtue through constant practice and familiarization so that it becomes spontaneous. What we find is that the more we develop concern for others' well-being, the easier it becomes to act in others' interests. As we become habituated to the effort required, so the struggle to sustain it lessens. Eventually, it will become second nature. But there are no shortcuts. (in Gyatso 2000: 124–25)

The message here is clear: the way to become virtuous is through practice. Virtues/values are known and understood through their expression through deeds and behaviours, rather than words and laws.

This philosophy of *achieving* peace by *being* peaceful is in tension with the dominant belief that universal material prosperity is the foundation of peace. In emphasizing the person rather than the product in *Small Is Beautiful*, Schumacher raises an important question about the consequences of "Age of Reason" explanations for acquiring peace:

> Gandhi used to talk disparagingly of "dreaming of systems so perfect that no-one will need to be good." But is it not precisely this dream which we can now implement in reality with our marvellous powers of science and technology? Why ask for virtues, which man may never acquire, when scientific rationality and technical competence are all that is needed? (1974: 18)

This is a haunting question, one that raises science fiction images of a world consisting of "Stepford wives" and robots from an Isaac Asimov novel. What would the world look like if people operated solely on the basis of scientific rationality and technical competence rather than from a human centre governed by values and virtues?

This is not, of course, to condemn the many contributions of science and technology to our well-being. However, a discussion of values invites overall questions of morality, and moral posturing can also be problematic. James Gilligan warns of the downside of value judgments in criminal justice issues:

> I have often heard people explain a person's violence by saying, "He must just be evil...." But moral and legal judgments about violent behavior that deem it "bad" or "evil" or "guilty" are *value judgments* about it, not *explanations* of it. (1992: 91–92)

There is a difference between using values to judge others and using values to guide one's own actions. Gilligan's point is that, in order to understand violence, we must disabuse ourselves of the notion that value judgments are sufficient in themselves to solve problems and understand instead that problems require more holistic analyses of causation. Taking this further, we might consider punitive responses to what we might think of as evil actions to be, themselves, evil. Speaking of Nel Noddings' work, Roger Bergman notes (2004: 159) that "evil and moral evil are renamed in three ways. Firstly, as 'pain and the infliction of pain, [second, as] separation and the neglect of relation, and [third, as] helplessness and the mystification that sustains it' (Noddings 1989: 103)." This could well be a description of a harmful event, a school disciplinary response or a criminal justice sanction. If the response to harm is more harm, what are we teaching and what do we learn?

In their discussion of universal core values within the processes of peacemaking circles (one practical model of restorative justice), Kay Pranis, Barry Stuart and Mark Wedge comment that although people of different cultures, from various walks of life and with diverse religious perspectives may describe or emphasize values differently, "the type of value is always the same: positive, constructive, healing values — values supportive of the best in ourselves and others" (2003: 33). These core values transcend this specific model and can be applied to any process that aims for a restorative integrity.

Following is a list of ten core values offered by Pranis et al. (2003) in the context of peacemaking:

1. *Respect*: "honouring ourselves by acting in accord with our own values, honouring others by recognizing their right to be different, and treating others with dignity. We express respect not only in how we speak and act but also through our emotions and body language. Respect comes from a deep inner place of acknowledging the worth inherent in every aspect of creation" (35).

2. *Honesty*: "starts with self-honesty — owning our thoughts, feelings and actions. We lower our masks and let ourselves be as we truly are. Instead of dissembling to protect an agenda, we share our inner world and begin a dialogue aimed not at defending our perspective but at openly questioning it to discover a wider truth" (35).

3. *Trust*: "we learn to trust that we can work things out in a good way by acting in accord with our values. Trust begins with ourselves: trusting who we are and that we can follow through on what our values call us to do. Trust challenges us to take risks, first in exposing who we are and then in reaching out to others" (36).

4. *Humility*: "with humility, we honor another's voice by holding a listening, receptive posture. As we do, we experience who a person is in an open non-judgmental way…. Humility also grows from recognizing our own limitations. We don't know what may be true for others or what their experiences may be…. Humility calls us to focus more on discovering the wider truth than on advancing our own needs" (36–37).

5. *Sharing*: "opening ourselves to others and allowing our relationships with them to develop as they will… we need to release the urge to control people and situations. Sharing calls us to shift our stance from angling for control to recognizing the interests of others" (37).

6. *Inclusivity*: "actively seeking to involve everyone whose interests are affected… [w]e respect others' contributions and strive to incorporate their

concerns into the outcomes, even if laws or circumstances don't require it…. [Inclusivity] inspires a generosity of spirit that draws everyone in instead of keeping some out" (39).

7. *Empathy*: "understanding each other through our stories reduces the distances separating us and inspires compassion. As we learn more about the paths each of us has walked, the urge to judge others falls away, and we find meaning in giving and receiving empathy. Whereas pity can feel condescending, empathy expresses the equality between ourselves and those who suffer it" (40).

8. *Courage*: "holding values and living them are two different things…. We need courage to find our own paths and to grant others the space to do the same, especially when we or they stumble…. Courage doesn't mean the absence of fear but the ability to acknowledge fears and to go forward in spite of them. Courage carries us beyond fear and apathy" (41–42).

9. *Forgiveness*: "emerges from the dynamics of each individual's healing journey, which generally begins with learning to forgive ourselves…. Forgiveness involves a much deeper experience of finding inner peace along paths unique to each person…. With forgiveness, we avoid the self-destructive effects of anger and hatred" (43–44).

10. *Love*: "we need love to develop our connection with everyone and everything. Love deepens our awareness that we're not separate, however much we may appear to be. All the values contribute to our ability to love, while love in turn expands our ability to embrace other values. We may not be able to sustain whole, unconditional love, but as we work with our values our capacity to love expands. As it does, love becomes a healing force in our lives" (44).

This may sound, on the surface, to be a tall order. Of course our actions are never always, and in every way, consonant with our values. But if we hold these values as the benchmarks of our accountability — to ourselves and to each other — we are more likely to keep them foremost in our deliberate consciousness and are therefore more likely to act on them. This is true in our personal, daily lives as it is in our participation in restorative justice processes.

The values listed above emerge in many other writings as well. Braithwaite suggests a framework for RJ values based on existing international covenants and declarations, including respect for fundamental human rights (2000a: 438–39). Hal Pepinsky (2000c) addresses inclusion as a specific value with implications for power. He suggests that when an event triggers a process, inclusion means you lose control of that process by giving ownership of it to the people affected by it. This, he summarizes as "giving way to vulnerability, to attachment to outcome" (2000c: 482), further explaining how inclusion affects the idea of predetermined agendas in the example of violence:

In plain terms, the scary thing about violence, including that in crime and criminality, is that actors remain goal-directed, mission-bound, sticking to a preset agenda no matter who gets hurt or left out along the way. The actor may be a single person, group, organization, or even a direction in movement of all humankind collectively. This remains my definition of violence, applicable to all levels of human interaction. I define remaining fixated on any substantive social outcome or agenda as my ultimate social problem.

By definition, then, the antithesis of violence is altering one's objective or agenda out of compassion for others whom one's actions affect. Insofar as this give-and-take or mutual accommodation takes place in interaction, I call interaction "responsive" and postulate that "peace" is "being made." I also refer to this process as "participatory democratization," "balanced conversation" or "discourse." Insofar as we make peace — establish trustworthy relations and build community and personal responsibility — we let go of attachment to outcomes. We are violent insofar as we hang onto objectives or substantive agendas. This has become the dependent variable in my own theorizing, replacing crime and criminality. (in Sullivan 2003: 70)

Pepinsky's analysis of inclusion has many implications for the criminal justice processes to which we are accustomed, such as that the concept of violence is much broader than the physical assault of one by another and that inclusion can reduce violence by truly opening to the thoughts and experiences of all those affected by an event and eliminating foregone expectations.

The issue of power and control is also raised in the value of fairness, which most of us associate with justice. Drawing from the earlier work of Thibaut and Walker (1975), Rob Neff (2004) talks about achieving justice in child protection work, where the tension between the needs of the child, parents and state often yields dissatisfying outcomes. Neff notes Thibaut and Walker's argument that people judge actions as fair when both process and outcome controls are addressed. Neff adds that "this argument has been supported by a series of experiments which have consistently demonstrated that how one perceives the fairness of a procedure is largely a function of the amount of control that he or she has over the process and is an important determinant of satisfaction with the outcome of a procedure" (2004: 141). There is a recognizable connection between the values of inclusion and fairness here.

The value of forgiveness is often contentious, conjuring expectations of victim obligations to offer forgiveness to offenders. Many things are wrong with this assumption, but given its proliferation we examine in greater detail what others have said about forgiveness. At the outset, we begin with the assumption that forgiveness is a voluntary act by the victim; it is essentially a decision by the victim to release the hold the offence has on them, a choice that can only be made by the victim and in a period of time that works for them. A common error is to reduce forgiveness to a commodity, something that is given by the victim to the offender, who then somehow benefits. We cannot demand or forbid victims to forgive their offenders, recognizing of course that the terms "victim" and "offender" are interchangeable designations for those of us fallible humans who are not saints. When experiencing harm, victims need autonomy in their recovery process; they need to be the "deciders," supported by caring individuals and communities. In order to encourage the process of recovery — often referred to as "healing" — victims need to make their own decisions about forgiveness. The work of forgiveness is that of the person harmed; it is of primary benefit to them, with only secondary benefits flowing to the perpetrator of the harm.

Katy Hutchison, a prominent British Columbia advocate for RJ from a victim's perspective, describes the power of forgiveness is "a gift." The following passage from her book, *Walking After Midnight*, recalls the scene in which she had to tell her four-year-old twin children that their father was dead, having been killed the night before:

> Sitting across the kitchen table from Emma and Sam, I tell them, "Somewhere underneath all this we will find a gift. I cannot imagine right now what it will be, but I promise we'll find it. And when we do, we will hold it close to our hearts. Maybe one day we will be able to share the gift." Wordlessly, they both nod. (2006: 27)

A much later chapter in her book, titled "Finding the Gift," recounts the story of Katy's reconciliation encounter in Matsqui Institution with the man responsible for her husband's death. This passage articulates Katy's own beliefs at this stage of her forgiveness process:

> This is the heart of the matter. I believe that when something happens to us in life — whether it is something that is put upon us or something we bring on ourselves —we all have a responsibility to roll up our sleeves and clean up the mess. Sometimes this means we find ourselves working alongside the very person or people who caused the harm. But what of it? Why do we back away and say, "I do not have to do anything with or near this person," when the potential for such profound change and healing exists? What more powerful alliance could there be than that between those responsible for and those most affected by the harm? (202–203)

Victim autonomy, it would seem, also includes the notion of everyone's responsibility to participate fully in their own recovery. For Katy Hutchison, this is part of the "gift" of forgiveness.

Other perspectives consider the benefits and obligations of forgiveness to the perpetrators of harm. What becomes of forgiveness when the conflict is between groups of people rather than between individuals? This is a chief concern of truth and reconciliation commissions, commonly associated with post-conflict societies such as South Africa. Writing about Hannah Arendt on collective forgiveness, Pettigrove (2006) treats forgiveness as benefit more to the receivers than the givers. The concept of *invitational forgiveness*, as described by Govier and Hirano (2008), includes the idea that victim forgiveness requires that the victim believe the offender is likely to acknowledge their wrongdoing and need to atone.

Finally, recent research indicates that forgiveness yields health benefits to its proponents. After conducting a study of fifty-six people using an imagined burglary scenario, Charotte Witvliet and her colleagues conclude:

> Imagery of justice—especially restorative—and forgiveness each reduced unforgiving motivations and negative emotion (anger, fear), and increased prosocial and positive emotion (empathy, gratitude). Imagery of granting forgiveness (versus not) was associated with less heart rate reactivity and better recovery; less negative emotion expression at the brow (corrugator emg); and less aroused expression at the eye (lower orbicularis oculi emg when justice was absent). When forgiveness was not imagined, justice-physiology effects emerged: signs of cardiovascular stress (rate pressure products) were lower for retributive versus no justice; and sympathetic nervous system responding (skin conductance) was calmer for restorative versus retributive justice. (2008: 10)

If forgiveness is good for one's well-being, as this suggests, RJ practice should include meaningful efforts to create the supports and safety necessary for forgiveness to flourish.

Values Education

Given the seemingly insatiable proclivity for curriculum delivery and testing in education systems, teachers tend to offer instruction as formal lessons. But Arthur Dobrin points out that the cultivation of morals and ethics in students cannot be relegated to didactic instruction alone:

> In recent years, many have pushed to teach morality to children in public schools. In fact, real moral lessons are taught all the time but not necessarily in classes designated as such. Generally, real

> moral lessons are not those found in the syllabus but discovered in
> the demeanor of the staff and the structures and procedures of the
> school itself. (2001: 274)

A discussion of the role of restorative justice in maintaining civil society echoes Dobrin's assertion that "moral lessons are embedded in the very relations in the school" (275). Morrison, for example, concludes in her studies of restorative justice in the schools that, "strong institutional investment that enables the capacity for individuals to participate in communal life is the cornerstone of building responsible citizenship" (2001: 209). In other words, responsible citizenship cannot be reduced to curriculum alone but must be experienced and reflected daily in the workings of the institution itself, from its policies to the conduct of its staff.

The idea that we must, as Gandhi implored, "be the change we wish to see in the world" is a consistent theme in the peace literature. Richard Quinney, a veteran criminologist and primary influence in the peacemaking tradition of academic thought on crime and social control, suggests:

> If human actions are not rooted in compassion, these actions will
> not contribute to a compassionate and peaceful world.... The means
> cannot be different from the ends; peace can come only out of peace.
> As A.J. Muste (1942) noted, there is no way to peace; rather, peace
> *is* the way. (2000: 26–27)

The implications of this for values education in social institutions are obvious. People — children, youth and adults — need to experience the home, school, workplace and other institutions as safe and peaceful places in which to work and learn. In order to *have* a peaceful environment, the people in it have to *be* peaceful. This means that there is a responsibility for modelling peaceful relations, as reflected particularly in the conduct and conflict management approaches of the teachers, administrators and parents.

The role of curriculum in schools, in particular, is also related to the development of responsible citizenship values. The idea that values of peace must be lived can be transferred to the processes by which curriculum is presented. When people take a more active role in their own learning process, the depth of learning increases. Merely establishing codes of conduct for people in any specific setting is problematic "if becoming responsible is to be thought of as more than mere compliance" (Rowe 2006: 521). Obedience to rules and laws may be achieved through external motivators such as punishments and rewards, as we learned in Chapter 2, but it is not a substitute for intrinsically motivated value-based conduct — conduct that is not dependent on carrots and sticks. However, external codes *can* be useful tools for cultivating and enhancing internal values: "School behaviour policies should be regarded as powerful learning contexts and need, in many cases, to be re-thought in terms of their own intrinsic moral characteristics and better linked with opportunities elsewhere in the school which provide authentic moral reflection and dialogue, an essential element in the development of moral responsibility" (Rowe 2006: 529).

Kristjan Kristjánsson echoes the idea that values education requires many strategies, arguing that modelling of good virtues is not sufficient for a full understanding of how to live a virtuous life:

> To be sure, we may "know a heap of things" about a virtue simply by seeing it enacted by virtuous persons, and following the example of the virtuous is, in fact, the way in which young people learn to be virtuous. If, however, we want to fully understand the nature of the good life and the role of the particular virtues in such a life, we need objective, exemplar-independent standards to help us grasp that truth. Merely pointing to role models or other good examples is not enough. (2006: 48)

In other words, as noted earlier, we don't learn by experience but by reflecting on experience. Moral education requires a context in which core values are the common practice and experience; however, to encourage reflection, it is also necessary to articulate these values in other ways. These might include policies or codes of conduct, as well as ongoing dialogue about what these values mean in everyday situations as they arise. A clear strategy for values education generally should be reflected in both initial and in-service training of teachers (Halstead and Taylor 2000). Many existing processes facilitate this strategy, such as direct instruction and special programs of study, discussion, Just Communities, collective worship, extra-curricular activities, involving children in rule-making, circle time, use of stories, personal narratives, peer mediation and the Philosophy for Children program.

Dobrin, too, considers the need for values clarification, suggesting that core values tend to fall into two categories: one encouraging "amicable relations by focusing upon equitable treatment" and the second "designed to prevent harm to the vulnerable" (2001: 277). He emphasizes equitable treatment and preventing harm of the vulnerable, and reflects sentiments of justice as an essential component of peace. While the emphasis on en-couraging amicable relations is about making peace, preventing harm of the vulnerable evokes the value of justice. In the educational context, this means that clarifying values in the teaching of peace must include attention to the concept of justice. We follow this interesting conversation in more detail in the next section.

Offering another perspective on values, this time in an Australian context, Braithwaite (2001) looked at a study conducted in the 1970s and summarizes a list of 125 values into two "major value orientations or values systems," one based on harmony and the other on security. Calling this a "value balance model" (V. Braithwaite 1998), she added the caveat that individuals may be prone to prioritizing harmony or security rather than attempting to balance these values. The nexus of neurobiology and moral development presents support for the security-and-harmony model, adding the element of imagination. This is expressed in the "Triune Ethics Theory," which Darcia Narvaez and Jenny Vaydich explain as

> an attempt to integrate current findings across subfields of the social and neurobiological sciences, addressing the central motive and emotional states identified by Moll et al. (2005). Triune Ethics Theory suggests that three types of affectively-rooted moral orientations emerged from human evolution. Arising out of biological propensities, the three motivational orientations can be significantly shaped by experience. The Ethic of Security is focused on self-preservation through safety and personal or in-group dominance. The Ethic of Engagement is oriented to face-to-face emotional affiliation with others, particularly through caring relationships and social bonds. The Ethic of Imagination coordinates the older parts of the brain, using humanity's fullest reasoning capacities to adapt to ongoing social relationships and to address concerns beyond the immediate. Each "ethic" has neurobiological roots that are apparent in the structures and circuitry of the human brain. (2008: 304–305)

In summary, Dobrin identifies two core values, one encouraging "amicable relations by focusing upon equitable treatment" and one preventing "harm to the vulnerable," while Braithwaite demonstrates that two systems, one based on harmony and the other on security, underpin values generally. It would appear that harmony (amicable relations based on equality) and security (preventing harm, especially of the vulnerable) are core values from which other values, thoughts and actions emerge, while a third ethic, imagination, opens up possibilities for change, adaptation and creativity.

Care and Justice

The realm of morality theory in the late twentieth century was enriched by the contributions of two scholars who wrote about moral development from the different standpoints of justice and care. Lawrence Kohlberg (1981) developed a cognitive justice morality focused on moral reasoning, summarized in his model of the stages of moral development:

Level 1 (Pre-Conventional)
> Obedience and punishment orientation
> Self-interest orientation

Level 2 (Conventional)
> Interpersonal accord and conformity
> Authority and social-order maintaining orientation

Level 3 (Post Conventional)
> Social contract orientation
> Universal ethical principles

He noted that, although these stages are incremental and sequential, individuals might not progress through all stages. These stages of development reflect different capacities for understanding *justice*, the foundational concept in this model. As healthy children develop into adulthood, they mature through the stages of moral reasoning, from bald self-interest, through reflexivity to external motivators and ideally to abstract thought on values-based action.

In her book, *In a Different Voice* (1982), the other scholar, Carol Gilligan, posited a difference between masculine and feminine ways of thinking about morality. Gilligan challenged Kohlberg's model, arguing that morality could be differentiated into a morality of justice and a morality of care (Vikan, Camino and Biaggio 2005). Noting that the research subjects used in testing his model were mostly men, she tested her ideas with subjects who were mostly women and discovered that it was an ethic of *care*, rather than justice, that determined women's moral reasoning. Many scholars who have studied the works of Gilligan and Kohlberg conclude that both of these perspectives have merit, albeit with less emphasis on the gendered meanings. That is, both justice and care are important ethics in themselves and also correlate with the value orientations of security and harmony.

Justice

When each of us was small, our first experiences with conflict invited an encounter with the idea of justice. Perhaps we noticed that our siblings were getting more ice cream or a playmate in the sandbox had taken all the toys. Economic considerations see people as essentially egoistic and looking for the best deal for themselves. Relational considerations mean that we derive our sense of justice from comparative social judgments: "What do I have — compared to others?" (Schroeder et al. 2003: 384). This is the domain of distributive justice, in which we are concerned with the just allotment of resources among a number of people. But it is not quite as simple as the "divide and choose"[2] approach to instilling fairness in distribution. In criminal justice we are also challenged by other ideas. One example is the principle of less eligibility, introduced by Jeremy Bentham in the eighteenth century, which essentially states that prisoners should not be treated better than the poorest hard-working law-abiding people.[3] Here we are concerned with justice as deserts — what do people *deserve?*

Analyzing justice involves many issues and perspectives; what is common amongst these is their contextualization in larger institutional frameworks. Our experiences as children can be the basis for wider considerations of criminal justice policy. In the examples noted above, justice is calibrated and measured. Who has what? Are the allotments fair? Who decides how we work this out? "Justice is the first virtue of social institutions, as truth is of systems of thought" (Rawls 1999: 3). This observation reflects the conventional understanding of justice as an institutional characteristic.

The idea of justice as an individual *virtue* — a significant idea in the realm of education for citizenship and in the arena of criminal justice generally — is not understood uniformly even within a culture. Primarily, modern interpretations of "justice" have tended to see it "as a virtue of *social institutions*, and thus as relating to institutional decisions and public policy, rather than as a virtue of *individual persons* and their decision-making" (Kristjánsson 2003: 185). Yet justice is an important value for citizenship in democracies, particularly at the level of individual relationships, as a way of reducing conflict. The more individuals incorporate the value of justice in their day-to-day dealings with other people and as a standard for their own personal actions, the fewer civil and criminal conflicts will occur that require coordinated community and state intervention.

This focus on the personal dimensions of justice in legal institutions is echoed and extrapolated in the realm of formal education:

> There is no dearth of interest in justice in academic circles. Since the ancient Greeks, questions of justice have riveted the attention of almost every major philosopher. In the last few decades justice has come to the fore as a research topic in psychology and sociology and Kohlberg's interest in justice, understood as a rationally grounded, overarching moral principle, placed justice firmly on educational agendas. In the post-Kohlbergian era, two major trends in values education still extol justice as a fundamental virtue to be transmitted to students: Proponents of "citizenship education" highlight justice as a public, democratic virtue, while proponents of "character education" champion the virtuosity of justice as a personal, pre-institutional character trait. (Kristjánsson 2004: 291)

The suggestion that justice is a character trait first, and an institutional product second seems almost foreign. In the world today, justice is something that we are brought to or given to us, not a way of being. What does it mean to be a just person?

Kohlberg's work on moral development based on the ethic of justice is animated in the work of Just Community Schools, which are "participatory democratic institutions where each member, student and teacher alike, was an enfranchised participant in moral discussions on the school's justice issues" (McDonough 2005: 200). In these schools, participants' moral reasoning stages are raised as they use reason and consensus to wrestle with issues. The Just Community emphasis on interpersonal relationships is a necessary context for moral maturation and demonstrates that Kohlberg's model was not only cognitive but also relational.

Care

The subject of the ethic of caring in education was revived by Nel Noddings (1992), whose premise that "we cannot separate education from personal experience" (xii) suggests that the success of education on morality depends on an experiential context. Challenging the facts-and-skills curricula of traditional, liberal education systems, Noddings offers an alternative, caring paradigm of moral education in which relationships are essential. She outlines the following four components of education for a caring ethic:

- modelling (teaching by showing, not telling, students by "creating caring relations with them");
- dialogue (open-ended talk "about what we try to show" that connects us to each other);
- practice (opportunities to develop caring skills and transform schools); and
- confirmation (affirming and encouraging the best in others). (22–26)

In contrast to the Freudian, authoritarian perspective that morality begins in fear (and hence the seduction of punishment in moral education), Noddings argues that "morality is affected by fear, but it is inspired by love" (110).

Paul Smeyers argues that care is a central concept for education. Care involves trust, particularly in student-teacher relationships, to sustain a safe learning environment. In caring relationships, "the one trusted completes the trusting relationships by committing herself to live up to what is expected of her. Instead of commitments to principles, being trusted engenders commitments to the person trusting and this in return affects behaviour" (1999: 242). Education for responsible citizenship through care yields other conceptual reconsiderations, too. Summarizing Joan Tronto (1993), Smeyers notes:

> The most fundamental level of change in our political ideals that results from the adoption of a care perspective is, according Tronto,

in our assumptions about human nature: that humans are not fully autonomous, but must always be understood in a condition of interdependence. A second shift appears if we connect our notion of "interest" with the broader cultural concern with "need." Third, from the perspective of care, individuals are presumed to be in a state of moral engagement, rather than a condition of detachment. (1999: 246)

The virtues of care, therefore, afford a relational perspective on civil and social life. Education and criminal justice programming that purports to better prepare people for more responsible citizenship must include an ethic of care, which can only be engendered through relationships.

Interdependence, needs and engagement are also key concepts in both the thought and practice of restorative justice. Interdependence speaks of interconnection, an important RJ premise and a foundational belief in Aboriginal teachings (Ross 1996). Differentiated from adversarial justice, restorative justice focuses on needs rather than rights (Sullivan and Tifft 2005). Its processes are predicated on the healing potential of engagement among those who have harmed, those who have been harmed, and the communities to which they belong (Zehr 2002). The value of care is also consonant with the values of restorative justice. The description of restorative justice as a "way of life," as often articulated in contrast to its administrative descriptions as a program or system, is mirrored in Smeyer's and Sherbloom's descriptions of care:

As opposed to an ethic of justice, an ethic of care revolves around responsibility and relationships rather than rights and rules, and is tied to concrete circumstances rather than being formal and abstract. An ethic of care is best expressed as an activity rather than a set of principles and, more so than virtue ethics and communitarianism, it challenges conventional borders and oppositions in moral philosophy. (1999: 244)

The ethic of care is relational, underpinned by a psychology that includes character education, social-emotional learning and positive psychology. (Sherbloom 2008)

Moralities of both justice and care — incorporating both men's and women's ways of being in the world, recognizing the importance of experiential pedagogy and focused on values that uphold universal notions of good citizenship — hold significant relevance for restorative justice. Restorative justice, as Zehr notes, is a "kind of coherent value system" that would seem to be countenanced by ethics of care and justice. A study by Juujärvi, in which students from practical nursing, social work and law enforcement programs were surveyed on their care reasoning in real-life moral conflicts, demonstrates the complexity of moral reasoning:

> In a nutshell: the function of care reasoning seems to vary according to the type of dilemma. In transgression dilemmas, the concern seems to be about repairing and maintaining relationship after a transgression has taken place. In temptation dilemmas, care reasoning centres on selfish interests versus unselfishness in the context of a relationship. In turn, needs-of-others dilemmas focus on the dyadic relationship, with emphasis on the caring response. In conflicting-demands dilemmas, the balancing of the needs of all persons involved takes a central position, whereas in social pressure dilemmas, care is often expressed in the form of values and ethical principles. (2006: 207–208)

Here again, we see both justice and care in action in moral reasoning, in the focus on repairing relationships and balancing needs.

Values for Citizenship

The virtues of care are also those of democracy and are therefore "appropriate aims of public education" (Gregory 2000: 445). Maughn Gregory ascribes six virtues to Gilligan's ethic of care: acquaintance, mindfulness, moral imagining, solidarity, tolerance and self-care. These virtues represent awareness of other people our conduct may affect, consideration of the ways our actions affect others, inquiry and understanding, helping others, empathy with peculiarities and burdening others less by taking care of ourselves (447–50). Democracies may be defined by rule of law and equal justice, but the day-to-day reality of social living requires that we live "nicely together." As Gregory notes, "democracy imposes on its adherents the public obligation to treat one another with the consideration, respect, and sometimes the tolerance, that will allow all private pursuits (i.e., individual and collective pursuits that do not threaten democratic pluralism) to thrive" (458).

Healthy democracies require both character education and citizenship education. Wolfgang Althof and Marvin Berkowitz describe the differences and similarities between the two:

> Character education's knowledge focus is more on moral concepts, manners and civility, the citizenship education knowledge base focuses more on politics, government and the interdependencies of social life. The dispositions (personality traits, values and motives) of character education and citizenship education share many examples: social justice, honesty, personal and social responsibility,

equality, etc. Of course there are some character dispositions that are less central to citizenship and vice versa, but the overall set has great overlap. Many of the skills of character education also apply to citizenship education as they are basic social-emotional skills of self-management and social competencies required for effective social living. (2006: 512–13)

The RJ focus on values such as justice and honesty, as well as the pragmatic opportunities for taking personal and collective responsibility, would seem to be a good fit for democratic societies. In particular, the participatory nature of RJ processes affords citizens opportunities to revisit and practise values in situations of conflict, where values are often forgotten.

Contemporary governance is predicated on the assumption that people can be convinced to conduct themselves appropriately through the knowledge of rules and their enforcement. However, an unfortunate byproduct of this stance is the phenomenon of "bystanding" — passively witnessing anti-social acts without acting. Research on social exclusion demonstrates that the expectation of meaningful participation in social governance further enhances peoples' readiness to strategically intervene in conflict situations. In a study of five schools, Feigenberg et al. questioned what might cause adolescents to make choices about their own (bystander) behaviour in situations where a group created social exclusion:

> While not perpetuating a situation of exclusion may be a more socially or morally acceptable choice, our findings also suggest that a focus on rules did not influence adolescents to choose an upstanding strategy rather than bystanding. It was when adolescents perceived their action as presenting possibilities for prosocial change that they were more likely to recommend helping the victim. These adolescents interpreted opportunities for change in their social context and perceived possibilities for things to be different, or better, in the future. Adolescents who feel their social environment welcomes participation, and is open to being transformed, are more likely to get involved when they witness exclusion or other acts of injustice. (2008: 178)

This study reminds us of the story at the beginning of this chapter, in which students passively, albeit uncomfortably, witnessed their teacher bully a fellow student. The evidence from this study shows that, when people have an experience of ownership of the community context, where the expectation for meaningful involvement in that community is present and when social wrongs are evident, people will do the "right thing." The expectation of participation and willingness to act are heightened when individuals have the experience and capacity to do so. RJ processes help individuals to build that experience and capacity.

Francis Schweigert (1999) asserts, first, that there is a need to nurture a sense of obligation to the common good and second, that community-based RJ reforms as educational interventions can promote an ethic of concern and action on behalf of the common good. Schweigert argues that the learning of the common good "is occurring within a social situation of mobile individuals and changing communities," and "the American conscience is being formed as simultaneously accountable to two moral imperatives: the freedoms of civil society and the commitments of civic virtue" (167). On a pragmatic level, this perspective reframes conflict in the classroom from problem to opportunity and offers teachers a different strategy — the "art of ecological cultivation." According to Schweigert, "the educator's most distinctive expertise is the organisation of social space to facilitate learning. Consequently, a critical task for moral educators is to learn to recognize and then organize our society's most potent opportunities for moral learning — that is to see conflict and wrongdoing as opportunities for engagement rather than as occasions for exclusion" (179).

Recognizing opportunities for RJ in democratic social life, as Schweigert has done, requires a holistic perspective. With this perspective, RJ values can be the guiding force for our individual actions and institutional cultures from early childhood development through family and school experiences to the wider social world of work and civilian interaction. Healthy democracies must include ways for citizens to develop and practice RJ values, as Tifft explains through the lifetime work of Richard Quinney:

> To realistically address the social problems of our society, the specific decision making and economic arrangements of our society must be changed, and they can be. Social change is constantly occurring, life is process. Democracy, a real opportunity for those who wish to participate in the decision-making processes, especially investment decisions that affect everyone, can only be increased by altering the hierarchical power and participatory relations that currently restrict real consciousness and participation. If this were to occur, the state (if these arrangements were to be retained) would be forced to serve interests other than those of the persons who currently make public and private investment decisions in our society. (2002: 247)

An underlying message here is that if we do not participate in the processes that affect our lives, we end up with a default society. The meaningful participation demanded by RJ affords us the opportunity to articulate our needs in contexts that are based on listening and affirmation and to act collectively to remediate the social conditions that generate these needs.

Processes

Throughout this chapter, we talk about processes in the context of values. Two final examples are now offered, which manifest the nexus of values and process. The first of these is dialogue, the second evaluation.

The term "dialogue" is used generically as a reference to a conversation or discussion. Mediators and other RJ practitioners refer to dialogue as a more specific kind of process, a purposeful conversation "in which the participants are open to the possibilities that the views they hold when they come into the conversation may evolve over the course of it. It is a conversation that may occur on one occasion or on an ongoing basis. The heart of dialogue is a willingness to listen" (Sigurdson and Danielson 2005: 1). This willingness is guided by values such as respect, honesty, empathy, inclusion and so on. The conversation is intended to be a safe place for all participants to express their views, and the objective is not to win your point but to listen to a range of possibilities that lead to a collective understanding or agreement. Relationship, as Glenn Sigurdsen and Luke Danielson note, is a significant product of dialogue: "I do not see relationship as a condition or precursor to dialogue but an outcome of it. This point is most clearly evidenced where the environment is highly conflicted, where no relationship exists, and the challenge is to find a way through dialogue to build a relationship sufficient to start, and then sustain a dialogue. The dialectic between dialogue and relationship is dynamic, iterative, and fluid" (2005: 1). RJ, as we have learned, is about repairing and building relationships; thus, dialogue is perfectly suited to its purposes.

Interest in evaluating RJ programs and projects is growing. Most RJ programs require funding to operate, and funders want evidence to gauge the value of dollars spent. This poses interesting dilemmas for a holistic view of RJ, in which the benefits of RJ values and processes may be difficult to count empirically and, even if possible, may not be recognizable for many years, particularly in the case of paradigm shifts. Harry Mika (2002) covered some common issues underpinning the evaluation of RJ projects. The presence of *parachuters* — a common phenomenon in the RJ world — raises questions of detachment, exclusion, imposition of external mandates and lack of meaningful community engagement and investment. These concerns embody values that are antithetical to RJ itself and highlight the difficulty in maintaining consistency between values and process. Restorative justice is not something we "do" to others but a set of values by which we all strive to conduct ourselves, however imperfectly, in all of our thoughts, words and actions.

Conclusion

The story of Mr. Fisher reminds us that we all have a responsibility to make the world a better place, even (and perhaps especially) when the going gets tough. This is not easy, but it is essential if any meaningful change is to occur. Values are the touchstones that inform how we want to be in the world, as individual people and as citizens in a collective. Values are not just words posted on mission statements in the entranceways to municipal buildings, schools and prisons, but they are embodied in the very processes in which we learn, are governed and handle the inevitable conflict that arises when we interact. RJ affords us the values to consider and the processes that provide integrity to the values. This poses a challenge for contemporary democratic societies, in which people are seen more as consumers than as citizens.

Once again, considering the concepts inherent in conflict between different cultures often offers us an interesting contrast to our own ways. The European concept of crime is referred to by Navajos as "disharmony" (Zion and Zion 1993: 408). In this, we see traces of our previous discussion on value orientations, particularly Valerie Braithwaite's research on harmony and security. Crime is conceptualized as a disruption of relational harmony. As Yazzie (1994: 181) concludes, "the primary goals of the traditional Navajo system are to restore victims, and most importantly the rule breakers themselves to harmony."

Nils Christie's *Crime Control as Industry* included descriptions of advertisements in *Corrections Today*[4] as evidence of the burgeoning business interests in a carceral penal policy (2000 [1993]: 111–17). Each year I show my introductory restorative justice classes examples of the advertisements to demonstrate the nuances of this phenomenon. Over the years, a new advertisement featured in this trade magazine. A company selling razor wire and prison fencing headlined its copy with the word "security" in bold and capitalized letters, with a dictionary style explanation that followed:

se-cu-ri-ty
noun (Latin *securus*; without care)
Freedom from risk or danger; safety. 2. Freedom from doubt, anxiety or fear; confidence. 3. Something that gives or assures safety…

The simple Latin root definition of the word "security" as "without care" offers a metaphorical foil for ongoing dialogue in restorative justice. In the context of the definition that follows, it would seem that "without care" might more specifically be rendered as "without concern" — the state of being produced by effective security. In either case, the impression is that security frees the individual from care and concern about their own safety, presumably to self-actualize without fear. Missing from this explanation, however, are the implications for social life in a world of freedom from care. Caring is not the paranoid drudgery of individual and collective vigilance — it is an important ingredient in the development of social relationships. Caring for others is fundamental to human development. Indeed, as Noddings reminds us, "the German philosopher Martin Heidegger (1962) described care as the very Being of human life" (1992: 15). Freedom from care, therefore, is not necessarily a positive state.

In the context of the advertisement, security is represented by the images of razor wire and tall fences. This is a vision of security without care as a separation of people and lives. Freedom is juxtaposed to captivity, human subjects separated from human objects. This interpretation of security as separation holds profound implications for the health and very existence of relationships. But there is another version of the word "security" with very different connotations, one associated with care *attachment*. Early theorists in the area of human development link security with attachment:

> [The] sophisticated, competence-motivated infant us[es] the primary caregiver as a secure base from which to explore and, when necessary, as a haven of safety and a source of comfort.... [The] secure base concept is central to the logic and coherence of attachment theory and to its status as an organizational construct. (Waters and Cummings 2000: 165)

I show my students two images I once copied from a Google images search on the word "security." One image is that of a fence topped by barbed wire, denoting a vision of security based on detachment. The other image is that of a smiling little boy with a blanket wrapped around him, suggesting a vision of security based on attachment. Placing both images on a projector simultaneously, I ask: "What do you want more of?" Almost no one wants the fence and almost everyone wants the blanket; in other words, our preference is for security *with* care.

Notes

1. Virtue is moral excellence and promotes individual and collective well-being. See The Virtues Project at <www.virtuesproject.com>.
2. This refers to the common parenting approach to fairness in simple matters. For example, in cutting up a piece of cake for sharing with two children, one person gets to cut the cake and the other child chooses their piece. This encourages the cake cutter to cut the piece fairly in half, since the other party gets first pick of the pieces.
3. Bentham spoke more generally about poverty than prisons in the context of this principle of less eligibility, although the context of this principle has been most commonly punitive criminal justice. The specific reference to less eligibility is as

follows: "If the condition of persons maintained without property by the labour of others were rendered more eligible, than that of persons maintained by their own labour then… individuals destitute of property would be continually withdrawing themselves from the class of persons maintained by their own labour, to the class of persons maintained by the labour of others" (in Sieh 1989: 162). For a larger discussion of this principle in criminal justice, see Sieh (1989).

4. *Corrections Today* is the official publication of the American Correctional Association.

7

The Geometry of Individuals and Relationships

The Marked Man: Toilet Talk, Leaked Files, and a Swastika Tattoo — What's Ottawa to Do?

Michael Friscolanti

In the late 1990s, while locked away at Alberta's Drumheller Institution, Darren LeTourneau served a lengthy spell in solitary confinement. All alone most of the day, he did what most prisoners in the hole often do: he drained his toilet, stuck his head over the bowl and struck up a conversation with the inmate next door. For months, he and his unseen neighbour — a prisoner named Ron — chatted through the underground pipes, usually for hours at a time. They even played chess, mimicking each other's moves on their own separate boards. "We became pretty good friends," LeTourneau recalls. One day, after weeks of anonymous toilet talk, the pair finally met face-to-face. Locking eyes in the prison exercise yard, LeTourneau was speechless.

Ron was black.

For a man like Darren LeTourneau — a rabid racist with a huge swastika tattooed on his stomach — it doesn't get much worse than finding out your new best friend is actually your sworn enemy. From birth, LeTourneau had been raised in the ways of white supremacy, taught to despise any skin colour other than his own. When he got that repugnant tattoo, he was only 14 years old. "When I found out the colour of his skin I just didn't like him, and I didn't know why," LeTourneau says, remembering that day in the yard. Back in his cell, he sat silently for hours, trying to justify his life of bigotry. Disillusioned, he eventually went back to the toilet, back to Ron. "I told him who I was and my beliefs," LeTourneau says. "We just kind of worked through it together."

By the time he left solitary, LeTourneau had renounced racism. All that remained of his prejudiced past was his tattoo, the big black swastika splashed across his abdomen. In May 2001, he formally asked the Correctional Service of Canada to pay for its removal. The answer he received — yes, then no — is now the centre of a lawsuit that could cost the federal government a lot more than the $6,500 it would have spent to erase the tattoo in the first place. Officials at B.C.'s Mountain Institution (LeTourneau had since left Drumheller) originally agreed to fund the laser surgery, concluding that a swastika-free stomach would not only appeal to potential employers, but might help ease gang tensions inside the prison.

In February 2002, however, the *Globe and Mail* caught wind of the plan, informing taxpayers that they were about to pay thousands of dollars so a repeat convict — a car-stealing, gun-toting former neo-Nazi who once escaped from a Quebec jail — could shed a piece of his unsavoury past. The front-page article also cited internal progress reports, including one that described LeTourneau as a "manipulative" man who might be "trying to 'jump through the hoops' to get out of jail." In other words, the whole reformed racist thing might be a charade. Amid the crush of publicity (news agencies around the world picked up the story) corrections officials cancelled the surgery, declining to provide any specific reason. Even worse, other skinheads — in and out of prison — began to threaten their one-time associate. "It was a nightmare," LeTourneau says. "There are tons of people out there who don't really like me and wouldn't mind seeing me dead."

But he fought on, asking the federal privacy commissioner to investigate how his personal files ended up in the press. The commissioner sided with him, concluding that the leak was indeed a breach of his privacy. Last month — buoyed by the ruling — LeTourneau filed a lawsuit against Ottawa, demanding unspecified damages for the "humiliation" he endured after the "grave violation" of his privacy. If nothing else, he hopes a judge will force the government to pay for the surgery it originally promised. A spokesman for the Correctional Service of Canada said he could not discuss the case because it is still before the courts.

LeTourneau was released from prison on May 3, a few weeks after launching his suit. Now 28, he remains in British Columbia, working as an aluminum sider. "I won't step foot in a jail ever again," he insists. When contacted by *Maclean's*, LeTourneau was hesitant to even discuss his case, well aware of what happened after his last stint in the spotlight. He prefers to lie low these days, anxious to avoid any unwanted attention, or worse, unwanted visitors. "I'd love to get an apology, but that's never going to happen," he says. "The government never says sorry for anything they do wrong."

One thing is certain: don't expect to see Darren LeTourneau walking down the street without a shirt on. "It has ruined a lot of things in my life," he says of the swastika. "One way or another, it's coming off." (Friscolanti 2006, *Mclean's Magazine*)

❧ ❧ ❧

Really, universally, relations stop nowhere, and the exquisite problem of the artist is eternally but to draw, by a geometry of his own, the circle within which they shall happily *appear* to do so. He is in the perpetual predicament that the continuity of things is the whole matter, for him, of comedy and tragedy; that this continuity is never, by the space of an instant or an inch, broken, and that, to do anything at all, he has at once intensely to consult and intensely to ignore it. (Henry James, 1875)[1]

Although Henry James was referring to the problem of the novelist in curtailing unnecessary developments in a novel, the metaphor of a "geometry of his own" can help in appreciating an important dimension of restorative approaches to social problem-solving. Often understood as a criminal justice diversion or alternative measures program for young, non-violent, first-time offenders, restorative justice in fact holds deeper meanings about building peaceful communities. It is about communities becoming involved in pragmatic, values-based processes to help address the social justice issues underlying harm-doing in individuals and, more significantly, within the communities themselves. Communities are constituted by the relationships that bond them; restorative responses to harm-doing, criminal or otherwise, attend to the health of these relationships.

Our current criminal justice system operates on the basis of individuals who occupy different roles in the system — victims, offenders, police officers, lawyers, correctional personnel, to name a few. The geometry of James's "artist" in criminal justice is a circle drawn tightly around the culpable individual, in reference to individual responsibility. The doer of the crime is the cause of crime; therefore the solution to crime is found in responses to offenders, usually through punishment or "treatment." These responses are often found in incarceration, a practice that damages or severs any relationships the individual might have had. Where crime is understood as the problem of the criminal alone, crime prevention strategies tend to focus on the convicted.

The story of Darren LeTourneau, a swastika-tattooed white-supremacist prisoner in solitary confinement sharing his thoughts and time with an unseen black prisoner through a toilet telephone, is a cogent example of how individuals can be changed through relationship, even in adverse circumstances. The story also illuminates the limits of institutional responses to situations, particularly when the institution is so responsive to political influence.

A focus on relationships creates a new geometry to frame our understanding of justice. Zehr describes crime as a "violation of people and relationships" (1990). In this chapter we consider aspects of the individual and relationships between individuals. A key characteristic of restorative approaches is that they are relational; the well-being of individuals and communities is dependent on the health of their relationships. A focus on relationships enhances and energizes important harm prevention goals, by assisting individuals with personal healing needs that address what formal criminal justice systems refer to as criminogenic factors. Seriously engaged community groups offering restorative processes to people in conflict may also gather critical data about community capacity to prevent harm-doing, as well as follow-up analyses that attempt to realistically discern gaps and tears in community services and development strategies that contribute to overall harm prevention. These are the nuts and bolts of restorative justice, the theory in practice.

We begin with an overview of where we are now with specific reference to individuals and relationships in adversarial, retributive criminal justice and other institutional systems. We move on to a different conceptualization of individuals and relationships afforded by a restorative justice vision. In this part of the chapter, we rely heavily on indigenous views of individuals and relationships in the particular context of justice and healing as a preferred orientation for more generic RJ practices. Aboriginal approaches are particularly useful as a point of contrast for systems and processes with which most Westerners are more familiar.

The Individual and Relationships in a Retributive Paradigm

As has been noted, Western systems of criminal justice are predicated on the questions, "Was a crime committed?" "Who did it?" and "What do they deserve?" These queries not only demonstrate the strong offender orientation of the system but also highlight a focus on the individual. The processes involved, from pre-sentence reports to data for creating further files, are geared toward compiling profiles of individual law-breakers with attention to criminogenic risk factors. At a lower level, schools follow similar processes when addressing student rule-breaking; administrators process the cases, and the response is generally some form of punishment, sometimes involving exclusion (school suspensions). Consequently, the problem of crime or rule-breaking is perceived as the problem of the individual. The source of crime or harm is found in the offender; therefore the solution to crime or harm is to deal with that individual.

This is not to say, of course, that no attention is paid to the relationships shared by the individuals in question. In assessments of the individual, relationships are considered but are generally framed by the needs of the systems rather than the needs of society as a whole. If offenders have poor or nonexisting relationships with family members, this information is noted as an individual risk factor rather than a wider social issue. Great attention is paid to how to "correct" the individual with the appropriate program, with a minimal or nonexistent focus on addressing aetiological factors of crime or delinquency through community development. Indeed, the latter focus is generally seen as outside the mandate of criminal justice agencies and education systems.

This focus on the individual is a clear expression of the positivist school of thought in criminology. In this perspective, deviance is seen as being internal to the person (psychology) or innate to the person's being (biology). Stephen Duguid explains how this is different than the social contextualizing approach of sociology:

The approach of psychology has been quite different and with very different implications for the individual criminal. Instead of rehabilitation — returning the criminal to his or her pre-criminal state — the psychological approach centred the source of deviance with the individual rather than the context.... From their first forays into the world of deviance, psychologists and psychiatrists have tended to see the criminal deviant more in terms of someone who really cannot help himself.... Garland makes the point that this movement from subject to object has had a long and varied history of labeling, categorizing, and stigmatizing the criminal offender, including categories such as the degenerate, the feeble-minded, the inebriate, the moral imbecile, the habitual offender, and more recently, the psychopath. All of these labels presume the powerful effect of a "norm" from which individuals deviate.... These labels are all designed to allow us to somehow make sense of the "other," the small minority of marginal and troublesome souls that we find in our midst....

This image of most crime as essentially a "molecular event"... takes tremendous pressure off the social system concerned since much criminal activity that might have been attributed to poverty, racism, family breakdowns, or general anomie resulting from bureaucratized capitalism or socialism is now seen purely in individual terms, extracted from context. (2000: 28–32)

Duguid's observations, while made in the context of prison regimes, are easily generalizable to the criminal justice and school systems. The tools available to respond to harm within the retributive paradigm, whether we define this harm as crime or rule-breaking, are limited. Essentially, the response is some form of punishment. It is therefore essential for the process to generate a punishable actor, a person responsible who can be blamed, in order for retribution to "work."

An approach to crime and other harm-doing that focuses on the individual can be explained by the metaphor of a microscope. The criminal or harmful event is the first site of intervention; in our current system the intervention is shaped by a view that places individuals and their actions under a microscope to dissect and determine the pathological components. The problem of the harm is thereby addressed by assessing and treating the problems of a "deviant." Since the mandate of the system is only to deal with the individual charged under law or the person accused of rule-breaking, its response is necessarily directed to the individual.

Individuals are also significant in the retributive idea of deterrence, an idea predicated on the belief that individuals will be deterred from criminal activity by fear of punishments. The individual's actions are judged on the basis of the "reasonable man," with attention paid to the mental capacity of the person to form a *mens rea* or criminal intent. The assumption is that reasonable men will avoid criminal activities, however pleasurable or profitable, to avoid the pain of punishment. General deterrence refers to the notion that individuals generally will be deterred by the proclaimed punishments of other specific individuals convicted of offences. This is a key motivation for the meting out of harsher punishments at the top end of sentencing ranges in highly publicized criminal cases. Questions may be posed here as to the desirability of using individuals as a means to an end, rather than seeing them as ends in themselves.

We have already considered the idea that victims have been de-centred from criminal justice processes. Since the state is the legal victim in criminal cases, the role of actual victims is to act as witnesses for the state or as passive bystanders. Victims are given the opportunity to provide victim impact statements, but these are used for the purpose of ensuring punishment against the harm-doer. Again, victims are not seen as ends in themselves but are used as means to ends. There is no obligation in the retributive system to attend to the needs of victims, even if they have suffered significant trauma. Victims must seek assistance for their needs from services outside of the criminal justice system, and if they do not qualify for criminal injuries compensation they may not have the financial resources necessary for individual counselling or any other remedial responses.

The primary relationship of the criminal justice process is between the accused and the state. This relationship comes out of the belief that harmful acts and behaviours can be meaningfully addressed through a system of codified rules, regulated processes and state-administered punishments. Personal relationships are problematic in this system, which operates like an impersonal machine.[2] However, harmful acts are very personal events — to those who inflict the harm, to those who are victimized by them and to all those who are significant in the lives of both. The majority of those involved in interpersonal violence, for example, are young men who are acquainted with one another. Yet there is seldom attention given to the dynamics and complexity of the relationships or other personal background that caused the harm to happen, or what needs to be done to prevent a recurrence of the harm.

The British Columbia case of Matthew Vaudreuil, a child who was abused and finally suffocated to death by his mother in 1992, is illustrative. The case was studied by the Gove Inquiry into Child Protection (1995), which determined that Ministry social workers had visited the home on many occasions in three cities over the course of six years, but no one had protected the child. Matthew's mother was herself a product of the child welfare system. Judge Thomas Gove came up with a list of 118 recommendations for improving the child welfare system and new procedures for improving accountability and communication between professionals, which resulted in the creation of the Ministry of Children and Families. None of the experts in this new Ministry, however, were to have a personal relationship with the children or their parents. While they might live in the community where their clients also reside, they would be expected to maintain their professional distance. Indeed, almost fifteen years later there is not much improvement in child welfare in British Columbia. In 2008, the province's children and youth representative, Mary Ellen Turpel-Lafond, reported that the deaths of many children in the care of the new Ministry were due to the inexperience of social workers, high caseloads, insufficient supervision and ineffective training (CBC News 2008).

People who have the benefit of a community are much less likely to fall subject to the depersonalizing treatment of state agencies. In a healthy community, people are aware of one another's problems and help each other out in times of need or crisis. By contrast, people who are channelled through social welfare and criminal justice agencies are dehumanized. Punitive educational, social welfare and criminal justice agencies further isolate and stigmatize them. When we look to find justice through laws and formal processes governed by rules and the meting out of punishments, we extinguish the hope of strengthening the relationships between the individuals involved, and between individuals and their communities.

We live in a highly bureaucratized state. Criminal justice professionals have noted the increasing preponderance of paperwork demanded by the system. Police, parole and probation officers, in particular, spend less time "on the beat" and with their clients because of the paper responsibilities of their work. Ruth Morris, a noted Canadian penal abolitionist, recounted a conversation about justice with Sakej Henderson, of the Native Law Centre in Saskatchewan. Henderson said:

> At a meeting of Justice Ministers in Canada they agreed that the Canadian criminal justice system has failed and continues to fail. The aboriginal people call the Justice Ministers the "Keepers of all the bad experiences." My grandfather used to say, "You really think you can make angels out of assholes with a piece of paper?" (in Morris 2001: 118)

Henderson's grandfather made an important point. Laws, rules, directives, reports, etcetera — the "pieces of paper" — cannot effect changes to people and communities that may be necessary to address and prevent crime. It is only through relationships and community that aberrant or destructive behaviour can be grappled with, worked through and changed. Laws may be necessary to keep institutions accountable, but people are more likely to feel an emotional connection to another human than to an institution, and intrinsic accountability is cultivated through relationships rather than institutional commands.

Unfortunately, relationships that could have a constructive bearing on either a victim's or accused's problems are discouraged or even forbidden by penal and social welfare policy. Victim support workers are required to limit the content of their interactions with victims of crime in order to avoid being subpoenaed as witnesses themselves and to preserve the integrity of the formal system. Moreover, a police victim support worker may pass the case to a crown counsel victim support worker (if there is one), who then passes the victim on to a clinical therapist, resulting in sparse continuity of relationship and little basis for trust between the victim and the support workers.

The law-breaker is similarly passed from one criminal justice professional to another, down the line from arrest to post-release from incarceration. Criminal justice employees and community volunteers are repeatedly counselled to establish firm boundaries in their relationships with prisoners in order to maintain professional distance. All relationships are monitored to guard against any exchange of sex, money or drugs. Although volunteers may form meaningful relationships with people in prison, they do so under surveillance and as targets of suspicion. Family members often cannot afford the travel for prison visits. Many prisoners have no visitors at all. Visits are treated as a privilege, not a right, and when problems arise in the prison, visits may be cancelled. For prison authorities, the value of prisoners' familial relationships or friendships for longer term community reintegration is overshadowed by the more immediate interests of prison security.

In summary, any system based on the philosophy of retribution treats the individual as the sole locus of the problem and thus the focus of intervention. This often involves punishment and exclusion, as if problems will disappear if we simply outlaw them. In this context, relationships are viewed with suspicion, whether the concern is that the "offender" will compromise the one in relationship with them or that the "offender's people" are just a nuisance to the enterprise of correction. The retributive paradigm wrenches individuals out of their social, emotional and spiritual contexts, leaving dysfunctional communities, families and social practices intact.

Individuals in a Restorative Justice Paradigm

Individuals are as much a focus of restorative approaches as they are in the retributive system. However, given that restorative processes are anchored in core values that guide the integrity of intervention activities, individuals are treated as subjects rather than objects. Individuals are seen as ends in themselves, not as means to other broader criminal justice ends.

The clear answer to the first question of restorative justice — "who was harmed?" — is the individual victim. Fully restorative processes are attentive to the unique and specific needs of each victim. As each person comes to the criminal event with their own life history and experiences, their individual responses to harm will vary. Their needs will be different, and thus the support and services offered to them will also be different.

As with individual victims, the lives of those who cause harm will each be unique. Holistic approaches to accountability take into account the context of the individual's life, not to excuse but to understand how harms occurred. The case of *R. v. Jacob*, in which Judge Barry Stuart locates the crime within the accused's lifetime of unsuccessful institutional interventions, presents a good example of the importance of contextualization in our efforts to understand causes of problems. People who cause harm commonly experience shame and despair after the event, and processes that attend to core values will be sensitive to their particular needs. Restorative processes ideally strive to create an environment that is safe enough for those who have harmed others to be able to interact from their core values instead of from positions of defensiveness and avoidance. In Chapters 8 and 9 we consider in greater depth how two key psychological phenomena — trauma and shame — affect individuals and the restorative approach.

Notions of the individual in RJ must be sensitive to cultural differences. In Canada, the issue of Aboriginal people being overrepresented in criminal justice-involved cohorts is a primary example. As noted by Richard Dana, the American Indian self "has more fluid and permeable boundaries and contents that not only include the individual, but more typically contain the family, extended family, tribe or community as well. In traditional individuals, this self may be further enlarged to contain animals, plants and places as well as natural, supernatural, or spiritual forces" (2000: 70–71). Here, the lines of separation between self and others and the environment are ambiguous; indeed, it seems that no such lines exist, in clear contrast to the concept of individuality so dear to Western cultures. Paul Krech echoes this observation: "The value of setting one's self apart from the crowd has never sat well in Aboriginal communities, and has often led to a growing alienation from one's people. The foremost of indigenous values are related to group, family, and community welfare" (2002: 80).

At the same time, the individual in some form does exist in Aboriginal cultures. Zion's observation that Navajo justice was (and is) more concerned with the "wholeness of the person, a peaceful community and adjusting relationships than it is with punishing people" (1995: 6) affords this recognition. But Krech expresses an immediate caveat about the relativity of the individual to others. For example, a respect for self in Aboriginal cultures is grounded in healthy respect for others, intimating the individual's connection to community (78). These ideas are explored in more depth later in the chapter in the African concept of *ubuntu*.

Peter D'Errico offers a particularly helpful comparison between Aboriginal and Western societies:

> There are great differences between an indigenous community and a society built on what I came to call "market individualism." An indigenous community provides a pragmatic interpersonal context for individual life: How will what I do affect others? Who am I in relation to others? This context is immediate, palpable, reflecting an awareness in the moment, as opposed to a rationalized conception of "shoulds" and norms. I felt community as a concern by others for me. (1999: 385)

"Market individualism" is perhaps most baldly expressed in the once popular pyramid marketing schemes that ask new sales "members" to use their network of relationships to sell products for the company. Relationships between individuals are seen as opportunities to make money, which is the grease to the wheels of individual survival. In more rabid capitalist societies, people may be less concerned about how their actions affect others than what others can give to them.

James Zion and Elsie Zion (1995) suggest that individualism is a key barrier to the evolution of restorative justice in Western societies:

> How can indigenous peoples help the liberal state to learn from indigenous community justice and understand community alternatives to liberalism? This challenge makes us think about the first, because they are related. The problem is individualism. The modern state evolved in a climate where central authority and power was assumed by a few.... The challenge is to define individualism in a context where people form relationships with each other (perhaps in small neighborhood groups), define their common needs, and make plans to see them. (1993: 364)

Again we see individualism defined in a community context, wherein the role of community is integral to the constitution of the individual. D'Errico's observation of indigenous individuality emphasizes the *feeling* generated by community connection — we act or don't act in certain ways according to how this might affect our relationships with others, because we don't want to jeopardize the community connections that make us feel good. Community, in this sense, means grassroots interpersonal engagement, not the meaning associated with community as anything that isn't government. "Putting 'feeling' first in a search for justice does not threaten individuality and human freedom; on the contrary, it demands that law be assessed in light of what it means to those affected. Individuality is rooted in the history of human experience…. Individuality is endangered not by community discourse but by the state's seizure of community" (D'Errico 1999: 392).

Relationships in a Restorative Justice Paradigm

The Western epistemologies of science and reason are well established in our modern criminal justice systems. The dominance of positivist criminology in mainstream practices is found in the ways that conflict is processed as well as the focus on an individual's criminogenic factors in sentencing and treatment. Rupert Ross explains how Aboriginal ways of knowing, based on connections and relationships, differ from Western approaches:

> [Aboriginal science] appears to be a somewhat different emphasis from the one Western science makes, at least in its most recent past. Milton M.R. Freeman, professor of Anthropology at the University of Alberta, explored that difference in an article about traditional ecological knowledge:
>
> > The methods of [Western] science are essentially reductionist, that is to say, they seek to understand organisms or nature by studying the smallest or simplest manageable part or sub-system in essential isolation…. The non-Western forager lives in a world not of linear causal events but of constantly reforming, multi-dimensional, interacting cycles, where nothing is simply a cause or an effect, but all factors are influences impacting other elements of the system-as-a-whole.

That passage struck a chord with me. I recalled, for instance, studying plants in high school. We learned about their cell structure, photosynthetic processes, root systems, reproductive systems and so forth. We did not, however, learn much about how they contributed to the other plants, birds, insects, soils and animals that shared their meadow, or vice versa. It was, as Freeman suggests, a reductionist approach, focused not so much on the relationships *between* things as it was on the characteristics *of* things.

By its relative silence on the connections between things, it worked to create the opposite impression. Nothing seemed to be an essential part of anything else. Rather, all "things-out-there" became separable resources to be extracted (or ignored, poisoned, paved over, etc.) at our whim. In that frame of mind, it would never have occurred to me to consider accommodating myself to the realities of *their* equilibria. Instead, they were there to accommodate mine. It was clearly a

human-centered, human-dominated universe that I was being taught
to see, even though no one ever said it. (1996: 62–63)

Ross's observation demonstrates the hurdles we must encounter in attempting
to envision a justice that sees crime as "a violation of people and relationships" (Zehr 1990: 181). It suggests that the ways we think about crime and
the protocols of response to it are affected in the same manner as the ways
we conduct ourselves with each other.

In Aboriginal teachings, the goal is not crime prevention but rather
peacemaking, an approach that underscores cultural norms. Native ethics
and rules of behaviour exemplify peacemaking norms that begin with individuals in relationships. We have already been introduced to some facets of
Aboriginal culture and justice that differentiate it from the modern criminal
justice system. Clare Brant addresses the reasons for the development of
these rules of conduct for suppressing conflict in Aboriginal communities:

> The individual and group survival of this continent's aboriginal
> Plains, Bush, and Woodlands people required harmonious interper-
> sonal relationships and cooperation among members of a group.
> It was not possible for an individual to survive alone in the harsh
> natural environment but, in order to survive as a group, individuals,
> living cheek by jowl throughout their lives, had to be continuously
> cooperative and friendly. (1990: 534–35)

These rules or concepts include non-interference, non-competitiveness, emotional restraint, sharing, a particular understanding of time (to act when "the
time is right" rather than by a clock), attitude toward gratitude and approval,
protocol and teaching by modelling. This approach, developed through centuries of experience, calls for individual behaviour in interactions with others
that reduces reasons or opportunities for conflict. While not suggesting that
a full-scale adoption of these rules or concepts in wider Canadian society is
possible or perhaps even desirable, Brant's article presents several interesting
ideas that invite consideration in a view of restorative justice as peacemaking.

Rupert Ross also notes how the difficulties of individuals surviving alone
in the Canadian natural environment worked as deterrence to anti-social
behaviour:

> In traditional times… deterrence was accomplished without much
> man-directed intervention. In the first place, the social group was
> the extended family, with the result that any harm done was harm
> to family members. Secondly, Mother Nature was the great enforcer,
> for anti-social conduct almost by definition diminished the capacity
> of the group to maintain bare survival in the woods. If man failed,

Mother Nature punished. The overriding threat was banishment from the group, banishment into the wilds where, without the help of others, there was every likelihood of death. It was critical to each person that he maintain the welcome of the group, for without it he was lost. (in Green 1998: 31)

The motivation to repair harm resulting from anti-social conduct, then, came in the form of the relationships between those who caused harm and their extended family members. Harm-doers were motivated to embark on a healing journey in the benefit to self-survival found in the relationships that formed their community.

Thomas King, Guelph University professor and author/actor of the popular CBC radio show *Dead Dog Café* explains the meaning of the Aboriginal term "all my relations":

"All my relations" is the English equivalent of a phrase familiar to most Native peoples in North America. It may begin or end a prayer or a speech or a story, and, while each tribe has its own way of expressing this sentiment in its own language, the meaning is the same.

"All my relations" is at first a reminder of who we are and of our relationship with both our family and our relatives. It also reminds us of the extended relationship we share with all human beings. But the relationships that Native people see go further, the web of kinship extending to the animals, to the birds, to the fish, to the plants, to all the animate and inanimate forms that can be seen or imagined. More than that, "all my relations" is an encouragement for us to accept the responsibilities we have within this universal family by living our lives in a harmonious and moral manner. (1990: ix)

Again we are reminded of the key value orientation of harmony in relationships and the perception of the individual as a part of a whole. In this belief system, it is not possible to extract the individual from their relational context and treat them as a separate unit.

In the restorative justice paradigm, relationships between real people are the focus of intervening processes. As discussed by Zehr (1990), crime is primarily a violation of people and relationships, not the laws and the state. Crime may involve physical or other injury and affect our sense of trust with others. This damage needs to be repaired, and many in restorative justice practices equate justice with healing. A peaceful, safe and just society begins with individuals who are at peace with themselves living in peaceful interaction with others, with cultural mechanisms for working out conflict within the community. A peaceful, safe and just society does not begin by fiat or government statute.

Ross (1996) and others make reference to the centrality of relationships in traditional Aboriginal responses to harm-doing. The focus was on healing social relationships, akin to *tsedaka* justice, described by Bianchi and covered in Chapter 3. Robert Yazzie and James Zion note the Navajo expression to describe someone who shows disrespect by his actions: "He acts as if he has no relatives" (1996: 162). When relationships are not right between individuals in a community, the community itself is affected. Conflict can be seen as an opportunity to see what is not working in our relationships and to gather in a process that is motivated by a desire to find out what is wrong and how to fix it.

The importance of relationships in restorative justice is also underscored by the de-centring of professionals, who (as Christie notes) have "stolen" the conflict and have become the primary players in responses to it. Professional relationships come burdened by professional distancing and often without intimate knowledge of the communities in which their clients live. With virtually no connection to the community, social workers, therapists, police officers, lawyers and so on prescribe and deliver programs of treatment to be followed by the convicted person.

Consistent with social control theories, it makes sense that people bonded to a community or an extended family will have a stake in those relationships. It is primarily relationships — not laws or sanctions — that deter criminal or harmful activity. When people do offend despite these bonds, restorative justice processes look at both the harmful deed and the relationships that are affected, and determine how those relationships can be strengthened for the benefit of all. This is particularly important in situations where the community is unhealthy. The good of the individual is inextricably linked to the good of the community and vice versa. Michael DeGagné (2007: 53) observes, "Community healing is a necessary complement to individual healing. Restoring networks of family and community support is essential to stabilize the healing of individuals who continue to carry the burden of childhood trauma and family disruption."

Pepinsky (2000a) suggests that empathy is an important tool for building healthy relationships and generating greater safety from personal violence. His article challenges the effectiveness of obedience in encouraging truly peaceful behaviour. If we return to our earlier discussion of punishment in Chapter 2, we may see some parallels in these themes. While punishment may cause damage to relationships, empathy helps to build them. Unfortunately, punitive political climates can undermine the development of empathy in criminal justice matters, in which empathy is typecast as a misguided sentiment of "bleeding hearts" and leniency.

Finally, we may consider the role of relationships in restorative justice program development. Susan Sharpe notes that a feature of strong restorative justice programs is "open and collaborative relationships with those who have the potential to significantly affect the program's operation, focus, and ultimate success" (1998: 54). While different communities place emphases on different relationships, strong programs generally build effective relationships with some formal justice system officials as well as with the community at large. In other words, attention to relationships in RJ is not limited to those within the "case" itself — a specific "geometry" within which relations are circumscribed by institutional limits — but to relationships between the RJ facilitators and institutional personnel.

Holistic Visions of the Individual and Relationships

We have made liberal use thus far of indigenous perspectives of individuals and relationships. Direct translations of Aboriginal words into English can be difficult since there may be no comparable words for some concepts. Zion draws on many of the ideas introduced in this chapter and Chapter 6 — harmony, respect, relationships, love — in his explanation of problematic translations of words like "justice":

> One of the most important things about indigenous community justice… is feelings. It is relationships. It is Navajo k'e and Zulu *ubuntu*. It is Cree *ki-ah-m*. All three are difficult to translate into English. *K'e* is a Navajo word which translates as "respect," "friendship," "reciprocal relations," "solidarity," and even "love." K'e is related to *hozho*, or the "perfect state," as Chief Justice Robert Yazzie explains. (*Hoxho* is usually rendered as "harmony," but it means a situation where people and things in relations — all reality — are functioning together as they should.) How can you develop a legal procedure based on "the perfect state"? Navajos are trying to tell us that justice is respect in relationships. (1999: 367)

The pervasive interconnectedness of indigenous culture described in this passage also intimates a general sense of communal well-being derived from harmony. Harmony can be explained through the example of the medicine wheel. Almost all North and South American native spiritual traditions hold the medicine wheel as a central concept. This is expressed in many relationships of four — for example, four grandfathers, four cardinal directions — that can be used to see and understand ideas (Bopp, Bopp, Brown and Lane 1985: 8–17). In this approach, healing the effects of harm on the individual requires attention to the four aspects of our nature: the physical, mental, emotional and spiritual. The medicine wheel symbolizes balance in the development of all these aspects, which is the foundation of individual health. Likewise, when the medicine wheel is used to understand the dynamics of the family or community, the four "interrelated dimensions of activity and potentiality that are constantly at play" are dominant thinking patterns (mental), human relations (emotional), physical environment and economy (physical), and cultural and spiritual life (spiritual) (Bopp and Bopp 2001: 25–28). To bring a neglected or damaged part back into balance with the other parts requires healing and nurturing of the person, family or community.

One possibility for the difficulty in offering meaningful translations is that concepts such as *k'e*, *ki-ah-m* and *ubuntu* denote a spiritual component that is not familiar in Western societies. Barbara Wall offers an example: "At its core, Navajo philosophy is inherently spiritual; it speaks of the connection of all things; it focuses on unity, equality, and harmony in balancing the spiritual, physical, emotional, intellectual and familial needs of the community and all of creation" (2001: 532–33). Connection is a spiritual process as well as emotional (affective). It is the source of harm, healing and more.

The African concept of *ubuntu* was widely introduced to Western countries while the South African Truth and Reconciliation Commission was holding hearings to process the aftermath of years of terror and destruction during and following the dissolution of the Apartheid regime (Minow 1998: 52). Another African concept, *ukama*, provides an additional layer of meaning to a more holistic vision of individuals and relationships. Murove (2004) explains these ideas:

> Whilst the Shona word *Ukama* means relatedness, *Ubuntu* implies that humanness is derived from our relatedness with others, not only to those currently living, but also through the generations, past and future. When these two concepts are compounded in their togetherness they provide an ethical outlook that suggests that human well-being is indispensable from our dependence on and interdependence with all that exists, and particularly with the immediate environment on which all humanity depends....
>
> The concept of *Ukama* offers a general scope for understanding African ethics. In *Ukama* relationality permeates all spheres of existence. However, this relationality is further concretized in *Ubuntu* because the main presumption in *Ubuntu* is that the individual is indelibly associated with the community, and can only flourish in *Ukama* within the community. *Ubuntu* implies the inherent African appreciation of relationality or *Ukama*. (2004: 196, 203)

South African Archbishop Desmond Tutu, a key player in the Truth and Reconciliation Commission, describes *ubuntu* further: "A person with Ubuntu is open and available to others, affirming of others, does not feel threatened that others are able and good, for he or she has a proper self-assurance that comes from knowing that he or she belongs in a greater whole and is diminished when others are humiliated or diminished, when others are tortured or oppressed" (1999).

We can only imagine what a family, community, school, social service or criminal justice system would look like if it were based on the concepts of *k'e*, *ki-ah-m*, *ukama* or *ubuntu*. Imagining a different world, however, is an important first step toward creating an alternative one. These concepts seem to nicely wrap up the main themes of restorative justice and offer us a path toward realizing meaningful change. Our familiar Western approaches of shaming, exclusion and stigmatization pose challenges for the manifestation of RJ in action and will continue to do so without a shift in our fundamental thoughts of who we are in our relationships with others. RJ is not a matter of changing others. For both ethical and practical reasons, we can only change ourselves, and, in accordance with these relational concepts, the families, communities and society in which we have a place will also change.

Patricia Monture-Angus (1999) notes her "dance" with the notion that she is both a Mohawk woman and a lawyer, while trying to comprehend Aboriginal peacemaking in the context of Canadian law. Significant was her realization of the degree to which she "resists thinking like a lawyer" (158), intimating a contrast of justice paradigms between Aboriginal and Eurocentric thought. She refers to the "vitality and resilience of Indian law" (159), as a lived relational belief system in which there is constant curiosity and affirming of relationships, from social introductions to our connectedness to the earth and anything in between. This is not abstract law, but law as lived: "These [ancient kinship] relationships are the basic fabric of Aboriginal laws. Every time Aboriginal people greet each other, they are affirming the fundamental relationships that exist between them. It is, therefore, safe to say that Aboriginal people are affirming their legal relationships every day. It is part of the subtle ways of who we are" (159). The constant acknowledgement of relationships through social practices is the actualization, the living, of the law.

A more holistic view of individual people and relationships includes the idea of dependencies. Using Basil Johnson's *Ojibway Heritage* (1984), Rupert Ross (1996) explains relationships as dependencies rather than as hierarchies. The earth comes first, as everything depends on her, followed sequentially by the plants, animals and then humans. In this view, individual human survival depends not only on affirming one's relationships to other humans but also one's relationships to the animals, plants and the earth. We might recognize aspects of the Aboriginal view of relationships in the following critique of our more familiar scientific consciousness by Morris Berman:

The view of nature which predominated in the West down to the eve of the Scientific Revolution was that of an enchanted world.

143

Rocks, trees, rivers, and clouds were all seen as wondrous, alive, and human beings felt at home in this environment. The cosmos, in short, was a place of *belonging*. A member of this cosmos was not an alienated observer of it, but a direct participant in its drama. His personal destiny was bound up with its destiny, and that relationship gave meaning to his life....

Scientific consciousness is alienated consciousness: there is no ecstatic merger with nature, but rather total separation from it. Subject and object are always seen in opposition to each other. I am not my experiences, and thus not really a part of the world around me. The logical endpoint of this world view is a feeling of total reification: everything is an object, alien, not-me; and I am ultimately an object too, an alienated "thing" in a world of other, equally meaningless things. This world is not of my own making; the cosmos cares nothing for me, and I do not really feel a sense of belonging to it. What I feel, in fact, is a sickness in the soul. (1984: 2–3)

There is much to mull over in Berman's assessment of the less appealing effects of a scientific consciousness in terms of relationships. There are, of course, many positive effects of science for different aspects of late modern life, such as in health care and technology. But we have been reticent to acknowledge the negative aspects of this consciousness, particularly as Berman describes them. Alienated objects are by definition not engaged in meaningful relationships, since to be an object to is to be something "other than," and alienation itself is about a lack of relationships. The contrasting view of nature is, much like Aboriginal thought, holistic and interdependent, and because of this, imbued with meaning. Relationships are not abstract, clinical descriptions but affective, lived experience.

Conclusion

The thought came into [Fools Crow's] mind without warning, the sudden understanding of what Fast Horse found so attractive in running with Owl Child. It was this freedom from responsibility, from accountability to the group, that was so alluring. As long as one thought of himself as part of the group, he would be responsible to and for that group. If one cut the ties, he had the freedom to roam, to think only of himself and not worry about the consequences of his actions. So it was for Owl Child and Fast Horse to roam. And so it was for the Pikunis to suffer. (Welch 1986: 211)

This passage from James Welch's novel *Fool's Crow* — about the colonization of indigenous people in the Midwest of the U.S., in particular the Pikunis, one clan of the Blackfeet tribe — reminds us of the power of both disconnection and connection. It also asserts the value of the individual's membership to a community for true accountability. Characterizing this particular sense of accountability is the feeling of belonging to the group that motivates it. This is quite different from the rather perfunctory accountability individuals are expected to have to laws and institutions, which are abstract entities animated by professionals and public servants who are likewise limited by relationship boundaries.

Restorative justice starts with each of us as individuals and extends out to our relationships with others and to our communities. In a real way, the values of restorative justice speak to what Mark Kingwell refers to as the "virtues of a diverse political order": tolerance and sensitivity, civility and respect (2000: 89). Socrates asked, "What is the life worth living?" Kingwell answered, "We are, finally, happier not with more stuff but with more meaning: more creative leisure time, stronger connections to groups of friends, deeper commitment to common social projects, and a greater opportunity to reflect. In short, the life of the well-rounded person, including crucially the orienting aspect of life associated with virtuous citizenship" (218).

Relationships have a way of transforming us as individuals. The story of Darren LeTourneau at the beginning of the chapter illustrates this well. In the exceptional circumstances of the story, a man's commitment to white supremacist ideology was overcome by his personal engagement and fellowship with an unseen black prisoner with whom he had bonded in friendship. Imagine what else is possible, in potential relationships between disenfranchised youth and engaged adult members of a community or between an isolated harm-doer and the person they've hurt. Separation increases the distance between us; engagement brings us together. And in the engagement, we are afforded unexpected opportunities for personal growth that work towards greater community health.

However, the word "relationships" is often deployed in institutional policies in ways that denote the idea of working with others but devoid of emotional connection. Indeed, a hazard of institutional engagement on a relational level is that community-based RJ practitioners and participants must interact with specific people occupying certain roles within the institution, and these people often move within their respective institutions to different roles. While it is possible to establish the kind of relationship we have described in a community or family with an institutional role-taker, not all role-takers are open to this kind of relationship. It is perhaps more fair to say that the relationships encouraged are those between people and the institutions themselves, which is problematic. How does one have a relationship, the kind discussed in this chapter, with an abstract entity? This question holds particular resonance when considered within the subject matter of the next chapter, where we explore the affect of shame.

Notes

1. From the "Preface to the New York Edition," written by Henry James in his novel *Roderick Brown* (1986, orig. 1875).
2. Cheliotis argues that managerialism in the penal system has a "pernicious effect" on criminal justice professionals. He considers "the reasons why contemporary penal bureaucracies endeavour systematically to strip criminal justice work of its inherently affective nature; the structural forces that ensure control over officials; the processes by which those forces come into effect, and the human consequences of submission to totalitarian bureaucratic milieus" (2006: 397).

8

Psychology of Restorative Justice
The Shame of Being Yourself

Shame
Vern Rutsala

This is the shame of the woman whose hand hides
her smile because her teeth are so bad, not the grand
self-hate that leads some to razors or pills
or swan dives off beautiful bridges however
tragic that is. This is the shame of being yourself,
of being ashamed of where you live and what
your father's paycheck lets you eat and wear.
This is the shame of the fat and the bald,
the unbearable blush of acne, the shame of having
no lunch money and pretending you're not hungry.
This is the shame of the concealed sickness — diseases
too expensive to afford that offer only their cold
one-way ticket out. This is the shame of being ashamed,
the self-disgust of the cheap wine drunk, the lassitude
that makes junk accumulate, the shame that tells
you there is another way to live but you are
too dumb to find it. This is the real shame, the damned
shame, the crying shame, the shame that's criminal,
the shame of knowing words like "glory" are not

in your vocabulary though they litter the Bibles
you're still paying for. This is the shame of not
knowing how to read and pretending you do. This is
the shame that makes you afraid to leave your house,

the shame of food stamps at the supermarket when
the clerk shows impatience as you fumble with the change.
This is the shame of dirty underwear, the shame
of pretending your father works in an office
as God intended all men to do. This is the shame
of asking friends to let you off in front of the one

nice house in the neighborhood and waiting
in the shadows until they drive away before walking
to the gloom of your house. This is the shame
at the end of the mania for owning things, the shame
of no heat in winter, the shame of eating cat food,
the unholy shame of dreaming of a new house and car
and the shame of knowing how cheap such dreams are. (1988)

✄ ✄ ✄

Most of us will recognize ourselves in some aspect of Rutsala's poem. The affect of shame is innate to human beings, and we all feel it during our lives, as either a fleeting emotion or a chronic and sometimes debilitating condition. Shame is a source of violent conduct and self-injuring behaviours; it can be seen in the body language of slumped shoulders and downcast eyes. Shame is everywhere, yet barely acknowledged, much less understood.

One of the insidious features of the adversarial criminal justice system is its distorted and insensitive handling of human emotion. This is a curious phenomenon since, if crime is about nothing else, it is about the range of feelings evoked by actions that violate the person. While the emotion generated by crime is a key reason why crime is a staple of news and entertainment, in the courtroom the potential individual expression of human feelings is seen as a problem that must be managed by court officers to maintain order in the court. Victims may be advised by lawyers to keep their emotions in check when testifying in order to present the impression that their testimony is rational and coherent; accused people who exhibit feelings during their trials may be seen as manipulative. Yet it is simultaneously acceptable — even laudable — that our reactions to crime and criminal justice be intensely emotional. These actions tell us something about our culture and its institutions, but they also belie the simple observation that humans are fragile.

The nexus of emotions and criminal justice is an under-examined topic in criminology, given its focus on rationalities (De Haan and Loader 2002). The understatement of this subject can be explained, in large measure, by the newly established dominance of cognitive and behavioural psychology in criminal justice institutions, which focuses primarily on criminogenic assessments and prescriptive treatments. This approach is well suited to the control and security demands of institutional processes, as well as attending to the menacing liability prospects imbedded in legal and policy frameworks. Testing and test scores promise to meet the definitions of empirical "evidence" required by administrative and institutional rationalities. However, any meaningful attention to the psychology of emotions, as well as its links to biology and sociology, has been sidelined by this particular psychological slant. History and philosophy are other casualties of the techno-rationalization of institutional practices, which further limits our fuller examination of the relationship between emotions and criminal justice.

In eighteenth-century England, there were not yet any stationary institutions of criminal justice, and courts travelled between different communities. The *assizes* — the periodical sessions of the superior courts for trial of civil and criminal cases — were usually held twice a year in each community. Sometimes they were celebrated with a grand ball, and the sessions of the court were opportunities for the community to gather together in witnessing solemn events. Court was also theatrical: "In the court room the judges' every action was governed by the importance of spectacle" (Hay 1975: 27). This spectacle, furthermore, resembled more the theatre of the pulpit than that of the stage:

> In its ritual, its judgements and its channelling of emotion the criminal law echoed many of the most powerful psychic components of religion.... Moreover, there is some reason to believe that the secular sermons of the criminal law had become more important than those of the Church by the eighteenth century. (29)

Institutions of criminal justice began to replace those of the church in the display of moral authority and the transference of emotions and to gradually reduce the relevance of community-based conflict resolution practices. The court as "moral theatre" became the practice in which the emotion generated by serious conflicts became the property of the judge and the court — representing the citizens as a whole — rather than the parties to the conflict themselves. Yet displays of emotion by these parties and the community members in the gallery were probably more evident than they are today, with the management of emotion having become more institutionalized and rationalized.

Christie's (1977) claim that professionals had stolen conflicts from their rightful owners, as demonstrated in this historical example, implies two significant changes. First, people in conflict were left with no integrated ways to process their own emotions generated by the conflict, having acceded that to the judge. Second, the members of the community at large — also excluded from participating in the processing of the conflict — were not only likewise disarmed of their capacities to handle their own feelings in collective ritual, but their natural competencies in supporting and helping their neighbours began to erode (McKnight 1995). Having been shifted from participants to spectators, individual citizens became less active in the affairs of their own lives and of the larger community. How these changes have affected the interplay of emotions — specifically that of shame — and criminal justice through the lens of restorative justice is the focus of this chapter.

As has been noted, restorative practices are not necessarily restricted to the domain of criminal justice, although the focus of this book is mostly within that context. Interpersonal conflicts that violate the person or property may generally be conceived of as crimes, with the specificity of the acts determining where on the spectrum of criminal justice intervention they are placed. Restorative justice theory and practice have spotlighted two areas of psychological interest that we review in this book. The first of these, shame, was a foundational concept in one of the first theoretical offerings in the field, Braithwaite's *Crime, Shame and Reintegration* (1989), and continues to provoke discussion and debate. The second area is that of trauma, raised more recently by restorative practitioners working with cases of serious crime and violence (Gustafson 2005), which is the main topic of Chapter 9. Although emerging primarily in the arena of restorative justice, both psychological phenomena also hold enormous implications for retributive-adversarial justice processes.

Emotions and Criminal Justice

In his classic study of the history of manners, the civilizing process and the formation of states, Norbert Elias warns that investigations of human behaviour that focus on reason at the expense of emotion will be of limited value (1994 [1939]: 486). Since the 1980s, the concept of "emotional intelligence" has seeped into human science discourses, although criminology has been notably resilient in deflecting most potential incursions of theoretical attention to emotions. When attention to emotion is evident in criminal justice or national security endeavours, it is manifested in odd and distorted ways. In Canada, for example, federal correctional programs address emotions in prisoner behaviour,[1] although the emotional contexts in which these programs occur and the personal emotional health of individual correctional employees remain well out of focus. In the U.S., political obsession with a "war on terror" essentially amounts to war on an emotional affect,[2] a rather dubious military target by any standards. The broad capture and dutiful embrace of science and reason in criminological research and criminal justice institutions appear to have stunted any development of interest in emotions, with curious implications. As Sherman notes, "For three centuries, criminology has tried to make reason, rather than emotion, the primary method of justice. The results so far are modest, blocked by a paradox in social policy: *we presume that criminals are rational, but justice should be emotional*" (2003: 2, emphasis in original).

A discussion of shame in restorative justice, specifically, will be more fruitful if preceded by an exploration of the general conceptual terrain of emotions and criminal justice. In a thoughtful examination of this nexus, Susanne Karstedt (2002) observes the changing moral imagination of societies in which the ideas of shame and restorative justice have re-energized a return to thinking about emotions in criminal justice generally. She identifies three core problems and associated questions generated by this: "Are emotional reactions towards crimes 'natural' or 'primordial,' such that they need not only a proper but a prominent place in criminal justice which has been unduly ignored?" "Do emotions constitute our moral principles?" and "Should institutions elicit or even require 'authentic emotions' from individuals?" (301). In response to her first question and using contemporary examples, she opposes the position that emotional reactions toward crime are "natural," arguing that "the specific institutional and cultural pattern in which these emotions are embedded constitute and define the emotional reaction" (305). She similarly challenges the question of emotions as moral principles, instead suggesting that emotions are "consequences" or "expressions" of accepted moral principles rather than the premises on which those principles are based. Finally, she considers the thorny issue of institutions expecting authentic emotions and concludes that any such expectation can only be compromised by the fact that emotions are largely invisible: How can any person, let alone an institution, know how an "offender" or "victim" really feels about the harm in question, much less command them to authentically reveal these feelings?

These questions raise important issues related to the emotions generated by criminal justice matters, demonstrating the complexity of justice in practice beyond legal frameworks. Emotions cannot be legislated in or out of practice; justice processes cannot compel or guarantee individual authenticity. The private self and its public presentation do not necessarily coincide, so it is not surprising that the emotions may be "invisible," especially in the face of historically and culturally specific expectations about their expression. Outrage at injustices or grievous harms, whether blatant or invisible, is not the á priori basis of morality and thus not a justification for authoritative moral responses. Our emotions are not accepted as moral reasoning for our actions; even in court processes, emotion-based reasoning is at best seen as a mitigating or exacerbating factor. Emotions are not even universally experienced and expressed across all cultures and political institutions, which defies any claims about their status as "natural." The expectation that victims or offenders will express certain emotions in certain ways can distort or even derail justice processes when the parties involved do not conform to the expectations. This is well demonstrated in the cultural differences between Aboriginal peoples and European colonial North American societies; the Aboriginal ethics of non-interference and non-competitiveness that lead to emotional restraint figure significantly in the misinterpretation of Aboriginal ways in criminal justice processes.[3]

Yet emotions have a significant role in criminal justice, as they do in conflict resolution processes generally. The work of the Harvard Negotiation Project, manifested in the renowned book *Getting to Yes*, addresses the element of emotion in its strategy of conflict resolution: "In a negotiation, particularly in a bitter dispute, feelings may be more important than talk" (Fisher, Ury, and Patton 1991: 29). The authors suggest that emotions in conflict resolution processes can bring negotiations to an end; consequently, it is necessary to address emotions by first recognizing and understanding them, making them explicit and acknowledging them as legitimate, and allowing participants to release emotions by letting off steam (29–31). Criminal justice processes, however, are not based on negotiation or conflict resolution; rather, they are structurally adversarial and produce "winners and losers." In this context, emotions may be seen as indicators of individual authenticity or manipulation, while the processes are based on precepts of rationality and the objective application of law and legal procedure. There is no mechanism or strategy in formal court processes for accommodating the emotion of its participants, since the expression of feelings generated by the crime in question is irrelevant in the face of the dominating focus on demonstrable facts.

The role of restorative justice in motivating and energizing an interest in emotions in criminal justice has been recently acknowledged (De Haan and Loader 2002; Sherman 2003; Karstedt 2002), with the attention to shame as a primary example. In the remainder of this chapter, I discuss shame as a focal point of thoughtful and conscientious restorative practices, as well as a psychological variable to attend to in service of participants and in one's own conduct.

What Is Shame?

The research in neurophysiology and neuropsychology suggests that emotions are based on a fixed set of physiological mechanisms (Nathanson 2003: 2). Donald Nathanson describes the sequence of conceptual relationships related to shame as follows:

1. We use the term "affect" to represent any of the nine families of physiological mechanisms that underlie all emotion. The affects are a group of highly patterned muscular and circulatory actions primarily displayed as "facial expressions" but also as certain odors, postures, and vocalizations. It is the evolved role of the affect system to add meaning to information derived from other systems.

2. When we accept or pay attention to the affect that has been triggered by one of [these] mechanisms… it becomes what we conventionally call a "feeling."

3. The combination of an affect with our memory of previous experiences of that affect is given the formal name of an "emotion." I've suggested that affect is always biology, whereas emotion always represents biography. Each of us has the same nine innate

affects, but our life experience makes our emotions quite different. (2003: 3)

In this model, shame is considered to be an affect; that is, it is one group of physiological mechanisms that plays out as a feeling and is described as an emotion. The space between biology (affect) and biography (emotion) suggests an interlude during which the individual interprets physiological cues as having particular meanings.

In the 1920s, Charles Cooley considered "self-sentiments" in the context of social psychology within a construct widely known as "the looking glass self" (Cooley 1922), or seeing oneself from the point of view of the other. According to Cooley, this dialectic between self-perception and the perception of others motivates a tendency to self-monitoring: "A self-idea of this sort seems to have three principal elements: the imagination of our appearance to the other person; the imagination of his judgment of that appearance, and some sort of self-feeling, such as pride or mortification" (184). George Mead (1934) later argued that the individual was the product not only of biology but also of social interaction, as seen in the individual practice of role-taking. Later still, Erving Goffman (1959, 1963) elaborated on the idea of the looking-glass self by suggesting that embarrassment or its anticipation underpins most social interaction. Thomas Scheff and Suzanne Retzinger use the backdrop of this historical work to launch their thesis of shame as the "master emotion of everyday life." They see shame as "a class name for a large family of emotions and feelings that arise through seeing self-negatively, *if even only slightly negatively*, through the eyes of others, or even for only anticipating such a reaction" (2000: 4). They explain their conclusion that shame is the master emotion because of its "many more social and psychological functions than other emotions" (6–7). Three observations motivated this understanding. First, shame is central to the conscience, "since it signals moral transgression even without thoughts or words"; second, it comes in real or imagined threats to social bonds ("it signals trouble in a relationship"); and third, shame is key to the regulation and awareness of other emotions (7).

Richard Shweder offers a definition of shame that seems to incorporate most of these themes:

Shame is the deeply felt and highly motivating experience of the fear of being judged defective. It is the anxious experience of either the real or anticipated loss of status, affection or self-regard that results from knowing that one is vulnerable to the disapproving gaze or negative judgment of others. It is a terror that touches the mind, the body, and the soul precisely because one is aware that one might be seen to have come up short in relationship to some shared and uncontested ideal that defines what it means to be a good, worthy, admirable, attractive, or competent person, given one's status or position in society. (2003: 1115)

Perhaps it is because shame is an affect innate to humans that we can all recognize the experiences described here in the context of our own lives. Johann Klaassen expands on the definition of shame to include what catalyzes it, what its effects are and what strategies we have to move through it:

Shame has three salient features. First, a judgment of shame arises in cases of moral failure, faulty action understood as indicative of some morally important flaw in one's character. Second, it brings about a kind of self-doubt which can, at times, become an almost unbearable sense of self-distress. And third, shame is overcome when one alters one's moral character — when, through moral growth, one ceases to bear the shameful character flaw which brought about the original judgment of shame. (2001: 175)

Nathanson and colleagues' model of the "compass of shame" explains maladaptive responses to shame that are resorted to when we feel we cannot pay attention to what the spotlight of shame tells us about our actions. The compass includes the following four poles: *withdrawal* (moving from those to whom our inadequacy has been revealed); *attack self* (used when withdrawal is too lonely and we align with others seen as more powerful, even if unhealthy for us, such as an abusive partner); *avoidance* (the ways deployed to make the bad feelings dissipate, such as abuse of alcohol, drugs or sex); and *attack other* (reducing the self esteem of others so as to elevate oneself). Klaassen's "moral character" is the healthier self that emerges when the maladaptive strategies for responding to shame are addressed.

The words "shame" and "guilt" are often used interchangeably, but scholars working in this area have delineated differences. Paul Gilbert (2003), for example, asserts that guilt is not based on threats to the self or the need to defend one's self, as is shame; rather, guilt is based on concern for others. He also argues that, while shame can be associated with other-directed anger, guilt is not. In his view, the product of guilt is reparation and the product of shame is concealment (1206). The individual's relationships loom large, albeit differently, in the difference between the two: "The evolutionary root of shame is in a self-focused, social threat system related to competitive behavior and the need to prove oneself acceptable/desirable to others…. Guilt, however, evolved from a care-giving and 'avoiding doing harm to others' system" (1205). Cassie Striblen (2007) reinforces the view of shame as related to a person's sense of their shortcomings as measured against the standards of a group they belong to or wish to belong to. She further notes: "While shame is related to one's shortcomings, guilt is related to wrongdoing. Guilt arises when one has broken a rule whose authority one accepts" (478). These perceptions of the difference between shame and guilt, however, were not confirmed in one study of people charged with drinking and driving (Harris 2006); the author suggests this might be a unique outcome given the specific context for the study of particular emotions.

If we begin with the premises outlined by the authors above, then we agree that the individual is a social being and that, in social engagement with others, the individual formulates roles and expressions that to some degree take feedback — actual or anticipated — from those around them. Shame is a family of emotions (also including humiliation, embarrassment) that, by definition, is relational. One feels shame as an individual, but that shame is an affective response to a social situation. As Scheff and Retzinger point out, the way an individual manages shame depends on many variables, including culture. Western societies favour an individual rather than the relational orientation common in Aboriginal cultures, so shame in modern Western cultures takes on hidden forms (2000: 5). This understanding of shame suggests at least two important considerations for restorative justice and its process: that shame has a relational basis, and relationships are integral to both the management of shame and a theoretical understanding of restorative justice; and that the hidden or disguised shame in Western society poses certain practical challenges to the facilitation of restorative processes.

Shame and Violence

Norbert Elias's *The Civilizing Process* (1994 [1939]), a seminal work in the sociology of Western society, offers a rich history of manners, state formation and civilization that features shame (among other phenomena). The wealth of analyses in this book, based in large measure on post-medieval writings on manners, outlines a sociological framework for the discussion of shame. In a nutshell, Elias concludes that European standards regarding a number of human activities — specifically violence, sexual behaviour, bodily functions, table manners and forms of speech — shifted on the basis of increasing thresholds of shame. The changing expectations of individual conduct emanated from the court etiquette of privileged classes (hence the term "courtesy") and demanded a new form of self-restraint, particularly in the face of a growing repugnance for "unmannered" behaviour from wider society. Elias continues with the psychological implications of shame in the unifying theme of violence. The second volume of this work reveals how the state acquired monopoly of violence over the individual and how civilized conduct prohibited violent expression by the individual.

One primary source on manners used by Elias was written by Erasmus of Rotterdam in the mid-1500s. The number of times this particular work was published — it was reprinted thirty times and reproduced in more than 130 editions into the eighteenth century — are indicative of its significance at the time (Elias 1994: 43). The following passage exemplifies the kind of instruction Erasmus offered to the populace of nascent Western states:

> A well-bred person should always avoid exposing without necessity the parts to which nature has attached modesty. If necessity compels this, it should be done with decency and reserve, even if no witness is present. For angels are always present, and nothing is more welcome to them in a boy than modesty, the companion and guardian of decency. If it arouses shame to show them to the eyes of others, still less should it be exposed to their touch....
>
> To contract an illness: Listen to the old maxim about the sound of wind. If it can be purged without a noise that is best. But it is better that it be emitted with a noise than that it be held back.
>
> At this point, however, it would have been useful to suppress the feeling of embarrassment so as to either calm your body or, following the advice of all doctors, to press your buttocks together and to act according to the suggestions in Aethon's epigrams. Even though he had to be careful not to fart explosively in the holy place, he nevertheless prayed to Zeus, though with compressed buttocks. The sound of farting, especially of those who stand on elevated ground, is horrible. One should make sacrifices with the buttocks firmly pressed together. (106)

The unexpected candour of these descriptions is humorous given the serious tone of the instruction. Erasmus offered clear information about what needed to change in individual, personal conduct with respect to a bodily function in order for the person to be perceived as "well-bred." It would seem that these standards were new for the times, given the careful attention to details.

Elias notes that Erasmus's treatise, in the imposition of social restraint, "has precisely the function of cultivating feelings of shame" (110). Over several centuries, the raising of the threshold of shame was connected with an increased expectation of mental self-restraint in "civilized" people (447). The realization of this self-restraint in matters of bodily function was extended to social conduct, in which the will to act violently was also restrained. Elias argues that the cultivation of this self-restraint of violent impulses, which once saturated the population at large, was a necessary precondition for the formation of civilized states — which then paradoxically gained the monopoly of force:

> The moderation of spontaneous emotions, the tempering of affects, the extension of mental space beyond the moment into the past and

future, the habit of connecting events in terms of chains of cause and effect — all these are different aspects of the same transformation of conduct which necessarily takes place with the monopolization of physical violence, and the lengthening of the chains of social action and interdependence. It is a "civilizing" change of behaviour. (448)

So, beginning with recommendations for how to suppress the passing of wind so as not to be seen as shamefully ill-bred, the civilizing process extends to other areas of social life. In order to avoid the discomfort of shame, individuals in Western societies became habituated to considering how our impulses and will could affect our status in the eyes of others. Into the mix came a new attenuation to the concept of time — a consideration of how actions today might affect the interpretations of our reputation and relationships in the past and future.

From a sociological basis, we can see how increased shame thresholds became tied to the widespread expectation of individual restraint on violent conduct and the concomitant acceptance of state violence. We now turn to the psychological impact of the nexus of shame and violence and consider two key works: law professor William Ian Miller's examination of individual humiliation, shame and envy in cultures of honour; and psychiatrist James Gilligan's observations of shame and violence in the context of his work with prisoners convicted of violent crimes.

One of Miller's interests is in the heroic society described in the sagas of Iceland. In his words, the sagas "reveal, with unusual astuteness, the behaviors of a people who cared with the totality of their being about the public figure they cut and about the respect they elicited. These people could not contemplate self-esteem independent of the esteem of others" (1993: ix). His discussion of shame is inextricably linked with honour: "Shame is, in one sense, nothing more than the loss of honor.... Shame has its obvious role in the socialization of honorable people and in maintaining social control" (118–19). The idea of shame is at once individual (the person's affect) and social (the person's chosen context). In the following passage, honour itself is tied to violence:

> To simplify greatly, honor is that disposition which makes one act to shame others who have shamed oneself, to humiliate others who have humiliated oneself. The honorable person is one whose self-esteem and social standing is intimately dependent on the esteem or the envy he or she actually elicits in others. At root honor means "don't tread on me." But to show someone you were not to be trod upon often meant that you had to hold yourself out as one who was willing to tread on others....

In the culture of honor, the prospect of violence inhered in
virtually every social interaction between free men, and free women
too. (84–85)

Fortunately, we don't live in the kind of heroic society Miller found in the
Icelandic sagas — or do we? An anecdotal review of some of the most popular
Hollywood-created action movies would probably reveal some interesting
similarities in hero culture. Storylines follow familiar patterns, where what
is interpreted as an unjust act visited upon an honourable or decent person
is righteously avenged. Violence is usually integral to the story.

The shame-honour nexus is unfortunately not only the theme of commercial movies or Viking stories. James Gilligan has seen it vividly in his work
with prisoners convicted of violent offences in the U.S. In his book *Violence:
Our Deadly Epidemic and Its Causes* (1996), he drew heavily on the insights
gained from many years of psychiatric work with incarcerated violent men,
bringing him to the conclusion that "the purpose of violence is to diminish
the intensity of shame and replace it as far as possible with its opposite, pride,
thus preventing the individual from being overwhelmed by the feeling of
shame" (1996: 111). In the lives of these men — survivors of a lifetime of
abuse and neglect by so-called caregivers — the incentive for violence is to
regain the respect that was believed to be lost in some verbal slag, physical
confrontation or dismissive act. Gilligan notes that "the inextricable connection between disrespect and shame is emphasized by the anthropologist
Julian Pitt-Rivers, who concluded that in all known cultures 'the withdrawal
of respect dishonors… and this inspires the sentiment of shame.' In maximum
security prisons, this is the story of men's lives" (109–10).

Gilligan's work offers an often tragic account of the relationship these
violent men have with the prison:

The violence specifically provides (and a nonviolent crime could
not) a face-saving way of obtaining care. It is face-saving because
he does not have to acknowledge to himself or others that he
wants care, food, shelter, and everything they stand for. He can
believe, and everyone else can believe, that he is in prison for
precisely the opposite reason: because he is so active, aggressive,
and independent, so big and tough and strong and dangerous that
society was actually afraid of him, that he really wants to leave
the prison, and it is fortunate that they put those walls there and
patrol them with armed guards, or otherwise you can be sure that
he would escape as soon as he could. And, of course, the whole
of society and the criminal justice system, from newspapers and
politicians, to courts and prisons, unconsciously colludes with him
in concealing the real reason that he is in prison — namely, that

no one would take care of him anywhere else, and he himself is so ashamed of that, and of admitting his need for care and his inability to care for himself. So violent behavior accomplishes the return of the repressed wishes to be loved and taken care of by others, but in a way that is face-saving, so that a man who feels ashamed can tolerate letting those wishes be gratified; and it is face-saving because violent behavior is the mirror-image, the exact reversal, of those wishes. (119)

Gilligan's interpretation of the violent behaviour of some prisoners will resonate with those who have worked in this field. Too often, prisoners like those described, when on the verge of release, will engage in what seems like self-sabotaging acts that set them back in their sentence progress. Gilligan describes this in the context of *care* — or rather, lack of care — that began when the person was very young and continued throughout his life. By the time of incarceration, this lack of care, at least ostensibly, requires a security intervention.

It is unsettling to imagine the devastating feeling of shame derived from having no one who cares for you. If we understand the roots of violence in shame, our responses to violence must begin there. Currently, the correctional response to violence in both Canada and the U.S. is forcible restraint coupled with cognitive programming and psychometric risk assessment. Interventions inside prison focus on the individual's conduct and what they did to other people; rarely, if ever, do prison programs address what other people did to the individual along the way to his or her prison sentence. The criminal justice system in particular has a built-in incapacity to see people as complex creatures. You are either victim or offender, and "never the twain shall meet." Somehow, we believe that punishment is the tonic that will cure violence. Gilligan explains otherwise:

The conditions that increase or intensify feelings of shame (for example, punishment, humiliation) decrease feelings of guilt (that is, increase feelings of innocence). This psychological truth—the capacity of punishment to relieve feelings of guilt and to intensify feelings of innocence—is, as I stated previously, the basis of confession, penance, and the absolution of sins. It is also one reason why punishment stimulates violence. Shame, by contrast, motivates not confession but concealment of whatever one feels ashamed of. Conversely, the conditions that intensify feelings of guilt (successful aggression and ambition, victory in a competition) diminish feelings of shame (or intensify feelings of pride, to say the same thing in other words). (2003: 1173)

159

So, beyond the notion of punishment as the deliberate infliction of harm, Gilligan asserts that punishment is also a catalyst for violence by the one being punished. This amounts to a vicious cycle of harm from which there is no apparent exit. Public debates on criminal justice, education and parenting are mostly located on a punishment pendulum, where the debate is between "tough" or "lenient" punitive responses to law or rule-breaking. Stuck in the rut of this self-imposed punitive framework, our creativity in any efforts to meaningfully address the problems (that is, in such a way that they might be fixed) is stunted.

Shame provides a different lens than behaviourism through which to examine violence and how to prevent it. To this point in the chapter, we have considered shame as an innate affect in all people; how this shame is managed includes historical, cultural and personal perspectives. We have seen that the shifting of shame thresholds over the centuries resulted in a growing state monopoly of violence accompanied by diminished social tolerance for individual expressions of violence. But shame can also be a source of violence, a way of responding to perceived disrespect and dishonour. Punishment provokes more shame and, if the punished have maladaptive ways of dealing with shame, generates even more violence. What are the policy implications of this to criminal justice? Are our current processes sufficient to address the phenomenon of shame? Since shame has been shown to be a key source of violence, and a recurring political claim is to bring safety to communities, should shame be considered a part of any criminal justice policy-making? An uncomfortable possibility is that our current criminal justice processes actually exacerbate shame and thus generate violence. Problem-solving thinking requires greater creativity in the search for alternative lenses and ways to consider reducing harm. Restorative beliefs constitute a different paradigm of thought through which to consider the same problems.

Shame and Restorative Justice

Criminology is multi-disciplinary, and as such it culls theories and research from a variety of disciplines, primarily sociology, psychology, biology, law and more recently, geography and education. In attempting to understand "crime," criminology dips into these disciplines to pull together ideas that collaborate to produce explanations that are not only "testable" but may garner evidence to influence criminal justice and social welfare policy. We might ask the deeper question of motivation for the different directions to which this evidence leads. For example, criminological research may be directed toward better police operations techniques, prison practices or sentencing strategies. This book suggests that the question of motivation is ethically bound to the notion of common interests and that these interests amount to individual and communal safety. While the aforementioned examples may well be intended towards the goal of safety, they are often predicated on larger theoretical or "commonsense" ideas that lack empirical foundation or omit consideration of relevant factors that challenge the status quo. Shame and trauma are two such factors, both of which may be better understood through the different, multidisciplinary lens of restorative justice.

One of the earlier theoretical works on restorative justice, *Crime, Shame and Reintegration*, introduced the idea of shame as a key component of collaborative processes. Its author, John Braithwaite, integrated the emerging family group conferencing model of social welfare and youth justice of New Zealand with his work on corporate crime, in which he focused on the variable of shame, highlighted in the New Zealand processes. However, his interest was less on shame itself (an emotion or affect) than on *shaming*, which he defines as "all social processes of expressing disapproval which have the intention or effect of invoking remorse in the person being shamed and/or condemnation by others who become aware of the shaming" (1989: 100). In Braithwaite's opinion, the problem with modern retributive criminal justice systems is that shaming is stigmatizing rather than reintegrative: hence, the opening to restorative justice approaches. In many respects, this treatise has been a landmark contribution to the larger field of criminology, where the construct of "reintegrative shaming" has opened new theoretical approaches to understanding crime and criminal justice responses. As Braithwaite himself later notes, "The theory of reintegrative shaming is an explicit attempt to integrate the insights of control, subcultural, opportunity, learning (e.g., differential association) and labeling theories of crime" (2000b: 296). Braithwaite's concept of reintegrative shaming has begun to resonate in the field of education and schooling, where colleagues are applying the concepts of his work in the form of shame management through reintegration to school discipline and to bullying (Ahmed et al. 2001; Morrison 2006).

In Australia in the 1990s, the notion of reintegrative shaming was introduced into the family group conferencing model, which was being adopted by police agencies and emerging private conflict transformation services and ultimately made its way to North America. In the U.S., this was initially manifested in the work of Real Justice, a company that held conferencing training sessions for people working in the fields of criminal justice and education. In Canada, the Royal Canadian Mounted Police (RCMP) were trained by the now defunct Australian company Transformative Justice Australia; the first conferencing attempts using reintegrative shaming occurred in Sparwood, British Columbia, and extended to other RCMP detachments, mostly in B.C.[4] Community volunteers, police officers, teachers and school principals were common consumers of conference training, which generally took one to two days. An introduction to reintegrative shaming was a component of the training, demonstrating the application of Braithwaite's theory to practice.

Fissures in the reintegrative shaming construct became clear to me a few years ago while participating in a meeting of restorative justice mentors in British Columbia. A colleague recalled a conversation with a police officer who had recently been introduced to the conferencing model in anticipation of the impending invocation of the *Youth Criminal Justice Act* (YCJA). The YCJA requires the police to deploy measures similar to "cautioning" and conferencing. He recalled the officer's spontaneous feedback on this restorative justice model: "The best thing about it is the *shaming* part." Whatever was intended in the idea of "reintegrative shaming" was demonstrably vulnerable to distortion in the particular standpoint of this officer, whose paradigm of justice was, by virtue of his profession, clearly retributive. In the context of his work and his framework of understanding, to shame a young person meant scolding them — and he seemed enthused about the prospects of doing so. Restorative justice is about healing harms, not creating new ones, and this perception of shame means that some non-offenders in the conference are now deliberately acting in ways meant to hurt the offender. The distinction between stigmatizing and reintegrative shaming, however well articulated in theoretical expression, was blurred in practice.

The conceptual and practical significance of shame as an emotion might be rescued by discontinuing the use of the term "shaming," which seems hopelessly vulnerable to misinterpretation and misapplication. Two reasons underpin this approach. First, shame is an emotion that holds enormous implications for practices in the criminal justice system, as well as those related to school discipline. As we have seen, the theory and research on shame lends itself to a serious reconsideration of current criminal justice and disciplinary practices, while at the same time opening possibilities for restorative interventions that may be more helpful in moving toward our universal interests of safe and connected communities. Second, the misunderstanding and misuse of shame as an action (as in *shaming*) can result in dangerous and distorted interventions that may exacerbate the presenting problems, thus moving us further away from these universal interests.

If the goal of restorative justice is to heal harms, it is probably counterproductive to respond to harm in a manner that further harms. Reintegrative shaming is a process that assumes the person at its focus would be supported within the community's fold: "Reintegrative shaming means that expressions of community disapproval, which may range from mild rebuke to degradation ceremonies, are followed by gestures of reacceptance into the community of law-abiding citizens" (Braithwaite 1989: 55). The goal of an adversarial justice system is to find the guilty person and punish them. Using shame to stigmatize makes the accused person a pariah and casts them out of the collective without any robust ritual equal to a trial to signify the ending of the punishment. In the case of sex offenders, it has been suggested that stigmatizing approaches can exacerbate an inclination to sexual interference by socially isolating the perpetrator, while reintegrative approaches better protect the children from further assaults (through affected community awareness) and the perpetrator from vigilantes (McAlinden 2005). The difference between the two in reintegrative shaming theory is not about whether to shame or not to shame, but about what happens afterwards. However, Nathanson (1997) notes that while reintegrative shaming theory assumes that shaming in a conferencing process "works" to change behaviour if it is followed by community reacceptance, in fact "the mutative force is *empathy*, not shame" (16, emphasis added). Nathanson explains that community members in the circle express who they are and the harm-doer feels shame at offending the people in the circle. Realizing that they're "not in, they're out," the harm-doer wants in.

Studies conducted on reintegrative shaming theory (RST) have covered different aspects of the process. In their research on high school delinquency, Ibolya Losoncz and Graham Tyson (2007) found that shaming may not affect predatory crime as predicted in the theory. However, they did find large support for the focus on the difference between stigmatization (harmful) and reintegration (beneficial) (175). A study on drinking and driving, as part of Australia's RISE (reintegrative shaming experiments), examined the effect of RST and procedural justice on recidivism and support for the law over four years (Tyler et al. 2007). These results demonstrated that "treatment" (i.e., the consequences of the arrest, whether an RJ intervention such as community service or a punitive one) did not seem to affect recidivism in either the group processed under RJ or the group under the retributive system. Yet they did find that treatment "did affect people's orientations toward the law, with those who attended conferences viewing the law as more legitimate and believing that breaking the law would create more problems in their lives" (565).

Lening Zhang and Sheldon Zhang's test (2004) of Braithwaite's reintegrative shaming theory with "predatory delinquency" also produced mixed to weak support for the theory. Their findings did not support the idea that reintegrative shaming could predict future predatory behaviour; however, they did find that parental forgiveness and peer shaming had significant effects on reducing the likelihood of being involved in predatory offences again. Earlier, Carter Hay (2001) tested reintegrative shaming theory with adolescents and parental use of shaming, resulting in findings that were "neither uniformly supportive nor unsupportive" of the theory. He notes that, similar to the evidence discussed in Chapter 2, moral and reason-based sanctions were better with adolescents than coercive or intimidating sanctions. Hay suggests that RST might be correct in asserting the harmful effects of stigmatization, but that shaming itself might not be the source of that stigmatization even when reintegration is absent (148).

Finally, the emphasis in restorative justice on victim involvement has cast a light on the role of shame in victim responses. It seems natural to assume that a harm-doer might feel shame; we might even hope that a person committing a transgression against another feels the effects of conscience and then of shame for having the capacity to hurt another. What is less understood is that those who have been transgressed often experience shame, too. Intuitively, we would think that an innocent person victimized by another doesn't "need" to feel shame because they have done nothing of which to be ashamed, but this is not necessarily so. Shapiro (2003) considered the plight of concentration camp and torture survivors: "It seems that the very condition of subjugation has the opposite effect; it intensifies or adds to feelings of shame. In other words, it is not only the experiences these people were forced to endure or the actions they were forced to perform but their very helplessness and inability to resist that is reason for shame. It is the fact of subjugation itself that is damaging to self-respect" (1132).

A subjugated individual, then, loses their sense of personal autonomy. We have already considered the idea that shame is about the self and how the person is viewed by others. Klaassen (2001) added that shame is about failures and faulty character traits. In the context of Western societies, which value strength, assertiveness and self-reliance, it is not difficult to see how victims might also experience shame. To be weak in a survival-of-the-fittest culture feels shameful. It can also lead to maladaptive responses to shame, as Nathanson describes in the "compass of shame." We can see how today's shamed victim can become tomorrow's violent aggressor.

Conclusion

> We live in an atmosphere of shame. We are ashamed of everything that is real about us; ashamed of ourselves, of our relatives, of our incomes, of our accents, of our opinions, of our experience, just as we are ashamed of our naked skins. (George Bernard Shaw, *Man and Superman*, 1903)

There is a deep sense of shared sadness in Rutsala's poem, with which we began this chapter. The recognition of the effects of shame in our own lives seems inescapable once identified and understood. As a normal human affect, shame is part of our individual and collective make-up. It is curious that, until quite recently, almost nothing has been said about shame in criminal justice literature and only then through the lens of restorative justice. It would seem that the realm of criminal justice is replete with examples of shame-based behaviour, not only for harm-doers but also for those who have been harmed and everyone else around them. The insights gained from understanding shame would go a long way toward helping us address the hurts and pains of human interaction.

Sandra Bloom (1997) notes that emotions, overall, have an important role in our thinking processes, which portends significant shortcomings in reason-based criminal justice protocols. Humans' cognitive imperative requires us to categorize and organize information, and when this does not happen we become confused and conflicted. Affect (emotion) keeps us aware of this disruption to cognitive processes, requiring resolution or prolonged emotional distress (41–42). Our criminal justice processes might expect people accused or convicted of crimes to be accountable purely on the basis of the "reasonable man," but what is reasonable for individuals depends in large measure on what they come to the crime with. Robin Karr-Morse and Meredith Wiley note that the effects of excessive shame in early childhood, particularly during the first year of life, change the brain's basic biology such that the emerging individual expects little sensitivity from others and shows less concern for relationships with others generally. The result is a person more likely to experience "severe emotional disorders associated with the underregulation of aggression and an impaired ability to empathetically experience the emotional states of others" (1997: 197–98). The dynamics of shame-humiliation always accompany child abuse (Schore 1996), a common theme in the biographies of individuals convicted of prolific and/or violent offences. Indeed, shame is also a *product* of transgression, where the victim of harm may feel exposed and devalued by the aggressor. Gerrit Glas used the example of a Polish aristocrat who had survived the Warsaw ghetto and who, in a documentary, is initially unable to speak when asked of his ghetto experiences, to demonstrate the effects of shame on the bearer's spontaneity. He notes: "Intense shame... seems to be related to experiences that cannot be shared with and tolerated by others — at least not in the imagination of the person who feels shame" (2006: 183). In this way, shame can been seen as a catalyst for keeping secrets, where the holder of the secret is unable to seek help for the personal effects of their victimization.

It seems remiss to omit an understanding of shame in our calculations of what to do to create healthier societies. Criminal justice practices would seem to only exacerbate shame and, therefore, its effects. Restorative practice, at least in theory, incorporates this understanding into its processes. However, maladaptive responses to shame are often the catalyst for harm-doing and signal the need for our attention to wider social practices such as childrearing, teacher conduct in classrooms and recreation, as well as criminal justice.

Notes

1. As part of its "Living Skills" program, prisoners may also be prescribed the "Anger and Emotions Management Program," and the follow-up "Anger and Emotions Management Maintenance Program." See <http://www.csc-scc. gc.ca/text/prgrm/correctional/living_skills_program_e.shtml>.

2. According to emotion researcher Donald Nathanson (1994) fear-terror is one of the nine innate human affects.
3. Brant (1990) describes native ethics and rules of behaviour in order that psychiatrists not misinterpret Aboriginal cultural norms in the context of mental health. Three of these ethics — non-interference (discouraging coercion), non-competitiveness (suppressing conflict) and emotional restraint — promote self-control and hinder violent feelings.
4. For more details on the RCMP history with conferencing see Chatterjee and Elliott (2003). The author took the conferencing training with Transformative Justice Australia in Vancouver in 2001.

9

Psychology of Restorative Justice
Trauma and Healing

"Mom Is Lying. Mom Is Hurting Me.
Please Call the Police."

Bruce Perry and Maia Szalavitz

Back in 1998 most of [our trauma] work was based at our large clinic in Houston. James, a six-year-old boy became one of our patients. Our work in his case was not therapy; I had been asked to provide expert input on his complex situation. James taught me a great deal about courage and determination, and reminded me how important it is to listen, paying close attention to the children themselves.

James was referred to us by a judge who had received so many different opinions about the boy's situation that he hoped we could clarify what was going on. A child's legal advocacy organization was worried that he was being abused by his adoptive parents. Numerous therapists and Child Protective Services, however, believed that he was such a troublemaker that his adoptive family had needed a break from him. Teachers reported unexplained bruises and scratches. The boy had been adopted before his first birthday by a couple who had also taken in three other children and had one biological child. James was the second oldest....

According to his mother, Merle, James was incorrigible and uncontrollable. He frequently ran away from home, he tried to jump out of moving cars, he attempted suicide and wet his bed. By age six he had been hospitalized numerous times, once after jumping from a second storey balcony. He lied constantly, especially about his parents, and he seemed to enjoy defying them. He was being prescribed antidepressants and other medications for impulsivity and attention problems. He'd seen numerous therapists, psychiatrists, counselors and social workers. His mother said he was so unmanageable that she called Child Protection Services on herself, pretending to be a neighbor concerned that his mother could not handle him and that he was a danger to himself and his siblings. The last straw was an overdose of medication he'd taken that had landed him in an intensive care unit. He was so close to death that he had to be flown to the hospital in a helicopter for rapid treatment. Now he'd been taken to a residential treatment center to give his mother a "respite." The judge had been asked to determine what should happen next.

CPS caseworkers and several therapists believed he had Reactive Attachment Disorder (RAD), a diagnosis frequently given to children who have suffered severe early neglect and/or trauma.... It is marked by a lack of empathy and an inability to connect with others, often accompanied by manipulative and anti-social behavior. RAD can occur when infants don't receive enough rocking, cuddling and other nurturing physical and emotional attention. The regions of their brains that help them form relationships and decode social cues do not develop properly, and they grow up with faulty neurobiology, including an inability to derive pleasure from healthy human interactions....

Fortunately, RAD is rare. Unfortunately, many parents and mental health workers have latched onto it as an explanation for a wide range of misbehavior, especially in adopted and foster children.... The therapists and the mother's description of James's behavior did seem to fit the diagnosis. But there was something decidedly odd about James's records. When he was in the hospital or in a residential treatment center, he was well behaved. He didn't try to run away, didn't threaten suicide. His behavior in schools was unremarkable aside from some minor aggression toward other boys, nothing like the out-of-control demon his mother consistently complained about....

When I met James, I instantly liked him.... He was engaging, behaved appropriately and reciprocated eye contact and smiles. In fact, he laughed and joked with me and seemed to like my company. Stephanie, his primary clinician on our interdisciplinary team, felt the same way about him. After four sessions we had planned to stop seeing him because we felt we had enough information for our evaluation....

James had endeared himself to Stephanie and me and, as we discussed him, I realized that he could not have genuine RAD.

We began to look more closely at his records and at the different versions of the events contained there....

Now we learned that medical staff had been suspicious of Merle almost every time she'd had contact with them. As REMS [emergency medical services] workers fought frantically to stabilize the boy... she'd sat calmly, sipping a soda, her hysterics and worry about the child mysteriously ended, even though his survival was still far from assured. At the hospital, upon being given the good news that he would pull through, Merle shocked the doctor by asking that the boy be removed from life support. One ER nurse suspected her of tampering with the medical equipment. As soon as he was conscious and his mother was not present, James told hospital staff, "Mom is lying. Mom is hurting me. Please call the police."

Suddenly, James's behavior made sense to us.... It was clear to me that James had run away because his mother was harming him, not because he was defiantly misbehaving. Running away is uncommon among children his age, even those who are abused: even the most severely battered and neglected elementary children tend to fear change and strangeness more than they fear losing the only parents they have ever known. They prefer the certainty of misery to the misery of uncertainty. The younger the child, the more important familiar people and situations usually are. Many such children have begged me to return them to violent and dangerous parents. But James was different. His behavior was that of someone seeking help, not of someone who had difficulty forming attachments and relationships....

James's case plunged me into the heart of one of the key conflicts in child psychiatry: although the patient is a child, he is not the one that gets to make most decisions about his care and treatment, and he is often not the person who provides the initial information about the case.... James's case had been framed as that of a "difficult" child with "behavior problems." But he was really a courageous, persistent and ethical child who'd been placed in an impossible situation — one in which his every attempt to help himself and his siblings was framed as evidence of his "bad behavior." (Excerpts from *The Boy Who Was Raised as a Dog*, 2006: 203–208)

❧ ❧ ❧

The story of James is a sadly familiar one to frontline workers and therapists in the realms of social service, education, mental health and criminal justice. Although Canada is a signatory to the U.N. Convention on the Rights of the Child,[1] it has not materially honoured many of its commitments to the Convention's articles. Notably, the Canadian government has made no progress in eradicating child poverty, which the House of Commons pledged to accomplish in 1989. It goes without saying that the plight of abused children has also faded on the radar screen of children's rights. Given our proclivity for criminalizing social problems, the lens of behaviour analyses tends to see children's disruptive actions as evidence of their individual deviance rather than as symptoms of broader harms visited upon them. David Finkelhor (2008) notes that while juvenile delinquency is a large priority in academic research and government policy, children are more likely to come to the attention of authorities as victims than as offenders. And when we do see that children are being abused, our response focuses more on prosecuting and punishing the perpetrators than on healing the victimized children. This attention on the individual deflects our interest in the broader context in which problems and harms arise.

In this chapter, the focus is on the psychological phenomenon of trauma, which has become a notable variable in both harm and healing. Restorative processes focusing on serious crime have generated evidence suggesting that meaningful, trauma-informed approaches to the harm produced by violent acts is of great value (Gustafson 2005). Using this aperture, we can see the implications of trauma for the subject matter of criminology generally. Understanding how trauma relates to the concerns of social institutions such as the family, schools and criminal justice system offers fresh opportunities to respond more holistically and effectively to acts and behaviours that compromise individual and collective well-being. Our existing social institutions are not particularly well constructed to recognize and address the evidence and implications of trauma, and it becomes easy to see that, when in conflict, the needs of these institutions are viewed as more important than the needs of the people they were meant to serve.

We begin by asserting the healing focus of restorative justice, a necessary precursor to addressing the harm of trauma. An approach to harm, criminal or otherwise, that seeks to heal rather than hurt — either directly or indirectly — is particularly conducive to responding to trauma in helpful ways. To broaden our understanding of trauma, we continue by explaining what it is. We touch on the biological components of psychological trauma, followed by a consideration of how trauma emerges and is reflected in both victims and perpetrators of harm. Further, we discuss the role trauma plays for professionals and laypeople engaged in emergency and criminal justice work and the implications of this for the individuals involved as well as the administration of justice. Finally, we look at what we can do about trauma in the twenty-first century and how this challenges conventional responses to harm in Western societies.

Restorative Justice as Healing

Underlying [a restorative justice] understanding of wrongdoing is an assumption about society: we are all interconnected. Many cultures have a word that represents this notion of the centrality of relationships. Although the specific meanings of these words vary, they communicate a similar message: all things are connected to each other in a web of relationships. The problem of crime, in this worldview, is that it represents a wound in the community, a tear in the web of relationships. Crime represents damaged relationships. In fact, damaged relationships are both a cause and an effect of crime. Many traditions have a saying that the harm of one is the harm of all. A harm such as crime ripples out to disrupt the whole web. Moreover, wrongdoing is often a symptom that something is out of balance in the web. (Zehr 2002: 19–20)

In Howard Zehr's view, harm is the concern of the individual and the community, in a concrete rather than an abstract sense. When we think of harm, we are more focused on the specific experiences of real people. In centring the concept of harm, approaches to justice become more oriented to meeting the needs of those harmed and those who have acted in ways that have produced harm. This requires the support of the community, which is obligated to address the larger social justice issues and "other conditions that cause crime or create unsafe conditions" (Zehr 2002: 30), with a view to further harm prevention. Zehr and Mika's "signposts of restorative justice" (Zehr 2002: 40–41) could be interpreted as guidelines for "doing no further harm" while addressing harm that has already occurred. The language of punishment is not in these guidelines; in its place is the directive to "recognize that while obligations may be difficult for offenders, those obligations should not be intended as harms, and they must be achievable" (40). Again, we are reminded how important it is to continually revisit restorative processes by connecting practice with core values, particularly respect (36).

Relationships are key to understanding harm, as is a focus on the core value of respect. In *A Healing River* (Douglas and Moore 2004), Donald Nathanson recounts the Lewis Carroll story of the walrus and the carpenter walking down the beach, and the walrus requesting that the carpenter stop introducing him to so many oysters because it is hard to "eat someone you've been introduced to"; in other words, it is more difficult to inflict harm on those we know than those we not only do not know, but treat as objects. Barb Toews and Howard Zehr note:

> Maintaining the crime experience in the hands of experts contributes to othering and the creation of social distance between offenders, victims, and the rest of society.... Once we create this sense of otherness and social distance, we are able to do things to them that we would not otherwise be able to do if we saw their uniqueness as individuals. As Christie (1982) has pointed out, it is this sense of social distance that allows us to deliver pain to offenders and to ignore and/or blame victims. (2003: 262)

In order to reduce harm, then, it is essential to focus on the development of healthy relationships.

In restorative justice the response to harm is motivated not by the quest for punitive consequences for individual offenders but for healing of each individual affected by the harm as well as the collective healing of the community in which the harm occurred. If the term "healing" is defined as making something sound or whole, restoring it to health, then the goal of post-harm intervention is holistic restoration. The metaphor of a stone dropping into a pond creating concentric circles of ripples describes the effects of harm and the consequential paths of potential healing. In justice, to move toward equilibrium is to heal what has been broken by the stone's rupture of the pond's surface. In restorative justice, this means that great attention is paid to needs — of the person harmed, the harm-doer and the community — in order to determine what healing options may be required. As healing must be considered on a case-by-case basis, there are no magic overall prescriptions or predetermined timelines that can govern the process. Joe Solanto, in *A Healing River*, refers to the flexibility required to work with victims to ensure that healing processes are safe and proceed on their own rhythm. Jamie Scott suggests that the healing mandate of restorative justice may put it in conflict with the retributive system's schedule and should therefore be considered "a separate piece of work."

Sharpe (1998: 9) notes that part of healing the harm is reparation, which might include acts such as the return or replacement of stolen property or an apology. Taking responsibility for one's actions in a concrete and direct way, while being supported in ways that reflect core values, is a healing approach to "paying for one's crimes." In this sense, healing is about "making things right" between people in relationships that are damaged or broken. If this is not done, a history of brokenness may ensue and become a catalyst for new harms: "History cannot be changed, but sometimes it can be healed. History must be healed if mankind is to survive" (Consedine and Consedine 2001: 205).

Restorative or transformative justice has also been described as "healing justice," as explained by Breton and Lehman:

> [Restorative justice] preserves what's meaningful in life, starting with issues of safety, self-worth, self-respect, and mutual understanding. Instead of being reactive to events, this model uses events as opportunities for everyone to feel heard, to share hurts from injustices, to rebuild trust in ourselves and each other, and thereby to restore relationships. More than restoring even, healing justice uses instances of hurt to enhance bonds between people and to build communities. The process of working through pain creates an understanding of each other that inspires compassion for our shared human condition. (2001: 13–14)

In other words, justice isn't about abstract standards of legality but about serving human well-being and making our relationships work well. Through the process, we come out of our pain and discover potentials we did not know we had. This not only brings healing but builds self-esteem. If justice does not include healing processes, the pain generated from harm can become chronic (14) and may manifest in a variety of other physical and psychological ailments.

Perhaps the greatest contribution to the emphasis on healing in justice has come from Aboriginal traditions. A native perspective on healing is offered by Patricia Monture-Angus, a Mohawk sociology professor at the University of Saskatoon: "Healing is... about taking responsibility. It is about re-learning how we are supposed to be. Without knowing what traditional responsibilities are, then the right to self-determination really means nothing. Healing is about learning to act in a good way" (in Ross 1996: 219).

The process of healing is not straightforward or prescriptive, but there are common themes. In his consideration of two different Aboriginal community approaches focused on healing, Rupert Ross notes that both projects used the language of restoring, teaching and helping (1994: 249). In addition to the immediate, short-term healing needs of the parties affected, these approaches toward community healing were also aimed at the causes of the crime or harm (Ross 1996: 218). This involves a great deal of attention and planning, as Yazzie and Zion (1996: 168) note about Navajo culture:

> Planning is a major Navajo justice value that is sometimes ignored in state practice. Nahat'a, or planning process, is very practical. Non-Navajos sometimes mock traditional practice. For example, there are Navajos who look in the future using a crystal. A non-Navajo might ridicule that, but Navajos explain how it is done. When you hold a crystal in your hand, you see that it has many facets. You examine each closely, and upon a full examination of each side of the crystal you can see it as a whole. That describes nahat'a, where the parties closely examine each facet of the dispute to see it as a whole.

Aboriginal communities are serious in their efforts to understand the causes of crime, both to fairly address the needs of all of the parties to the specific harmful event and to regain understanding of communal responsibilities through traditional teachings.

What Is Trauma?

Since restorative justice is about healing harms, it is helpful to consider a practical understanding of harm. That is, what is the effect of the violation represented by harm on the person who experiences it? This would seem to depend on two things: the character, intensity and duration of the harm; and the particular individual's capacity, dependent on their own life experience, to "handle" the harm. For example, a broken house window from a misdirected softball might produce very little discomfort for someone inclined to perceive the event as an accident, apart from the nuisance involved in repairing it. However, for someone whose house has already been burgled or who has had some other related negative experiences, a broken window might produce a greater psychological reaction. This suggests a need for flexibility and curiosity in restorative processes, so that everyone understands *what* needs to be healed for every person to go on in a good way.

The *DSM-IV*[2] defines a *traumatic event* as that which involves "actual or threatened death or serious injury or a threat to the physical integrity of self or others" with a response of "intense fear, helplessness, or horror" (American Psychiatric Association 1994: 427–28). Judith Herman's clinical psychiatric work with female victims of gender-based violence in the early 1990s drew attention to symptoms attributed to the phenomenon of trauma. Herman (1997: 33) describes *psychological trauma* as "an affliction of the powerless," which "call[s] into question basic human relationships" (51). Further, she reports that traumatic events "breach the attachments of family, friendship, love and community. They shatter the construction of the self that is formed and sustained in relation to others. They undermine the belief systems that give meaning to human experience. They violate the victim's faith in a natural or divine order and cast the victim into a state of existential crisis" (51).

Trauma research had its seeds in the 1970s. Throughout the 1980s and 1990s, the many U.S. veterans of the Vietnam and Gulf Wars who were suffering major mental health problems as a result of their roles in combat provided impetus for continued research. In 1980, the term "post-traumatic stress disorder" (PTSD) was introduced in the third edition of the *DSM* (Flouri 2005: 373), mostly to deal with Vietnam veterans. However, community-based studies have more recently revealed that PTSD occurs in approximately 8 percent of the adult population at large in the U.S. (374). Manifesting in a pronounced way within an identified population (combat soldiers), PTSD was initially explored in a relatively narrow context. Simultaneously, research on violence against women from a feminist standpoint produced the construct of "battered woman's syndrome," a constellation of symptoms and factors that strongly resembled those of "combat stress." In combination, these two psychiatric research streams — of combat soldiers and victims of violence against women, all suffering similar symptoms — have been the chief contributors to the study of trauma in the past twenty-five years.

Within the military, officers such as Lieutenant Colonel David Grossman have drawn attention to PTSD.[3] Previous recognition of the debilitating personal effects of combat warfare on particular individuals was reflected in terms such as "soldier's heart" (American Civil War) and "shellshock" (World War I). In the following passage, Grossman's military perspective reveals important cues about the character of and responses to trauma:

> The extraordinarily high firing rate [by American soldiers in Vietnam] resulting from modern conditioning processes was a key factor in our ability to claim that we never lost a major engagement in Vietnam. But conditioning which overrides such a powerful, innate resistance has enormous potential for psychological backlash. Every warrior society has a "purification ritual" to help the returning warrior deal with his "blood guilt" and to reassure him that what he did in combat was "good." In primitive tribes this generally involves ritual bathing, ritual separation (which serves as a cooling-off and "group therapy" session), and a ceremony embracing the warrior back into the tribe. Modern Western rituals traditionally involve long separation while marching or sailing home, parades, monuments, and the unconditional acceptance of society and family.
>
> After Vietnam this purification ritual was turned on its head. The returning American veteran was attacked and condemned in an unprecedented manner. The traditional horrors of combat were

magnified by modern conditioning techniques, and this combined with societal condemnation to create a circumstance which resulted in 0.5 to 1.5 million cases of post-traumatic stress disorder (PTSD) in Vietnam veterans. This mass incidence of psychiatric disorders among Vietnam veterans resulted in the "discovery" of PTSD, a condition which we now know has always occurred as a result of warfare, but never in this quantity....

Atrocities, the intentional killing of civilians and prisoners, must be systematically rooted out from our way of war, for the price of these acts is far, far too high to let them be tolerated even to the slightest, smallest degree. This means that we enter into an era of transparency and accountability in all aspects of our law enforcement, peacekeeping, and combat operations. This also says something about those who are called upon by their society to "go in harm's way," to use deadly force, and to contend with interpersonal human aggression. These individuals require psychological support just as surely as they require logistical, communications, and medical support. Thus, as our society enters into the Post-Cold War era, the fields of psychiatry and psychology have much to contribute to the continuing evolution of combat, and to the evolution of our civilization. (Grossman n.d.)

In this passage, Grossman remarks on the significance of post-battle rituals for the health of returning warriors and how the absence of welcoming messages and support for Vietnam veterans contributed to the prevalence of PTSD in these soldiers. He extrapolates on this idea in his book *On Killing* (1995), in which he argues that those soldiers who experienced the worst of warfare but had significant individual support on return recovered more quickly than those who did not have that support. This is reified by a study demonstrating the mitigating effect of high levels of perceived support from family and friends and low levels of disengagement from social relationships on PTSD scores in civilians who had suffered from violence committed in communities (Scarpa et al. 2006). The individuals' relationships with primary people in their life, as well as their relationship with the wider community, were key to their healing. Grossman's warning about PTSD indicates his concern about the effects of the disorder on the actions of frontline enforcement personnel. The implications of PTSD are wide-reaching.

Eve Carlson and Constance Dalenberg's (2000) conceptual framework for the impact of trauma on individuals is useful for outlining areas of study that are valuable for informing social, education and criminal justice policy. One other psychological phenomenon of interest to this area of study is shame; the post-trauma emotions of shame and guilt find expression in a range of avoidance behaviours, such as isolation, detachment, withdrawal, cancellation of appointments, surrender of responsibilities, emotional constriction and so on (Wilson, Drozdek and Turkovic 2006: 138). Trauma and trauma-induced behaviour and thought patterns are also passed on intergenerationally and well beyond the original events, as in the examples of Holocaust legacies and war-displaced refugees (Lev-Weisel 2007).

Two other areas of related interest deepen our insight into the aetiology of harmful actions. Sheryn Scott (2007) observes that multiple traumatic experiences over a lifetime tend to increase the severity of PTSD symptoms and that adults who were sexually abused as children are more likely to develop PTSD than those who have not had these experiences. It has also been argued that psychological trauma differs according to the source of the trauma (LaMothe 1999). Whether the trauma occurred as a result of natural events or at the hands of other people is said to affect the healing of the trauma sufferer. "Malignant trauma" — that which is experienced through the violence of another human being — "is the result of five interrelated experiences of loss: (a) shock associated with the loss of expectation of help; (b) loss of control over the integrity of one's body; (c) loss in the belief that the other is obliged to respond to a cry; (d) loss of trust associated with the experience of betrayal; and (e) loss of another's commitment to recognize, respect, and respond to one's desires and needs" (1193). People afflicted with PTSD are thus often victims of sexual and other physical violence, with the consequence of experiencing fractured trust in relationships with other people. These significant issues might be addressed through restorative practices.

Biology of Trauma

One way of viewing trauma is through its biological effects. Research on the effects of serious trauma on small children and babies (during the human's most active time of brain development) demonstrates specific effects in brain chemistry: "When stress is especially severe or prolonged, permanent changes may occur in hormone levels that alter the brain's chemical profile and affect patterns of information processing. The result may be maladaptive behavior patterns, including both aggression and depression" (Karr-Morse and Wiley 1997: 156). Trauma also refers to the physical injuries sustained by violent acts. Nature and nurture seem indistinguishable as causal factors in crime when the effects of trauma are a mix of both experience and physiology.

In *A Healing River*, psychologist Joe Solanto outlines the psychological manifestations of trauma and describes the effects of trauma on a person's biology and brain chemistry. He offers some ideas, based on kindness and safety, to help the sufferer of trauma-related disorders. His clinical observations of trauma echo those of Eldra Solomon and Kathleen Heide (2005), who note, "Traumatic experiences cause traumatic stress, which disrupts homeostasis" (52). They summarize the biological effects of trauma on brain function as follows:

> Traumatic events overwhelm the brain's capacity to process information. The episodic memory of the experience may be dysfunctionally stored in the right limbic system indefinitely and may generate vivid images of the traumatic experience, terrifying thoughts, feelings, body sensations, sounds, and smells. Such unprocessed traumatic memories can cause cognitive and emotional looping, anxiety, PTSD, maladaptive coping strategies, depression, and many other psychological symptoms of distress. Because the episodic memory is not processed, a relevant semantic memory is not stored and the individual has difficulty using knowledge from the experience to guide future action. (54)

This summary reminds us of the impact of emotion on cognitive functions, discussed in the previous chapter on shame. It also generates questions; if we layer this knowledge of the trauma-affected brain over criminal justice expectations, many anomalies arise. For example, how reliable are the testimonies of eye-witnesses to traumatic events, subject as they may be to unprocessed episodic memories? How well does a perpetrator of violence reason? How might untreated PTSD affect the performance of police officers discharging regular duties after experiencing severe violence?

Claims to mitigating variables such as PTSD in determining individual culpability for acts of violence and other harms can sometimes elicit contempt. The claim that violently victimized children often become violently offending adults commonly draws the response that not all people who were abused as children become abusers themselves. On the surface, this is true. But research gains in the early twenty-first century have offered us some understanding on why this is true, and these reasons have little to do with mere cognitive "choosing" to be good or bad in spite of one's life experiences. The key concept here is "resilience," or why some people bounce back from terrible experiences and live relatively successful lives in spite of them, while others don't.

Biological research has demonstrated that resilience — or more precisely, decreased resilience — can be explained by an interaction between certain genes and the environment, in an area of research known in the field as GxE (Caspi et al. 2003). In the case of resilience, when a particular variation of the gene 5-HTT is combined with an adverse environment (a violent home, for example), the individual can experience a psychological response such as depression. Why? The 5-HTT gene is comprised of two alleles. An allele is one member of a pair or series of different forms of a gene; an individual's genotype for that gene is the set of alleles it possesses. Each allele can be one of two sizes — long or short. A person's 5-HTT gene comprises one of the following combinations: two long alleles, two short alleles, or one of each. Alleles release serotonin, which is a neurotransmitter that plays an important role in the human brain's ability to modulate anger, aggression, body temperature, mood, sleep, human sexuality, appetite and metabolism. Adequate levels of serotonin in the brain help to mitigate the psychological effects of adverse or traumatic events. The presence of one or two short alleles appears to affect serotonin delivery; indeed, people with at least one short 5-HTT allele are prone to depression. People with two short 5-HTT alleles, especially those who have experienced a traumatic event, have an even higher likelihood of experiencing depression. Those with two long 5-HTT alleles, on the other hand, have a good chance of bouncing back from the traumatic events; that is, they are more likely to demonstrate resiliency. As can be seen, the gene does not "cause" depression on its own, but it can make a significant difference to a person whose environment presents mistreatment or several life stresses.[4] This is an example of the connection between nature and nurture.

Much of the research done in this area uses data from a longitudinal study conducted by the Dunedin Multidisciplinary Health and Development Research Unit at the University of Otago in New Zealand (Dunedin Study Website n.d.). This project began in 1972 when 1,037 babies were enrolled; almost 96 percent of the subjects (972, excluding eighteen who had died) returned for their most recent assessment in 2003–2005. Many insights about human development have been and will continue to be gained from this ongoing endeavour. For example, Avshalom Caspi et al. used data from the Dunedin Study to consider the role of genotype in the cycle of violence in maltreated children: "A functional polymorphism in the gene encoding the neurotransmitter-metabolizing enzyme monoamine oxidase A (MAOA) was found to moderate the effect of maltreatment. Maltreated children with a genotype conferring high levels of MAOA expression were less likely to develop anti-social problems" (2002: 851). MAOA facilitates the brain's ability to utilize serotonin, which affects resiliency to the effects of trauma. This finding adds to our understanding of resiliency, but it also reveals a genetic susceptibility to behavioural problems when the child is both maltreated and has a low-activity MAOA genotype. In this particular study, only 12 percent of the male birth cohort fit this latter description — but they accounted for 44 percent of the cohort's violent criminal convictions.

In other words, when it comes to human development and behaviour, biology matters. The previous examples speak to the genes-environment nexus and shed some light on the concept of resilience. Given human history of the twentieth-century, however, there is a risk in highlighting a genetic component of deviant behaviour. This is a central reason why the emphasis should be placed on the inter-variable effect of an individual's genes and environment. The genes alone do not foreshadow problems in the individual's future; they only matter if the individual's environmental conditions are extremely adverse and relational support is low. The evidence has been established: "In the past 10 years... research has demonstrated that exposure to trauma and violence has a causal, environmentally mediated, adverse effect on risk for outcomes such as anti-social behavior, substance abuse, and a wide range of adult psychopathology" (Koenen 2005: 509). People with these problems often end up in our criminal justice system, whether as perpetrators, victims or witnesses. A restorative, healing approach to the events that normally result in institutional intervention must then take into account the individual's life course to that moment, the person's resilience and the physical and emotional environment in which the person lives.

Our state institutions of criminal justice, education, health and social services operate primarily on the basis of cognitive rationality and morality. Individuals' culpability and capacity are assessed in order to determine appropriate interventions. Morality is the justification for our interventions, and a compassionate, inclusive, democratic perspective directs the "rehabilitation" or moral education component of our interventions. The problem is that these aspects are not the *only* ones at play in the individual's behaviour; there are physical dimensions to behaviour, as demonstrated in the biological evidence noted above. There are emotional dimensions, too, which are related to the physical; as Nathanson (1994) points out, emotion has a biological component called "affect." Emotions propel behaviours that can be maladaptive and even destructive. Heide and Solomon (2006) list the bio-effects of Type III trauma (complex PTSD) on the brain: childhood trauma interferes with normal brain development and can cause long-term changes in the brain as seen in EEG abnormalities in abused children; traumatic memories get trapped in the limbic system, which remains on red alert; childhood trauma causes long-term changes in the endocrine system (a positive feedback loop intensifies aggressive behaviour); and trauma causes a disconnect between the mind and body. They also noted that neglect can be more damaging than abuse, resulting in weak to negligible attachments, which also affect neuro-physiology. Ultimately, the authors pose the difficult questions that almost all other researchers ignore: "Research findings raise the question to what extent individuals with complex PTSD should be held accountable for violently explosive behaviour. Are Type III trauma survivors responsible for inexplicable violence if they are essentially in a survival mode when they attack others based on past events? Is it morally defensible to find these defendants culpable for their behaviour if scientific findings provide convincing evidence that individuals cannot process and evaluate information when they are in this hyperaroused state?" (229–30).

Trauma: Survivors and Perpetrators

The phenomenon of trauma is interwoven in the lives of both survivors and perpetrators of violence. Restorative interventions deployed with conflicts involving violation of the person and their property must be mindful of this possibility. Actions might not make sense, rationally or morally, and a trauma-informed assessment of a conflict's aetiology can sometimes help to explain what, on the surface, seems incomprehensible.

For example, the manner in which a traumatic event occurs affects the victim's response. Research has shown that there are different trauma responses between victims of crime and victims of industrial accidents (Shercliffe and Colotla 2009). Using the MMPI-2,[5] researchers found that, although the profiles for PTSD sufferers as crime victims or industrial accident victims were similar, crime victims scored higher on clinical scales measuring worry, depression and suspicion (355–56). Morality seems to factor into this difference. The researchers asked: "Why would a traumatic event involving a criminal act cause more psychological distress than an accident? One possibility is the attribution of blame for the incident to a specific person (in fact this is why the individual suffering the attack or assault is usually called the 'victim,' whereas the other is the 'perpetrator,' thus implying differential presumption of blame)" (356). The source of crime victims' particular distress indicates a breach of trust in their experiences of human relationships.

Victim service programs first emerged in the 1970s, largely from the efforts of women's groups (informed by feminist analyses) to offer triage support to women harmed by sexual assault or spousal violence. These services generally took the form of twenty-four-hour crisis lines, transition houses and counselling support. In the 1980s, more generic victim service agencies became established, often through the aegis of criminal justice institutions such as the police, courts and corrections. Both of these victim-serving streams continue to function in North America, supplemented by other community-based agencies. In a study of 660 victims, consisting of those who used and those who did not use victim services, Barbara Sims et al., examining the efficacy of such programs, noted:

> One of the major goals of victim services is to improve the ability of the victim to deal with the stressors associated with the victimization experience. In the present study, no statistically significant differences were found between users and nonusers of victim services when it comes to the psychological functioning scores of victims, a finding that supports Davis's (1987) claim of 15 years prior. Rather, it was the degree to which victims reported possessing adequate and sufficient coping skills in their day-to-day living that significantly predicted higher scores on victims' well-being. (2006: 401)

The goal of assisting the victim in dealing with their victim experience is, as the authors note, significant. A quick purview of victim service agencies in British Columbia, as an example, reveals the parsimonious attention to this aspect of the work. "Emotional support" is noted in the work of both police-based and community-based victim assistance programs (funded by the Ministry of Public Safety and Solicitor General). However, most of the listed activities of the programs seem to be anchored in measures to smooth the victim's path through the formal criminal justice system, such as offering information about how the system works and important court dates, helping victims to fill out forms and providing referrals to other agencies for counselling, housing and so on (Ending Violence Website n.d. and Police Victim Services Website n.d.).

Crime victims are the obvious potential sufferers of PTSD, and efforts have been made — particularly through the work of feminist advocates — to shield some victims from the retraumatization of adversarial court systems. This was particularly the case for victims of sexual assault, who were often aggressively cross-examined by defence lawyers. In North America, this resulted in several variations of rape shield laws, which limit a defendant's ability to cross-examine sexual assault complainants about their past sexual behaviour and prevent the media from publishing their names. However, not all victims suffer trauma in subsequent criminal justice interventions. For example, research on other kinds of crime trials suggests that offender trials do not generally retraumatize victims (Orth and Maercker 2004). While the trial itself might not trigger most victims, traumatized victims can carry subsequent feelings of wanting revenge depending on the variance in post-traumatic intrusion and hyperarousal (Orth, Montada and Maercker 2006: 238).

One measure of predicting future offending behaviour is early victimization. Researchers (for example, Leschied et al. 2008) acknowledge that a significant risk of adult offending is related to early childhood factors such as family violence, where the child is either the direct victim or a witness to violence from a caregiver. This is indicated in research on youth in the criminal justice system. Exposure to violence as a witness or recipient has been found to increase the risk for young adult criminal activity (Eitle and Turner 2002). Youth involved with the criminal justice system are significantly more likely to have been traumatized than other adolescents in the school system. A study of 152 adolescent court referrals, half boys and half girls, suggests a prevalence of trauma in both groups — girls (75 percent) and boys (51 percent) (Krischer and Sevecke 2008).

Much of the research in this area has involved incarcerated adults. Donald Dutton and Stephen Hart's (1992) study of 604 Canadian prisoner files reveals that men who were abused as children were three times more likely to be violent than men who were not abused. Another study of trauma experiences and mental disorders, involving thirty-nine forensic patients and 192 prisoners, reported a high frequency of traumatic events in both groups' backgrounds — forensic patients at 78 percent and prisoners at 75 percent — with dissociative symptoms being more common among prisoners (Timmerman and Emmelkamp 2001). Research also provides support for the relationship between violent behaviour and interpersonal traumatic events in a sample of thirty-nine women prisoners (Byrd and Davis 2008). Women prisoners present high levels of previous trauma exposure, high rates of substance abuse and clinically significant levels of depression and PTSD (Green et al. 2005). The authors of this study note: "There is an increasing understanding of the fact that many women in prison or jail for committing crimes are crime victims themselves" (146). Another study of prisoners, drugs and childhood abuse effects demonstrates strong evidence of a "cumulative abuse effect" for both men and women prisoners (Messina et al. 2007). Researchers examining PTSD, drugs and recidivism in prisoners note differences in the effects of trauma between men and women prisoners, with men experiencing most of their trauma while incarcerated and women experiencing more trauma on return to their communities (Kubiak 2004).

The results of these studies confirm what most attentive criminal justice professionals already know — that people who have been repeatedly harmed often take on the role of the harm-doer (Falshaw 2005). The criminal justice proclivity to strictly delineate the roles of victim and offender seems to be an institutional and conceptual convenience rather than a reflection of actual experiences. This lack of systemic insight is evident in a study on PTSD and prisoners in which the researchers looked at 103 relevant research articles on mental disorder in prisoners and found only four that offered criteria affording *any* analysis of PTSD (Goff et al. 2007). The authors note: "The prevalence of PTSD in prison populations might be expected to be higher than in the general population, and the omission of reference to it in such an apparently comprehensive review of prisoners is puzzling. Failure to identify and treat PTSD among prisoners could be a factor predisposing to suicide and self-harming behaviour in prison and, indeed, to recidivism" (153). Perhaps more to the point, the interventions of so-called correctional systems are predicated on the basis that offenders are somehow different than non-offenders, and consequently these interventions target behaviour on the surface of the criminal role. Louise Falshaw suggests: "Fear that the abuse will be used to legitimize the offending may be a reason that a history of abuse in offending behaviour treatment may not currently be given sufficient significance" (2005: 429).

Trauma: Professionals and Others

For the curious, the effects of trauma on people who have been processed through the criminal justice system should raise important questions. But there is another dimension to this trauma-informed scenario: the effects of violence and devastation on the people employed in systems mandated to undertake emergency responses or help those affected by severe violence post-trauma. In the first case, the worker is exposed to multiple, first-hand experiences of violence; in the second case, the exposure is secondary, or vicarious, traumatization. In either case, the experience of trauma may impact the individual's ability to perform their duties effectively and can carry over into the individual's personal life outside of work.

Police officers are an obvious launch for this discussion. The work of policing often entails encounters with situations that are volatile or require officers to attend to the aftermath of violent crime scenes. One study of eighty-four police recruits in Canada found that, while previous trauma did not increase biological distress during circumstances of acute stress, when combined with low social supports, previous trauma was associated with ongoing psychological distress (Regehr et al. 2007). In an Australian study of 103 police officers, researchers examined the impact of trauma disclosure on the psychological health of the officers; the findings demonstrate that officers who held back emotional disclosures of the trauma experience were more likely to suffer psychological distress and traumatic stress (Davidson and Moss 2008). One symptom of PTSD, according to the *DSM-IV*, is "irritability or outbursts of anger," a factor considered by another study of PTSD in police officers. The authors of this study found that "trait anger" (a trait pre-existing the individuals' choice of police work) was a risk factor for later PTSD symptoms, but also that these symptoms were associated with increases of "state anger" (hostility in the moment of police work) (Meffert et al. 2008). Research on police officers in Northern Ireland, who developed PTSD as a result of their work during the political "troubles" of the past, shows that a strong sense of *shared identity* mitigates the effects of trauma — a factor also known to underpin conflict (Muldoon and Downes 2007). Similar to the police, prison workers and prisoners are directly vulnerable to many of the traumatic life experiences listed in the *DSM-IV*, notably violent personal assault or being taken hostage, and secondarily as witnesses to the serious injury or death of another person as a result of violent assault (Freeman 2000).

Vicarious, or secondary, trauma has been identified as a possible risk for professional and lay people working with cases in which trauma is significant. Vicarious trauma is defined as "the response of those persons who have witnessed, been subject to explicit knowledge of or had the responsibility to intervene in a seriously distressing or tragic event" (Lerias and Byrne 2003: 130). Research shows that mental health professionals and trauma therapists with personal histories of trauma experience the most distress in their work (Buchanan et al. 2006; Pearlman and MacIan 1995). Birck (2002) reported very high PTSD symptoms among both mental health professionals and administrative staff working with torture victims. In work with sex offences, it has been found that clinicians with shorter time in the field report higher levels of vicarious trauma (Way et al. 2004), due to lack of experience or skills in managing this phenomenon in their role. While not everyone working in the field is affected, sex offender therapists who work in secure prison settings have reported high levels of vicarious trauma (Moulden and Firestone 2007). Both professionals and lay people in "helping" fields are particularly susceptible to vicarious trauma, because the very attributes that bring them to the work are those that make them vulnerable: "A desire to help survivors of traumatic events, exposure to traumatic material of survivors, and empathy are the foundational factors in the development of secondary traumatic stress" (Salston and Figley 2003: 172). Jury members can also experience psychological harm as a result of viewing and hearing traumatic evidence (Robertson, Davies and Nettleingham 2009).

While there is no question that trauma challenges one's mental health, it is clear that individuals respond differently depending on their innate resilience, previous life experiences and both emotional and physical supports. Some people are able to go further, reporting post-traumatic growth following violent experiences. Post-traumatic growth has been described as "positive psychological change experienced as a result of the struggle with highly challenging life circumstances" (Tedeschi and Calhoun 2004: 1). It has also been found that professionals' individual coping styles do not directly influence their symptoms of secondary traumatization in their work with trauma survivors (Killian 2008). Some research in these areas shows that many emergency professionals experience post-traumatic growth if they have extraverted personalities, are well trained and work in organizations characterized by a climate of care and support (Paton 2005). Other research demonstrates support for one component of this finding: the ambulance personnel most resilient to trauma were found to be those who were extraverted, open to experience, agreeable and conscientious (Shakespeare-Finch, Gow and Smith 2005).

What Can Be Done?

Trauma research is relatively new, with about twenty-five years of work drawn from neuroscience, genetics, biology, clinical psychology and psychiatry. It is only recently that criminologists have been curious to see the potential for trauma in their subject matter, and then mostly through the lens of restorative justice. Given its focus on harm and healing rather than crime and punishment, it is easy to see how a restorative lens could attract and accommodate a trauma focus within its gaze. The question of what can be done, within this context, largely depends on what lens we use to view the problems currently recognized as crime and deviance.

From a criminology perspective, there is ample evidence of the effects of trauma on individuals, their families, their communities and the broader social world. Yet our crime-and-punishment lens has not been so receptive to its implications. One reason for this was explained by Arrick Jackson et al.:

> Because of the inability of the field of criminology to develop research paradigms, the fields of criminology, sociology, and psychology must rely on middle-range theories as research programs, a reliance that subsequently leads to many topics being researched, tested, and debated among the respective fields to the exclusion of the others.... This conclusion can be found in the most recent literature on violence and trauma... where the authors discussed topics (violence and trauma) that are, for the most part, dependent on each other, yet they exclude important discussions about the other. The study of trauma cannot advance unless it first develops theories and empirical research that incorporate the field of violence and vice versa. (2005: 473)

Given the problem-solving perspective of restorative practices, the inclination to exclude factors or topics on the basis of rigid conceptual distinctions and enormous methodological challenges is not a significant issue — unless, of course, the restorative intervention is enveloped by a larger institutional imperative. The capacity for trauma-informed RJ processes to unpack the several layers of meaning that underpin violent acts affords a better understanding of a person's actions. Violence takes many physical and emotional forms, and the earlier it is inserted into a person's life experiences the more it affects that person's later behaviour.

What can explain our reticence to act meaningfully and helpfully when people are seriously harmed? Gail Ryan (2005: 134) notes: "Resources flow toward problems, more than prevention, perpetuating reactive rather than proactive strategies. Preventing the risks associated with children becoming violent and abusive is possible. The impediments are a matter of priorities and competing needs, not a lack of knowledge." We need to pay much more than lip service to the overall well-being of every child in a society, not just the ones who have the luck to attract sufficient help. Political dysfunction ensures that this situation continues, with public money pouring into police agencies, courts and correctional systems while it is only trickling into community-based social services and education. Another reason for our reticence is that to accept the knowledge on violence and trauma reviewed in this chapter is to be confronted with myriad structural problems posed by current institutional mandates. Criminal law is based on a belief in *mens rea* and the "reasonable person." Laws reflect a society's morality, and a breach of these laws summons various cognitive interventions to encourage or coerce the law-breaker to think reasonably and make better choices. Yet individuals are more than thinking, physical beings; they are emotional and spiritual beings as well. Furthermore, to rely wholly on cognitive interventions is to compromise our results; in the case of chronic traumatization (such as that of combat veterans, battered spouses and sexually abused children), social-cognitive information processing theories do not work (Kaysen, Resick and Wise 2003). Promising treatments for PTSD lie in the realm of psychological counselling, particularly with trauma-focused cognitive behavioural therapy and eye movement desensitization and reprocessing therapy (Bisson et al. 2007). Unfortunately, within the current retributive framework, interventions for "offenders" are generally rooted in what they did to other people and not what was done to them, so therapeutic PTSD interventions for violent prisoners are rare.

The story of James at the beginning of the chapter was relayed by a psychiatrist with rich experience in working with trauma-affected children. Bruce Perry's experiences with children who have been chronically neglected and abused — including a cohort of children rescued from the Waco, Texas, Branch Davidian compound before it was raided by government authorities — have led him to perhaps the most important conclusion for this chapter:

> Trauma and our responses to it cannot be understood outside the context of human relationships. Whether people have survived an earthquake or have been repeatedly sexually abused, what matters most is how those experiences affect their relationships — to their loved ones, to themselves and to the world. *The most traumatic aspects of all disasters involve the shattering of human connections.* And this is especially true for children. Being harmed by the people who are supposed to love you, being abandoned by them, being robbed of the one-on-one relationships that allow you to feel safe and valued and to become humane — these are profoundly destructive experiences. *Because humans are inescapably social beings, the worst catastrophes that can befall us inevitably involve relational loss.*
>
> As a result, *recovery from trauma and neglect is also all about relationships — rebuilding trust, regaining confidence, returning to a sense of security and reconnecting to love.* Of course, medications can help relieve symptoms and talking to a therapist can be incredibly useful. But healing and re-covery are impossible — even with the best medications and therapy in the world — without lasting, caring connections to others. Indeed, at heart it is the relationship with the therapist, not primarily his or

her methods or words of wisdom, that allows therapy to work. All the children who ultimately thrived following our treatment did so because of a strong social network that surrounded and supported them. (Perry and Szalavitz 2006: 231–32, emphasis added)

The key here, of course, is relationships — as a source of both trauma and healing. People affected by harm from any perspective respond more quickly when buoyed by relational support, be they victims, offenders, police officers or therapeutic clinicians. Since relationships are foundational to restorative justice, there is greater hope for problem-solving through a restorative rather than retributive lens.

Conclusion

A lot of people would say it's a bad idea, on your first day out of prison, to go right back to stalking the tranny hooker that knocked out five of your teeth. But that's how I roll." (Phil, character in the movie *Choke*, 2008)

An understanding of trauma can help us to understand what makes Phil tick. He knows that stalking his assailant is wrong, has suffered the punishment meant to deter him, but goes right back to doing it because that's how he "rolls" in his trauma cycle. We could also say the same thing about the institutions we have created to deal with our problems in the first place. A review of institutional mandates and practices is revealing. For example, Judith Herman's important contribution to the literature, *Trauma and Recovery,* (1997), highlights terror, disconnection, captivity and child abuse as significant contributors to trauma; these factors could also be used to characterize the prison environment and the lives of those sentenced to it. This suggests that the work ahead involves much more than helping people to meet their needs. Institutions also need rethinking and reformulating.

Curiously, a review of literature on victims of crime reveals a noticeable absence of discussion on trauma. Discussion on crime victims specifically focuses on what is possible within the limits of the status quo, and this usually pertains to notions of rights, victim impact statements and so on. In sum, the presentations are limited by the needs of the criminal justice institutions rather than the needs of the people harmed.

Notes

1. As of December 2008, 193 countries have ratified the Convention, including every member of the United Nations except the United States and Somalia.
2. The *DSM-IV* is the fourth edition of the Diagnostics and Statistical Manual produced by the American Psychiatric Association. This manual is a popular

tool among mental health professionals, particularly in the United States but also in other parts of the world.

3. "Killology" is Grossman's term for his study of the psychology of killing.

4. For a simple read on the GxE phenomenon, see Bazelon (2006).

5. The MMPI-2 (Minnesota Multiphasic Personality Inventory) is a frequently used mental health test for identifying personality structure and psychopathology. It is the first major revision of the MMPI, and released in 1989. The test is used for adults.

10

Restorative Justice as Community Development and Harm Prevention

Mrs. Macleod

Michael Bopp

Fresh out of university, I found myself working with troubled children and youth in Dawson City, Yukon. Many of the young people I worked with were from First Nations families. I felt it was important for me to try to work with those families and with the community, but I really had no idea where to begin. For the most part, community people were not interested in even talking to me. I was just another white "social worker."

I started visiting an old lady named Mrs. Macleod. I would have tea with her, and try to tell her all about my many ideas for improving the community. She never said much, but she seemed to appreciate my visits. I noticed that her son and grandson were often absent for weeks at a time or absorbed in binge drinking. I saw she needed her wood chopped, so I started doing that every few days. I also did some shopping for her or drove her to the store.

One day I was having tea with her, and I was talking away about some idea I had for how to fix the community. She rarely said anything when I talked like that, but this time she leaned over the table and abruptly stated, "Why don't you just shut up and listen. You talk too much. You should listen."

I left soon after that embarrassed and confused. But gradually I realized how right she was. From that point on, listening became my main strategy. The more I listened, the more I learned.

I also came to realize that I was working with a serious handicap. I had entered the community thinking I was "the one who knows," the expert. And why shouldn't I think like that? I had completed years of university training, and had come to believe that one who has such advanced learning as I, was now a qualified expert or professional. That's what professional training is all about, isn't it?

What I learned from Mrs. Macleod and her community (and many communities after that) was that my training had not prepared me to know more about people's lives and community than they knew themselves. Nor did I have any idea how to connect my knowledge and skills with their real needs within the tangled web of relationships within which they lived.

Very gradually (because it is very hard to let go of a part of one's self that one believes is basic to one's identity) I became what my friends referred to as a "recovering expert," someone willing to apprentice himself to community people in order to learn how to serve them. (Bopp and Bopp 2001: 94)

⚹ ⚹ ⚹

This story of the eager young social worker and Mrs. Macleod may be familiar to anyone engaged in community development work as an outsider. Parachuting into a complex network of relationships with their own unique history and local conventions, such workers can experience hostility and resistance by community members suspicious of paid professionals. An under-resourced community plagued by inordinate levels of social problems can be resentful of an external "expert" who has no demonstrable commitment to that community.

Restorative justice can be an important perspective and toolkit for community development. This requires a ground-up, community-based approach, which uses conflict as an opportunity to see what is not working so well in the fabric of relationships within any specific community of people. Increasingly, we see the expansion of government institutions and their mandates encroaching on the terrain of lived community experience. These institutions are necessary partners in the background of intervention, originally the forces of last resort when small local groups could not manage their collective affairs. But at this time in history, our primary sources of intervention are institutions.

While state institutions are likely to see interpersonal conflicts and damaging interactions as crimes, rule-breaking and individual irresponsibility or culpability, restorative practices focus on the more encompassing concept of "harm." Harm means more than just physical injury; it also includes mental damage, hurt and moral injury. Its meaning is not captured in "crime," which refers to an act deemed to be illegal whether or not it causes harm to the harm-doer or other people. Harm can be seen in the violence of power, in the very systems we use to respond to violence. Dennis Sullivan and Larry Tifft talk of systemic violence and the challenge of creating systems that make it "easier for people to be good" (2005: 123). Apart from the implied violence of the hierarchical relationships within institutions, they often contribute to maintaining wider social conditions conducive to desperate and harmful interpersonal behaviour. Acknowledging that our social systems may also be significant *contributors* to harm, through unfair or unjust beliefs, policies and resourcing, we undertake a social justice perspective to harm.

Ruth Morris criticizes restorative justice theory for its lack of attention to social justice issues:

Restorative justice theory did not take into account the enormous structural injustices at the base of our justice systems, and the extent to which they function mainly to reinforce racism and classism. Any theory or method that ignores racism and classism that are basic to retributive justice is missing something very vital, and will serve to reinforce that racism and classism further, by not challenging it....

Distributive justice abounds everywhere, and most offenders are, more than the average person is, victims of distributive injustice. Do we want to restore offenders to the marginalized, enraged, disempowered condition most were in just before the offence? (2000: 19)

Morris's words echo the concerns touched on in this book about the semantic implications of the very term "restorative justice." They also raise concerns about the co-optation of the language of restorative justice and the distortion of restorative practices within the retributive system, which adds to her discomfort with the term.

At the heart of this concern is the lack of emphasis on social justice within restorative justice discourse. However, it is clear that, while there are many examples of such disregard, practitioners grounded in the values and principles of restorative justice will inevitably be sensitive to social justice concerns. As Jennifer Llewellyn and Robert Howse suggest, "restorative justice begins from the disequilibrium of a relationship in society, but what is ultimately to be restored is not the facticity of the relationship before disruption but an *ideal* of a relationship of equality in society" (1998: 3). When restorative justice practices are motivated by a community-building focus rather than a case-processing formal criminal-justice mandate, opportunities for encountering and addressing inequalities and social justice issues become clear.

In this view, social justice issues can be addressed from a basis in grass-roots community development rather than more structured, conventional approaches like crime prevention through environmental design. Social welfare issues must be addressed in order to get to the roots of individual harm: "Community organization must take social conditions into account before accepting target-hardening as a *fait accompli*. Deficient education systems, poverty, underemployment and unemployment, insufficient health care systems, and unplanned pregnancies exacerbate an already strained urban setting" (Klein, Luxenburg and Gunther 1991: 293–94). Harm-prevention strategies that operate within a crime-control model may be attractive in the short term, but failing to address the causes of social injustice "will merely result in a fight against an unconquerable foe (e.g., crime and its social consequences)" (294). Since individual stories of the effects of unjust social policy come from the ground up, the community is the first site of social action. Community justice begins with the assumption that most individual and group behaviours are regulated by informal control systems such as families, neighbours and community organizations rather than formal institutions such as the police or courts (Kruger 2007: 104).

In this chapter, we consider the many dimensions of the term "community." We examine what possibilities exist for community in restorative justice in diverse social contexts where it is used as a guiding philosophy and practice (schools, families, clubs, criminal justice agencies, workplaces and so on). Community also invites the review of another concept: "social capital," a way of defining the benefits of relationships to general well-being. We close the chapter by considering how restorative justice community-building lends itself to cultivating citizenship skills for engagement in a democratic society.

What Is the "Community"?

Perhaps there is no more contested a concept in the restorative justice literature, and beyond, than that of "community." Authors repeatedly acknowledge the difficulty in defining the concept. There is something intimate in the ideal of community, a sense of connectedness and belonging that is an unqualified good. Yet the ideal seems far away from what exists and is often referred to as community. This section presents a variety of angles from which to imagine the many dimensions of community.

The word "community" is derived from the two words "common" and "unity," intimating a shared common oneness with others, according to experienced Canadian community developers Michael Bopp and Judie Bopp (2001). A high degree of deliberate engagement is assumed in their particular use of "community" to refer to "any grouping of human beings who enter into a sustained relationship with each other for the purpose of improving themselves and the world within which they live" (2001: 13). In the same vein, McKnight suggests that community "comprises various groups of people who work together on a face-to-face basis in public life, not just in private" (1995: 118). Clear and Karp summarize this stream of definitions in their offering: "Community is an entirely practical concept, not merely an ephemeral term of art.... For each of us, community is the complex interlocking of human relationships upon which we rely to live daily life. In modern societies, these are diverse, multiple, and individual, but they are no less substantial for their variety" (1999: 60). There is also an element of social exclusion to this practical, utilitarian definition of community, with its implication that there are others outside of the particular and perhaps insular community (Woolford and Ratner 2008: 124).

Western cultures in the nascent twenty-first century have experienced transformations of traditional versions of "community." Visions of the friendly neighbourhood, with people sitting on their porches and engaging with one another, walking to local shops owned by other neighbours and keeping an eye on all the kids seem like fairy tales to most people. Today, "neighbourhoods" are more likely to be a collection of houses with neighbours engaging sporadically. Indeed, a study in New York showed that people felt stronger connections to their co-workers than they did their neighbours (Dahlin, Kelly and Moen 2008). Perhaps idyllic communities only exist in government discourses. Martin Mowbray's critique of the focus on idealized versions of community in Australian government representations suggests dubious intentions. In his argument, governmental renditions of community ascribed "only positive qualities to community" and "facilitated a move to depoliticize social problems"; furthermore, community programs were "represented as being bottom-up and directed at community self-determination [but] were in fact funded and managed within centrally determined regulations" (2005: 257). This phenomenon has been referred to as "the evident gap between communitarian aspirations and community reality" (Dixon, Dogan and Sanderson 2005: 5), an outcome of competing philosophies of knowledge and human behaviour. Governmental deployment of "community" falls into McCold's (2004) definition of the macro-community as the interests of society generally.

Although not directly articulated, what makes the idea of community so appealing are its emotional characteristics. "Community is a feeling, a perception of connectedness — personal connectedness both to other individual human beings and to a group" (McCold and Wachtel 1998: 72). Emotion is a key phenomenon in restorative practices, contributing to our understanding of the noticeable invitation to the expression of feelings and the impact of these feelings on the engagement process and outcomes. Nathanson, whose work we were introduced to with the concept of shame, offers an explanation of community on the basis of affect, the biological portion of emotion:

A community is a public group of people linked by scripts for systems of affect modulation. It is formed and maintained by the following rules: 1) Mutualization of and group action to enhance or maximize positive affect. 2) Mutualization of and group action to diminish or minimize negative affect. 3) Communities thrive best when all affect is expressed so these first two goals may be accomplished. 4) Mechanisms that increase the power to accomplish these goals favor the maintenance of community, mechanisms that decrease the power to express and modulate affect threaten the community. (1997: 15–16)

Nathanson's work suggests that an essential component of communities is the sharing (mutualization) of emotion (affect). Restorative processes aim to create a safe space in which emotions can be expressed and managed by the group. Emotional release not only partially unburdens the person suffering, but it adds a memory hook to the harm suffered by the person for the others in the circle. When people are emotionally connected, they become more deeply motivated to change conditions in their community that may be hospitable to harmful behaviours. A feeling of belonging to a group heightens their sense of responsibility and accountability to the group. According to Peter Block, community "is about the experience of belonging. We are in community each time we find a place where we belong" (2008: xii).

We can recognize the emotional aspects of individuals as significant to both community and restorative justice, but can the same be true of communities themselves? David Diamond, artistic and managing director of Vancouver's Headlines Theatre, pioneered a forum theatre that engages communities in issues that matter to them. He explains that theatre is one process by which the emotion of a community can be expressed:

> We know now that, if we don't express ourselves as individuals, if we keep our stories bottled up inside of us, eventually we will get sick. The stress will manifest as disease. The human body is, after all, an integrated system.
>
> I suggest that, in the same way our bodies are made up of cells that constitute the living organism, a community is made up of individual people that comprise the organism I call the living community. Communities are alive and need to express themselves just like people; if they don't, they get sick, just like people. The proof of this is all around us. As cultural life has become more and more consumer oriented, living communities have manifested more and more disease.
>
> Theatre, like all other forms of cultural expression, used to be ordinary people singing, dancing, telling stories. This was the way a living community recorded and celebrated its victories, defeats, joys, fears. As the Cartesian or mechanistic model took root, and later as colonialism spread across the planet, coinciding with the mechanization of capitalism, this primal activity of storytelling also evolved in a mechanistic way. Like many other things we can think of, cultural activity became commodified. It transformed from something people did naturally, "in community," into a manufactured consumer product. (2007: 19–20)

This vision of the living community is useful for understanding the potential of restorative processes, whether they are used to handle conflict or deal with the general affairs of the community. Story-telling, freed from the constraints of specific legal limitations in the courtroom, forms a significant component of restorative practices. In this way, RJ is about community development.

Understanding the many dimensions of community is necessary in order to develop it. Another dimension is political, a phenomenon often forgotten in efforts to express a precise definition of community. The political life of communities varies among them, so what works in one community might not be as successful in another. Mae Shaw outlines specific factors emerging through the political lens of community:

> How community is constructed politically provides the discourses and practices which frame the parameters of community development at any given time; its possibilities and its limitations. Politics expresses the totality of inter- relationships, involving power, authority and influence. Clearly community does not exist within a political vacuum, but reflects and reinforces the dynamics of power within particular contexts and times. (2007: 34)

An example of Shaw's argument is found in John McKnight's explanation of Alexis de Tocqueville's account of the nascent American democracy, based on the French count's visit to the country in 1831. A contrast of political realities between the European and American communal life forms the gist of the following observation:

> What [de Tocqueville] found was that European settlers were creating a society different from the one they knew in Europe: communities formed around an uncustomary social invention, small groups of common citizens coming together to form organizations that solve problems.
>
> Tocqueville observed three features in how these groups operated. First, they were groups who decided they had the power to decide what was a problem. Second, they decided they had the power to decide how to solve the problem. Third, they often decided that they would themselves become the key actors in implementing the solution. From Tocqueville's perspective, these citizen associations were a uniquely powerful instrument being created in America, the foundation stones of American communities.
>
> It should seem obvious that communities are collective associations. They are more than and different from a series of friendships. One can have a friendship with a labeled person in an institution, for example, but that does not mean the person has been incorporated into the community. A community is more than just a place. It comprises various groups of people who work together on a face-to-face basis in public life, not just in private. (1995: 117–18)

Modern examples of these associations are the non-profit societies that are formed to offer community-based support to targeted groups that are underserved within current political-social structures. The John Howard Society of New Brunswick, for example, contributes toward community development and the reduction of harm in communities through its locally responsive Resiliency Centre (Kelly and Caputo 2005). Associations can form around a variety of needs and interests, for example, sports leagues and book clubs.

In summary, community is a multi-dimensional concept that includes relational, affective, political, creative and collective aspects. They are the micro-societies in which we feel some level of engagement outside of our homes. In the following sections, we look at what community means for restorative justice and consider how this contributes to social capital and the building of citizen capacity in democratic societies.

Community in Restorative Justice

Since the publication of Christie's "Conflicts as Property" in 1977, the concept of community has had a significant role in restorative justice. Processes of responding to conflict that involve communal engagement offer us opportunities to experience the fabric of communal life, and to revisit and clarify collective values and norms. These processes offer experiences from which to mobilize and strengthen informal social control and social support (Bazemore 2005: 133). Community-based restorative justice cannot be limited to the mere processing of school or criminal justice cases that are deemed suitable by formal institutions. There is much to work with in the preparation and follow-up to these cases, if we are listening to the stories of community members affected by harm. Soon, cases bleed into communal phenomena that require our sensitive attention. We learn about how our individual, collective and institutional responses to harm help or hinder our progress towards greater communal health, and this understanding shapes the questions we ask in our efforts to respond meaningfully without causing further harm.

An advantage of restorative processes is the opportunity they present for civic participation in communal matters. Carolyn Boyes-Watson argues, "If we believe (as I do) that crime is a community responsibility as well as an individual responsibility, then it is necessary for citizens to see 'crime' up close and personal," an engagement that has the beneficial corollary of increasing institutional and professional accountability (2004: 687–88). This is not a new way of thinking but rather a recovering of old traditions. Restorative approaches to addressing the transgression of community norms are evident in historical studies (Weitekamp 1999). Absent the large formal institutions of social control familiar to us today, most historical communities would have had no choice but to be "up close and personal" in their experience of crime and other harms. However, in the twenty-first century, this is not necessarily the case. While formal institutions proliferate across the landscape, actual communities might be harder to find — making it difficult to bring the community into restorative processes (Walgrave 2002: 76).

But perhaps the unrealized expectations of ideal communities could be transformed into the seeds of real community through restorative processes. Community development strategies alone have not been able to incorporate members' involvement in making decisions about issues that affect them (Kurki 2003). The potential for restorative justice to engage community members in meaningful decision-making about their own matters also affords opportunities to *build* community. People who have real, as opposed to perfunctory, involvement in decision-making will have more investment in the results. Circle processes in particular are well suited to a variety of purposes that directly or indirectly build community. They can be used for curative purposes, as in responding to harm with a goal toward healing, and in preventative ways, to address larger issues through democratic dialogue (Pranis, Stuart and Wedge 2003: 209). As citizens become accustomed to participating in circles, they begin to make a paradigm shift in their way of thinking about harm and to become more attuned to values-based responses. Since restorative justice generally and circles specifically are about building or repairing relationships, community development is a logical outcome.

One of the strongest community-building tools in restorative practices is the practice of storytelling. We know people better if we know some of their stories. Fiona Verity and Sue King explain the significance of this kind of engagement for widening our understanding of each other and strengthening the community:

At a conceptual level a structurally informed analysis of conflict and intolerance within communities and the extent to which these dynamics impact on "choices" and the actions of individuals would broaden the potency of restorative justice in restoring damaged social relations and preventing crime. It would do this through widening the understandings of contributing factors and widening the actions that constitute restorative ones. Furthermore at a conceptual level there is much restorative justice practitioners could gain from engaging with the long-standing debates within community development about "community" and participation. For community-development practice restorative gatherings may be effective in localities where there is fear of past violence and conflict or potential violence. The structure offered through facilitated dialogue is clearly effective in promoting quite extraordinary healing exchanges between parties where harm has been done. (2007: 480)

One outcome of storytelling and dialogue is a greater collective awareness of the community's weaknesses and strengths. This leads to a deeper understanding of the social justice concerns that constitute the wider context of individual interpersonal harms (White 2003). Perhaps the participants will recognize repeated themes in the stories, such as the lack of parental support and attachment, substance misuse or stress from unemployment. People might become motivated to mobilize their energies and assets towards repairing the holes in the wider community net.

In a society where institutions have replaced organic community responsibility, it is difficult to convince people to participate in finding and implementing solutions. Responsibility amounts to minding our own behaviour and voting in public elections. We rationalize that the taxes we pay relieve us of the obligation to participate at any other level. Even if our own behaviour results in institutional intervention, we will probably have other professionals take care of our responsibilities. Institutions treat people as "cases" and conflicts as "files" and are governed by rules and policies that limit their mandates and flexibility. Fred Boehrer, a Catholic Worker in New York state, describes the effect of this on individual human beings very well:

> Since beginning our Catholic Worker house of hospitality, we have encountered many people who have been harmed by the process we ironically name "social services." There is little "social" interaction between people, and often, much needed "services" are not granted. In social work language, a person's name is replaced with a "case number." A person's set of experiences, dreams, and aspirations are reduced to a "case," which needs to be "managed." Social workers tend to be well-intentioned people who have been trained to wade through the bureaucratic waters to find some assistance for others. As much as they might strive to personally connect with persons in need, they encounter both systemic obstacles and voluminous caseloads. A person who is poor is seeking not just shelter, food, clothing, and health care. S/he is also looking for compassion and dignity. But can s/he find compassion in a system? Most of the time, that answer is an emphatic "no." A dehumanizing system, especially one filled with overburdened social workers, cannot adequately respond to people forced into poverty. How did we buy into the myth that the state, which creates the conditions through which people become poor, is even remotely interested in helping people move out of poverty? (2000: 218)

The necessary distancing of state institutions from the humans in the problem further serves to insulate the rest of us from the experiences of less fortunate members of our communities, a point made earlier in the chapter by Ruth Morris on the need for social justice in restorative justice. Apart from the effects this has on those seeking or needing help, this current approach encourages us to focus on ourselves more and others less. Goodwill contributions to community make less sense if we have learned to focus only on ourselves. Restorative justice asks us to do what John F. Kennedy asked of Americans in his 1961 inauguration speech: "Ask not what your country can do for you — ask what you can do for your country." This is known as "subsidiarity," the practice of subordinating one's personal interests for the good of the whole.

Schweigert (2002) argues that solidarity and subsidiarity are complementary principles of community development, that at some level we need to recognize that we're all in this together and none of us can survive on our own. He suggests that "community is possible only if the citizens pledge their unconditional loyalty and commitment to do good and avoid evil and to contribute their good life to the shared life of the community. A commitment to reciprocity is inadequate, since the survival of community requires the maintenance of community even in the face of injustice and injury" (2000: 38). We motivate ourselves to embrace subsidiarity in community development through the emotional connection of relationships. Restorative practices aim to provide safe spaces to repair, build and create relationships. When humans gather in this way, a community of care, which is a necessary condition for meaningful accountability, can emerge. Care and accountability are mutually reinforcing (Schweigert 2002), and both are essential to community development.

Restorative processes, then, are well suited for the purposes of community development. They afford opportunities for storytelling, clarification of norms, relationship-building and an accountability that is both meaningful and sustainable.

Social Capital

Another significant contribution of RJ to community development is captured in the concept of "social capital." In popular literature, Robert Putnam's book *Bowling Alone: The Collapse and Revival of American Community* (2000) put the concept of social capital at the centre of discussion on social bonding and community. Putnam notes that we once bowled in leagues, which were opportunities to engage with larger groups of people communally — but not anymore. As community associations, clubs and organizations disappear, there are fewer opportunities for people to engage with each other in the community. The less people engage, the less commitment they have to the collective. It should come as no surprise that, when people take more out of a community than they put in, the community's vitality is weakened. The main idea of social capital theory is that there is value in relationships and social networks. The essence of social capital is the recognition that social ties make our lives more productive. Alejandro Portes summarizes that "social capital stands for the ability of actors to secure benefits by virtue of membership in social networks or other social structures" (1998: 6).

Social capital has been explored from a variety of perspectives. The rational (economic) approach sees social capital in human action as economic action, with organized connections being strategic and functional. Contemporary work on social capital includes a critical (Marxist) view, in which it is argued that human action is generated in a context of shared, class-based social expectations. Political (democratic) views of social capital see it as a "technique of association" that includes trust, mutual obligations and common attitudes of cooperation (Lewandowski and Streich 2007). Social capital has been theorized in other ways, too: as collective efficacy, social trust and reciprocity, participation in voluntary organizations, and social integration for mutual benefit (McKenzie, Whitley and Weich 2002: 280). On the other hand, it has also been observed that social capital is vulnerable to the pressures of formal institutions, which can constrain collective action if they come into conflict with informal groups (Dhesi 2000).

It makes sense that our networks of friends, acquaintances and groups affect what happens for us as individuals (Mouw 2006). When we are looking for employment or an apartment to rent, putting the message out through our networks increases the chance that we might get what we need. Our personal connections with people in our networks help to warm the pathways to that job or apartment; the expectation that we provide references in our applications for accommodation or employment is a concrete example of the importance of social capital. Our membership in social networks offers the benefit of helping us expand our potential as individuals through our interaction with others (Murray 2000). Putnam (2000) took this idea further, suggesting that well-connected societies provide overall benefits to everyone, even to individuals who are poorly connected themselves. For example, the spillover benefits from living in a well-connected community are found in lower rates of crime, which result from people watching each other's houses and children, to the benefit of all, even those neighbours who are not particularly engaged in the community. Generally, however, networks involve mutual obligations and tend to foster norms of reciprocity. We experience specific reciprocity in relationships where we do things for each other in the expectation of being helped at another time. Generalized reciprocity means that I do something for someone else without expecting anything specific in return from that person, but with the expectation that someone else will do something for me down the road. Sometimes this is referred to in restorative justice as putting something back into the big circle. When generalized reciprocity is a society's norm, its members are more efficient than are those who inhabit a distrustful and fearful society.

Understanding that human beings need to live together affords important insights about human nature (Savage and Kanazawa 2002). Human beings are social animals; we require engagement for our physical, mental, emotional and spiritual survival. This kernel of truth is important for restorative practices, which capitalize on our relationships with one another. This need for engagement with others builds motivation to desist from behaviours and actions that would harm other members of the community (Katz 2002). The more attached we are to others, the more we feel accountable to them for what we do. The goal of civic engagement through participation in restorative practices is valuable not only for the skills we learn from it but for the opportunities it offers us for social connectedness.

David Faulkner defines citizenship as "a way of talking about people as human beings, in the context of their rights and legitimate expectations, and of their duties and responsibilities—to one another and to the state—in a liberal democratic society" (2003: 288). Citizenship occurs against a backdrop of rights and responsibilities, which should ideally be balanced in their expectation and expression. On one hand, we have rights to public services and protection from avoidable harm, both of which are within the purview of state institutions. On the other hand, we are expected to contribute to the well-being of our communities by taking care of ourselves, respecting the rights of others and making modest contributions to the welfare of all. Communities are the context within which the exercise of rights and responsibilities often occurs, yet ideas of community and social capital challenge the conventional political approach to the relationship between the state and the individual, and can imply communal self-reliance (291). Faulkner's argument holds many implications for restorative justice:

> The limitations of criminal justice as a means of preventing and dealing with crime should still be acknowledged, and should be met by the development of non-criminal methods of social intervention, and not by continually expanding the scope of criminal justice. Any public or political confidence in such methods points not to incorporating them into the criminal justice system, as instruments of the state and backed by criminal sanctions, but to reinforcing and legitimating them as matters of social and civic responsibility. Where the criminal justice process has to be engaged, the purpose should wherever possible be to promote beneficent forms of social capital, for example by the rehabilitation of offenders and support for their families and for victims. It should not have the effect of weakening them, or of creating relationships or networks which are socially destructive. (295)

There are important messages in this argument about the fate of restorative practices that are owned or governed by state institutions, especially the criminal justice system. Most current restorative justice literature contends with aspects of restorative practices as defined by state imperatives, and does so without major critique. It is agreed that RJ works better than formal criminal justice, but the emphasis is still on offenders. Victims have a role and certainly more potential for having their needs met when their involvement is less restricted, yet, in criminal justice based restorative programs, they are still largely used as a means to an end rather than as an end in themselves. In some parts of the world, community volunteers are largely absent from RJ processes, which are facilitated mostly by criminal justice, social service or education professionals. In general, with the exception of British Columbia, with its unique history of community-based RJ, community engagement with institutionalized restorative processes is largely treated as an afterthought. The opportunities to create or strengthen social capital beyond the immediate circle of people affected by a harmful act are often unrealized.

In the last section of the chapter, we consider what important meanings and skills are missed when we omit the value of social capital from restorative processes. This relates to the practical expression of the ideology of democracy — and democracies are where most restorative justice programs and practices currently emerge.

Restorative Justice as Democracy Building

The etymological roots of the word "democracy" are, literally, "people rule." Of course it is logistically impossible, if even desirable, for every citizen to be active in all decisions about a nation's business. For practical reasons, our society is organized on the basis of representational governance. In most democracies, all citizens of a certain age are entitled to vote in elections to choose their representatives, who are entrusted to make decisions on their collective behalf. Our approval or disapproval of these decisions is expressed in our efforts to re-elect or unseat our representatives. In other words, the average person's participation in the democratic life of a society can amount to the effort to vote whenever elections occur, usually peppered with a lot of grumbling in between.

As Western societies became more organized, professionalized and institutionalized, the role of the average citizen changed from one of activity to one of passivity in collective matters. Today, most citizens live private lives and most issues arise at a personal level. When they occur outside this domain we secure the services of a professional or seek recourse from institutions. Even when we want to have a greater say in the matters that affect us, we may find barriers to participation. Braithwaite asked: "How can citizens hack a path to the heartland of the democracy if the democracy has no strategy for teaching them how to be democratic citizens?... And democracy is something that must be taught. We are not born democratic.

We are born demanding and inconsiderate, disgruntled whiners, rather than born listeners" (1998: 3).

Restorative justice is a deliberative, democratic process that offers the potential for greater citizen participation in public matters than do the existing institutional structures. And, as Albert Dzur argues, participation usually denotes greater responsibility:

> Civic accountability is a kind of power-sharing. Because of the stigmatizing and other harmful effects of criminal penalties, crime control policy is something democratic citizens need to own up to by crossing the rationality and responsibility thresholds. Although we may still wish to punish, even after participating in dialogue oriented restorative justice forums, if the forums have been structured properly we will have good reasons and not just instincts behind our choices. Participation in criminal justice proceedings allows us to take up our democratic responsibility and own up to the values embodied in our collective use of the awful power of criminal justice. (2003: 302)

Where participation in RJ processes affords citizens greater understanding of specific issues that affect them either directly or indirectly, it also affords them the ability to communicate their views on community standards. Braithwaite uses the example of RJ with a victimless crime common to the B.C. culture:

> I have seen conferences in Australia on marijuana use where much of the discussion was around the inappropriateness of the police intervening through threatening to invoke the criminal law against the marijuana use. Justice under the restorative model is an emergent property of deliberative democracy. Citizens are given a space where they can contest laws they believe to be unjust or laws that might be just in some abstract sense but unjust in the practice of their enforcement in a particular context. Because citizens discover through deliberation whether they feel something should be done about a particular injustice, restorative justice builds democratic commitment to doing those things. The story about restorative justice building motivation to repair the harm is therefore a relational one, not just one of the individual psychology of being moved by the revelation of injustice. (2001: 229–30)

The idea of relational motivation is a theme that resonates throughout this book. Being involved in a process as an active agent builds commitment to future action. As the saying goes, the world is run by those who show up.

The idea that restorative justice can help to invigorate participation in democracy can be extended to a broader issue: the idea of RJ as something more expansive than just criminal justice. Our current systems of governance are based on categories of engagement that may not be the best fit for RJ. Aboriginal justice, for example, differs from RJ in that it assumes from the outset a holistic approach to problem-solving within communities. Shereen Miller and Mark Schacter suggest that RJ needs to extend to extra-legal contexts in order to achieve its fuller expression:

> What we need is not merely a model of "restorative justice," but a model of "restorative governance" — in which criminal justice plays only a small role…. Why restorative *governance?* Because the term "governance" is coming to be understood as a process by which entire societies address social problems…. The criminal justice system struggles daily to deal with the consequences of our collective social choices, that are in turn the product of our system of governance. To place the burden of social healing on the justice system is like having the proverbial tail wag the dog. (2000: 406, emphasis in original)

Restorative governance, in its broader expression, would include health care, education, social services and criminal justice (409). The focus would be on solving problems rather than processing criminal cases. This, of course, would challenge the "silo thinking" of public service delivery, where problems are classified as belonging to either criminal justice or social services or education, all of which examples are governed by different jurisdictions.

Community-based restorative justice in British Columbia generally operates under the aegis of non-profit societies, an example of the associations Putnam spoke of in his research on social capital. The connections between associations and democracy were explained by Archon Fung: "Associations enhance democracy in at least six ways: through the intrinsic value of associative life, fostering civic virtues and teaching political skills, offering resistance to power and checking government, improving the quality and equality of representation, facilitating public deliberation and creating opportunities for citizens and groups to participate directly in governance" (2003: 515). These outcomes form the very lived experiences of democracy beyond the ritual of casting a ballot — the essence of democracy rather than the symbol of it. Yet power struggles occur in the relationships between associations and government institutions over competing ideas of democratic governance. Beliefs in the value of participatory democracy can conflict with those of representative democracy, for example, in cases where contests over practice jurisdiction pit government policies against the community's wishes.

Restorative practices are especially amenable to participatory democracy. They are also more likely to invigorate the sense of civic responsibility in people that helps to build community. The potential of this aspect of restorative justice has been under-explored, having been shadowed by the general absorption of restorative justice programs under criminal justice imperatives. Martin Mowbray offers a critique of this relationship between community associations and government that summarizes the current state of affairs in Canada:

> If a government really wanted to empower localities, it would (1) substitute achievable and practical objectives for the customary pretentious, fuzzy and self-serving stated aims; (2) move beyond the dubious use of pilot, demonstration or trial projects and commit substantial resources on a long-term basis to universal (rather than selectively targeted) programmes; (3) fundamentally include local government, albeit with certain conditions; (4) relinquish close control in favour of arm's length mechanisms for ensuring that community programmes remain equitable and totally transparent; and (5) strive to ensure that the objectives of other government policies and programmes are at least consistent. However, cows might fly. (2005: 263–64)

Program sustainability is a lingering condition of community-based restorative justice initiatives. Sandi Bergen, co-director of the Fraser Region Community Justice Initiatives Association in Langley, B.C., characterized the fate of some organizations as "death by pilot project," the outcome of a system in which ideas are tried for short periods but not resourced to continue even if proven successful. Under a hierarchical and administrative system of governance, there is little capacity to respond to the will of local people. Participatory democracy would afford communities a greater say in how their tax money was spent, beyond sweeping and always changing partisan political mandates.

Restorative practices help to build capacity in communities by giving everyone opportunities to practise democracy, which in turn strengthens the community and gives breath to the ideal of political democracy; "The goal of community development is to 'democratize democracy' in a genuinely socially inclusive form" (Powell and Geoghegan 2005: 140). Perhaps government officials might mute their policies and agendas and attenuate to community interests. The social worker admonished by Mrs. Macleod in our opening story made the mistake of assuming he knew what the community he parachuted into needed more than the community did itself. Ideally, professionals and laypeople would work together. As Peter Taylor explains, "although the powerful expert, often an 'outsider,' is seen as a key player in change processes of many kinds, the recognition is growing that such change agents are most effective when they engage deeply with those most knowledgeable about a particular context, supporting their critical reflection on the issues that affect them, and helping them to identify approaches and resources needed to bring about a particular change" (2008: 359). Appreciative inquiry and action research are examples of approaches to community building that involve lay people and professionals working collaboratively. Lay people come from many perspectives and have valuable wisdom to share about their communities. In particular, it is important to engage people who have traditionally been excluded from participation. For example, one study on the Community Action Program for Children in Canada noted the value of encouraging robust participation by marginalized people, who have been generally disempowered by gender, economic and social circumstances (Van der Plaat and Barrett 2005).

In restorative justice, the involvement of lay people in the process is not uncomplicated. One review of youth offender panels in England and reparative boards in the U.S. suggests there might be tension between community involvement and victim participation (Crawford 2004). This can be a warning that restorative justice process models are merely tools to begin the work of untangling conflict and harm and must be flexible enough to meet the needs of all the participants, or at least those of the primary players. In the case of smaller encounters such as mediation, the opportunities for community development lie in repairing or building the one or two relationships in the smaller circle. In larger gatherings, such as peacemaking circles, communal objectives rather than individual incentives form the context for the discussion; the opportunity presented by the intervention is to rebuild a wider circle of relationships by fostering ideas of solidarity and cooperation through the democratization of decision-making (White 2000).

We finish this discussion with a review of Dzur's (2003) argument that attempts to clarify the civic implications of restorative justice theory, citizen participation, and criminal justice policy. He notes that it is necessary for researchers to analyze of the impact of RJ on public attitudes towards crime and crime control policy. The public will have to contend with the ambiguities of certain aspects of RJ, such as the scope of authority, the degree of lay participation and the inclination towards flexibility of RJ in practice. But the success of RJ will depend in some measure on the political effects of specific programs and how the public understands the particular work. Dzur further argues that RJ is animated by different dimensions:

> Restorative justice is more than a criminological argument about what societies need to do to have less crime. It is a theory of criminal justice, a normative critique of mainstream ideas and methods. Although restorative practices are held to be more effective at crime control and more efficient in terms of resources spent on crime con-

trol, these are not the most important grounds for advocates. More important than these for advocates are its moral grounds. Even if restorative practices were slightly less effective and efficient, they would still be choiceworthy because of their moral advantages. (282)

The kernel of this point amounts to a general theme in this book, that we must *be* the change we wish to see. Restorative justice processes must embody the values we claim to hold. If harm or crime is the result of people not acting from the basis of core values, then the response to harm/crime must reflect the core values we uphold; this is commonly known as practising what we preach. Dzur seems to believe that a favourable argument for RJ can be made to the public but that there will be difficulty in convincing people that punishment is less rational and less morally desirable (295). Since the three main questions for RJ seem to de-centre punishment, this is a considerable hurdle to clear. In explaining RJ to people who have never been engaged in an RJ process, it is easier to sell its features of greater personal accountability than the notion that people might be less inclined to punish harm-doers as a result of the process. This speaks to Durkheim's argument about punishment, discussed earlier in the book. It also suggests that the more citizens are engaged in restorative justice, the less they will hold on to sacred notions of crime and punishment. The response to Dzur's concern, therefore, is to expand citizen engagement.

Conclusion

The significance of community in restorative justice is expressed in many ways. RJ processes that are more broadly inclusive afford greater opportunities for the primary people affected by harm, as well as others in the wider community, to participate in decisions that affect them personally. This offers everyone the chance to tell their stories, to hear about what is happening in their community and to learn and hone conflict resolution skills. As RJ becomes more prolific in its use, more relationships based on truth, trust and transformation will be created. Greater social capital is a logical outcome of restorative processes, which help to build a community where there is greater harm prevention. Passive citizens can become active citizens, invigorating the ideal of democracy itself.

The story of Mrs. Macleod reminds us that the problems of communities must be addressed with the inclusion of those most affected. An unfortunate byproduct of modern Western societies has been the atrophy of citizen engagement in the matters of their own community. We have paid a large price for this "contracting out" of our attention and participation, as institutions have taken on an increasing load of the work.

More importantly, institutions are abstract entities. They cannot "care" in the same way that people in a community care. This is an important distinction for imperatives of "accountability," which is presumed to mean the taking of responsibility. In a system based on rule of law, responsibility can mean liability, which is to be avoided. But the accountability we seek is surely that which comes from within, the desire to not harm others because it affects our personal integrity and the consonance between our core values and our actions. The necessary context for meaningful accountability is care, and we need to enable communities to cultivate care (McKnight 1995). Restorative justice is a promising philosophy and approach to both engaging and rebuilding community and, in this way, preventing harm.

Conclusion

To Declare Yourself

Flight of the Hummingbird

Michael Nicoll Yahgulanaas

Here is the story of the great forest that caught on fire.

The terrible fire raged and burned. All of the animals were afraid and fled from their homes. The elephant and the tiger, the beaver and the bear all ran, and above them the birds flew in a panic. They huddled at the edge of the forest and watched. All of the creatures gathered, except one.

Only Dukdukdiya, the little hummingbird, would not abandon the forest. Dukdukdiya flew quickly to the stream. She picked up a single drop of water in her beak. Dukdukdiya flew back and dropped the water on the fire. Again she flew to the stream and brought back another drop, and so she continued — back and forth, back and forth.

The other animals watched Dukdukdiya's tiny body fly against the enormous fire, and they were frightened. They called out to the little hummingbird, warning her of the dangers of the smoke and the heat.

"What can I do?" sobbed the rabbit. "This fire is much too hot." "There is too much smoke!" howled the wolf. "My wings will burn! My beak is too small!" cried the owl.

But the hummingbird persisted. She flew to and fro, picking up more water and dropping it, bead by bead, onto the burning forest.

Finally, the big bear said, "Little Dukdukdiya, what are you doing?"

Without stopping, Dukdukdiya looked down at all of the animals. She said, "I am doing what I can" (13–30).

❧ ❧ ❧

The story of the little hummingbird doing what she can offers us an important message with which to end this book on restorative justice. A common criticism of RJ is that it is unrealistic and unlikely in the face of the massive systems of institutions and bureaucracies that govern most aspects of our social and public lives. All that is necessary is for us to believe that we do not have the ability or interest to become more engaged in the affairs of our community that affect us, either directly or indirectly, and the limit is there.

Several years ago, I was in Berlin, Germany, on university business and took some time to do a walking tour of the city. Our tour guide, an energetic young American with a history degree working in the finance industry in the city, took us to many sites of historical significance before the tour ended in a park. The grand finale of the tour was a lively description of the events leading to the fall of the Berlin Wall on November 9, 1989. Our tour guide was so animated in his presentation that he attracted many Berliners in the park, who casually joined our small group of tourists. The guide explained how citizens of other Soviet Bloc countries such as Hungary and Czechoslovakia had demonstrated for their countries' liberation and how this was putting pressure on the East Germany government to open the Wall. The Berliners who joined us nodded with recognition.

The climax of the story came in his recounting of the day itself and how the East German Party Secretary for Propaganda, Günter Schabowski, unwittingly made it happen. Schabowski had been on vacation while his colleagues were trying to come up with a counterfoil to the pressures being exerted on East Germany to open the border between East and West Berlin. They had decided to allow some travel between the two parts of the city for Czech refugees to cross, as well as for East Germans with certain papers for private travel for limited times beginning November 10. At a press conference on November 9, Schabowski was asked about the government's plans for opening the Wall. Just before the conference, an assistant had handed him a note that said East Berliners would be allowed to cross the border with proper permission, which his colleagues had decided during his absence. But there were no instructions on how to handle the information and the border guards had not yet been informed. When asked by journalists when the new regulations would take effect he made the assumption that it was the same day and replied, "As far as I know effective immediately, without delay." Tens of thousands of East Berliners who had heard the news live turned up at the checkpoints at the Wall, encountering confused border guards who had had no instructions from their leaders. Vastly outnumbered by these citizens, the guards let ecstatic East Berliners without identification through the gates, where they were greeted by thousands of West Berliners gathering on the other side. And with this joyous reconnection of fellow Berliners, the Wall "came down."

The story seemed almost surreal to someone who had grown up in the shadow of the Cold War. Did the Berlin Wall actually open up because of a bureaucratic error? "What happened to the hapless Schabowski?" I asked a native Berliner who had sat down beside me during the telling of the story. He laughed and said that the Socialist Unity Party of Germany tried to sue Schabowski for the mistake. Schabowski was later to denounce his former regime, and in the late 1990s he was sentenced to three years' imprisonment for the murder of refugees during his time in the Party; he was pardoned after serving one year. Today, remnants of the Wall stand in parts of Berlin as reminders of the political folly of forced separation and trying to control others through harsh and restrictive measures.

The power of people to act on their own behalf and towards change in this story amounted to a simple unorganized gathering of citizens eager to change the conditions of their daily lives. Even in the face of an austere and hyper-controlling government, a small opportunity in the form of a bureaucratic error when seized by the citizens morphed into large-scale change. Individuals have the power, even unwittingly as this story shows, to facilitate change that affects everyone.

In this book, we cover a broad and deep terrain. The purpose is to introduce the paradigm of restorative justice and to challenge some of the key assumptions we hold about conflict and its transformation in order to understand the many dimensions of RJ. The selection and organization of topics and material is the result of many years of introductory RJ course delivery in the School of Criminology at Simon Fraser University and intentional listening to feedback from students, teaching assistants, community practitioners, and new and old colleagues teaching this course over time. As such, it truly represents a collective effort.

In a nutshell, this formulation of restorative justice begins with where we are right now and what we can learn from this. One significant lesson is manifested in the idea of punishment and the belief that somehow punishment "works" to address the problems that called for it. A key argument supporting punishment is its connection to justice itself, which we opened as a concept that is much wider than we currently understand it to be. We posit a different idea in its place, that of restorative justice, which in theory can address much of the shortcomings of the punishment/justice nexus. We then consider the question of how restorative justice, which asks different questions and is based on the concept of harm, can co-exist with law in a democracy predicated on the notions of rule of law and crime. Significant features of restorative justice are outlined and supported, beginning with the critical emphasis on values and processes, followed by a discussion of the central focus on individuals and relationships. Based on these features and experience derived from restorative justice practices to date, we explore two psychological phenomena of harm and its response — shame and trauma. Finally, we discuss the important restorative justice element of community, as it relates to both these phenomena and how restorative practices might help to build a more robust, participatory democracy overall.

Where do we go from here? Shifting our understanding of harm and how to be more helpful in our responses as part of our overall efforts to create a more peaceful world is an important first step. The next task is to do something. The prospects are daunting in a world guided by political forces predicated on beliefs of retributive justice, exclusion and the implied violence of force. But we have to start somewhere. A mentor who had spent some time in Vietnam during the war once told me that her Vietnamese friends told her that the only permanent thing was change. Change is inevitable; the question remaining is what kind of change do we want and how do we get there?

Kay Pranis talks about shifting our paradigm from a Newtonian to a quantum physics model.[1] She suggests that if we recognize that we are all profoundly interconnected to each other and the earth that supports us, it will radically change the way we interact with each other. If we understand this concept, then there is no excluding, detaching, throwing away — whether it be a person who offends us or a plastic drinking cup. Restorative justice is a paradigm, a philosophy and an approach that helps us walk in a less violent way as individuals and as communities. It is based on the belief that we should act not necessarily because we think we will be successful at achieving the goal but because it is right.

Jamie Scott helped to found the Collaborative Justice Project in Ottawa, Ontario, through the Church Council on Justice and Corrections and was to become the project's first coordinator. He now works for the United Church of Canada to help address the Church's responsibilities to Aboriginal peoples affected by residential schools. One of his mentors was Hans Mohr, a law professor at Osgoode Hall Law School at York University in Toronto and former member of the now defunct Law Reform Commission of Canada, who died in 2008 at the age of eighty. One of Mohr's teachings, relayed to me in an email from Scott summarizes important ideas introduced in this book:

> Hans Mohr was always skeptical about the seduction of hope, that is, the naive idealism that we can fix all the world's problems and arrive at the "kingdom." He believed that such idealism leads to frustration, disillusionment and despair because our efforts rarely turn out as we had hoped. Human failings and systemic evil are always at play creating new and unforeseen problems out of our best intentions. Problems, suffering and injustice are part of the human condition. If it is to be sustainable, the motivation for our good works and activism, he believed, must come from a different place than idyllic hoped-for outcomes. When I asked him why then I should bother trying to work to change things for the better, he replied with three words that I have never forgotten, "To declare yourself." The motivation for our good work and activism is to [bear] witness to the principles, beliefs and values that we profess. He felt that that should be motivation and reward enough.

This message is familiar and is one that has been articulated by many different people: "*be* the change" and "there is no road to peace; peace *is* the road" are just two examples. This idea is at once both liberating and burdensome. We are free in that the power is within each of us to make a difference, and we do not have to convince institutions or politicians to make wholesale changes to laws and policies so we can be active agents in our own societies. But at the same time, this freedom requires us to be more responsible, not only for ourselves and to those to whom we are legally obligated but also to our neighbours and the community at large.

John Ralston Saul offers some useful observations about this in relationship to Canadian society in particular:

> How rarely do we link our ability to imagine with our ability to act. Perhaps that is because we confuse simply doing our job, managing situations or focusing on the short-term with the concept of action. Perhaps this is because so many of us are somehow employed or feel employed rather than feel that we are free to act. And that atmosphere of *order* impinges on our real desire as individuals, as citizens, to get things done.
>
> And yet we do imagine our society and we do know what ought to be done. And there is enormous energy caught up in that imagination.
>
> When Canadians are asked — as citizens, not as representatives of interest groups or as employees — what lies at the heart of their civilization, they are most likely to reply: fairness and inclusion. (2008: 303)

This essentially invites us all to name our identifying collective values and to act on them. Restorative justice is premised on the same invitation.

We equate justice with fairness, and inclusion is the very bedrock of a democratic society. Restorative justice is therefore a natural fit with who we are and what we want in collective life. There is evidence, as demonstrated in different ways throughout this book, that restorative justice also works — not only as a way of thinking but in practice — to bring us home to those values which define us as a democratic society. Restorative justice is not easy and absolute, but its flexibility and wider lenses make it particularly amenable to the dynamic, changing circumstances of the world in which we live today. And as imperfect human beings, we are bound to get it wrong along the way. At least these failures can become opportunities to see what's not working in our relationships and institutions and to imagine new responses, gauged by the values of our best selves.

Note

1. See youtube video at <http://www.youtube.com/watch?v=HtUDut7DLIE>.

References

Abbott, Jack Henry. 1981. *In the Belly of the Beast*. New York: Vintage Books.

Adams, Paul, and Susan M. Chandler. 2004. "Responsive Regulation in Child Welfare: Systemic Challenges to Mainstreaming the Family Group Conference." *Journal of Sociology and Social Welfare* 31, 1: 93–116.

Ahmed, Eliza, Nathan Harris, John Braithwaite and Valerie Braithwaite. 2001. *Shame Management Through Reintegration*. New York: Cambridge University Press.

Althof, Wolfgang, and Marvin W. Berkowitz. 2006. "Moral Education and Character Education: Their Relationship and Roles in Citizenship Education." *Journal of Moral Education* 35, 4: 495–518.

American Psychiatric Association. 1994. *Diagnostic and Statistical Manual of Mental Disorders*. Fourth edition. Washington, DC: American Psychiatric Association.

Archibald, Bruce, and Jennifer Llewellyn. 2006. "The Challenges of Institutionalizing Comprehensive Restorative Justice: Theory and Practice in Nova Scotia." *Dalhousie Law Journal* 29, 2: 297–343.

Aristotle. 1985. *Nicomachean Ethics*. Translated by T. Irwin. Indianapolis: Hackett Publishing.

_____. 1991. *On Rhetoric*. Translated by G.A. Kennedy. Oxford: Oxford University Press.

Ashworth, Andrew. 1993. "Some Doubts about Restorative Justice." *Criminal Law Forum* 4, 2: 277–99.

Auger, Mario. 2005. "Un Enfant de 7 Ans (A Child of 7 Years)." In Lee Weinstein and Richard Iaccoma (eds.), *Prison Voices*. Kingston, ON: John Howard Society of Canada.

Austin, James. 2001. "Prisoner Reentry: Current Trends, Practices, and Issues." *Crime & Delinquency* 47, 3, July: 314–334.

Austin, James, and Garry Coventry. 1999. "Are We Better Off? Comparing Private and Public Prisons in the United States." *Current Issues in Criminal Justice* 11, 2 (November): 177–201.

Barbalet, J.M. 2002. "Moral Indignation, Class Inequality and Justice: An Exploration And Revision of Ranulf." *Theoretical Criminology* 6, 3: 279–97.

Bazelon, Emily. 2006. "A Question of Resilience." *New York Times*, April 30.

Bazemore, Gordon. 2000. "Rock and Roll, Restorative Justice, and the Continuum of the Real World: A Response to 'Purism' in Operationalizing Restorative Justice." *Contemporary Justice Review* 3, 4: 459–77.

_____. 2001. "Young People, Trouble, and Crime: Restorative Justice as a Normative Theory of Informal Social Control and Social Support." *Youth & Society* 33, 2: 199–226.

_____. 2005. "Whom and *How* Do We Reintegrate? Finding Community in Restorative Justice." *Criminology and Public Policy* 4, 1: 131–48.

_____. 2007. "The Expansion of Punishment and the Restriction of Justice: Loss of Limits in the Implementation of Retributive Policy." *Social Research* 74, 2: 651–62.

Bergman, Roger. 2004. "Caring for the Ethical Ideal: Nel Noddings on Moral Education." *Journal of Moral Education* 33, 2: 149–62.

Berman, Morris. 1984. *The Reenchantmennt of the World*. Toronto: Bantam Books.

Bianchi, Herman. 1994. *Justice as Sanctuary: Toward a New System of Crime Control*. Bloomington, IN: Indiana University Press.

Birck, Angelika. 2002. "Secondary Traumatization and Burnout in Professional Working with Torture Survivors." *Traumatology* 7, 2: 85–90.

Bisson, Jonathan I., Anke Ehlers, Rosa Matthews, Stephen Pilling, David Richards, and Stuart Turner. 2007. "Psychological Treatments for Chronic Post-Traumatic Stress Disorder: Systematic Review snd Meta-Analysis." *British Journal of Psychiatry* 190, 2: 97–104.

Blau, James. 2001. "Heat." *Journal of Prisoners on Prisons* 11: 9–11.

_____. 2003. "Guilty." *Journal of Prisoners on Prisons* 12: 72–75.

_____. 2007. "New Boots." *Journal of Prisoners on Prisons* 16, 2: 11–15.

Block, Peter. 2008. *Community: The Structure of Belonging*. San Francisco, CA: Berrett-Koehler Publishers.

Bloom, Sandra. 1997. *Creating Sanctuary: Toward the Evolution of Sane Societies*. New York: Routledge.

Boehrer, Fred. 2000. "The Principle of Subsidiarity as the Basis for a Just Community." *Contemporary Justice Review* 3, 2: 213–24.

Bopp, Judie, Michael Bopp, Lee Brown, and Phil Lane. 1985. *The Sacred Tree: Reflections on Native American Spirituality*. Lethbridge, AB: Four Worlds Development Press.

Bopp, Michael, and Judie Bopp. 2001. *Recreating the World: A Practical Guide to Building Sustainable Communities*. Calgary, AB: Four Worlds Press.

Boyes-Watson, Carolyn. 2000. "Reflections on the Purist and Maximalist Models of Restorative Justice." *Contemporary Justice Review* 3, 4: 441–50.

_____. 2004. "The Value of Citizen Participation in Restorative/Community Justice: Lessons from Vermont." *Criminology and Public Policy* 3, 4: 687–92.

_____. 2008. *Peacemaking Circles & Urban Youth: Bringing Justice Home*. St. Paul, MN: Living Justice Press.

Braithwaite, John. 1989. *Crime, Shame and Reintegration*. New York: Cambridge University Press.

_____. 1993. "Shame and Modernity." *British Journal of Criminology* 33, 1: 1–18.

_____. 1998. "Democracy, Community and Problem Solving." Paper presented at the Building Strong Partnerships for Restorative Practices conference. Burlington, VT, August 5–7. Retrieved: <http://iirp.org/library/vt/vt_brai.html>.

_____. 2000a. "Decomposing a Holistic Vision of Restorative Justice." *Contemporary Justice Review*. 3, 4: 433–440.

_____. 2000b. "Shame and Criminal Justice." *Canadian Journal of Criminology* 42, 3: 281–98.

_____. 2001. "Restorative Justice and a New Criminal Law of Substance Abuse." *Youth & Society* 33, 2: 227–48.

_____. 2004. "Families and the Republic." *Journal of Sociology and Social Welfare* 31, 1: 199–215.

_____. 2007. "Encourage Restorative Justice." *Criminology* 6, 4: 689–96.

Braithwaite, Valerie. 1998. "The Value Balance Model of Political Evaluations." *British Journal of Psychology* 89, 2: 223–47.

_____. 2001. "Values and Restorative Justice in Schools." In Heather Strang and John Braithwaite (eds.), *Restorative Justice and Civil Society*. Cambridge: Cambridge University Press.

Brant, Clare C. 1990. "Native Ethics and Rules of Behaviour." *Canadian Journal of Psychiatry* 35, 6 (August): 534–39.

Brehm, S.S. 1981. "Oppositional Behavior in Children: A Reactance Theory Approach." In S.S. Brehm, S.M. Kassin, and F.K. Gibbons (eds.), *Developmental Social Psychology: Theory and Research*. New York: Oxford Press.

Brenner, Viktor, and Robert A. Fox. 1998. "Parental Discipline and Behavior Problems in Young Children." *The Journal of Genetic Psychology* 159, 2: 251–56.

Breton, Denise, and Stephen Lehman. 2001. *The Mystic Heart of Justice*. West Chester, PA: Chrysalis Books.

Brincat, Cynthia A., and Victoria S. Wike. 2000. *Morality and the Professional Life: Values at Work*. Upper Saddle River, NJ: Prentice-Hall.

Buchanan, Marla, John O. Anderson, Max R. Uhlemann, and Erika Horwitz. 2006. "Secondary Traumatic Stress: An Investigation of Canadian Mental Health Workers." *Traumatology* 12, 4: 272–82.

Burford, Gale, and Paul Adams. 2004. "Restorative Justice, Responsive Regulation and Social Work." *Journal of Sociology and Social Welfare* 31, 1: 7–26.

Byrd, Patricia M., and Joanne L. Davis. 2008. "Violent Behavior in Female Inmates: Possible Predictors." *Journal of Interpersonal Violence* 24, 2: 379–92.

CBC Nws. 2008. "No Improvements in Care since Death of 4 B.C. Children." April 16. <http://www.cbc.ca/canada/british-columbia/story/2008/04/16/bc-child-death-review.html>.

Camp, Scott D., and Gerald G. Gaes. 2001. "Private Adult Prisons: What Do We Really Know and Why Don't We Know More?" In David Schichor and Michael J. Gilbert (eds.), *Privatization in Criminal Justice: Past, Present, and Future*. Cincinnati, OH: Anderson Publishing Co.

Campbell, Duncan. 2000. "US Jails Two Millionth Inmate." *Guardian Weekly*, Thursday, February 17.

Carlson, Eve B., and Constance J. Dalenberg. 2000. "A Conceptual Framework for the Impact of Traumatic Experiences." *Trauma, Violence & Abuse* 1, 1: 4–28.

Caspi, Avshalom, Joseph McClay, Terrie E. Moffitt, Jonathan Mill, Judy Martin, Ian W. Craig, Alan Taylor, and Richie Poulton. 2002. "Role of Genotype in the Cycle of Violence in Maltreated Children." *Science* 297, 5582: 851–54.

Caspi, Avshalom, Karen Sugden, Terrie E. Moffitt, Alan Taylor, Ian W. Craig, HonaLee Harrington, Joseph McClay, Jonathan Mill, Judy Martin, Antony Braithwaite, and Richie Poulton. 2003. "Influence of Life Stress on Depression: Moderation by a Polymorphism in the 5-HTT Gene." *Science* 301, 5631: 386–89.

Cayley, David. 1996. "Prison and Its Alternatives." *Ideas*. Toronto: CBC Radio.

Chambliss, William J. 1999. *Power, Politics, and Crime*. Boulder, CO: Westview Press.

Chatterjee, Jharna, and Liz Elliott 2003. "Restorative Policing in Canada: The Royal Canadian Mounted Police, Community Justice Forums, and the Youth Criminal Justice Act." *Police Practice and Research* 4, 4: 347–59.

Cheliotis, Leonidas K. 2006. "Penal Managerialism from Within: Implications for Theory and Research." *International Journal of Law and Psychiatry* 29, 5: 397–404.

Chevigny, Paul. 2003. "The Populism of Fear: Politics of Crime in the Americas."

Punishment & Society 5, 1: 77–96.

Chirkov, Valery, Richard M. Ryan, Youngmee Kim, and Ulas Kaplan. 2003. "Differentiating Autonomy from Individualism and Independence: A Self-Determination Theory Perspective on Internalization of Cultural Orientations and Well-Being." *Journal of Personality and Social Psychology* 84, 1: 97–110.

Christie, Nils. 1977. "Conflicts as Property." *British Journal of Criminology* 17, 1: 1–11.

_____. 1982. *Limits to Pain*. Oxford: Martin Robertson.

_____. 2000 [1993]. *Crime Control as Industry*. Third edition. New York: Routledge.

Choke. 2008. Film. Directed by Clark Gregg. Distributed by Fox Searchlight Pictures.

Clark, Mary E. 2005. "Skinner vs the Prophets: Human Nature and Our Concepts of Justice." *Contemporary Justice Review* 8, 2, June: 163–76.

Clear, Todd R., and David R. Karp. 1999. *The Community Justice Ideal: Preventing Crime and Achieving Justice*. Boulder, CO: Westview Press.

Coben, James, and Penelope Harley. 2004. "Intentional Conversations about Restorative Justice, Mediation and the Practice of Law." *Hamline Journal of Public Law and Policy* 25, 2: 235–334.

Cohen, Stanley. 1972. *Folk Devils and Moral Panics: The Creation of the Mods and Rockers*. New York: Basil Blackwell.

_____. 1985. *Visions of Social Control: Crime, Punishment and Classification*. Oxford: Polity Press.

Consedine, Robert, and Joanna Consedine. 2001. *Healing Our History: The Challenge of the Treaty of Waitangi*. Toronto: Penguin.

Cooley, Charles H. 1922. *Human Nature and the Social Order*. New York: Scribner's.

Cousins, Mark, and Athar Hussain. 1984. *Michel Foucault*. New York: St. Martin's Press.

Crawford, Adam. 2004. "Involving Lay People in Criminal Justice." *Criminology and Public Policy* 3, 4: 693–702.

Criminal Code of Canada. 2000.

Curtis, Dennis, Andrew Graham, Lou Kelly, and Anthony Patterson. 1985. *Kingston Penitentiary: The First Hundred and Fifty Years*. Ottawa: Ministry of Supply and Services Canada.

Dahlin, Eric, Erin Kelly, and Phyllis Moen. 2008. "Is Work the New Neighborhood? Social Ties in the Workplace, Family, and Neighborhood." *The Sociological Quarterly* 49, 4: 719–736.

Daly, Kathleen. 1999. "Restorative Justice and Punishment: The Views of Young People." Paper presented to the American Society of Criminology Annual Meeting, Toronto, November 17–21.

_____. 2002. "Restorative Justice: The Real Story." *Punishment & Society* 4, 1: 55–79.

Dana, Richard. H. 2000. "The cultural Self as Locus for Assessment and Intervention with American Indians/Alaska Natives." *Journal of Multicultural Counseling & Development* 28, 2: 66–82.

Davidson, Ann C., and Simon A. Moss. 2008. "Examining the Trauma Disclosure of Police Officers to Their Partners and Officers' Subsequent Adjustment." *Journal of Language and Social Psychology* 27, 1: 51–70.

Davis, R.C. 1987. "Studying the Effects of Services for Victims in Crisis." *Crime & Delinquency* 33, 4: 520–31.

De Haan, Willem. 1990. *The Politics of Redress: Crime, Punishment and Penal Abolition*. Boston: Unwin Hyman.

De Haan, Willem, and Ian Loader. 2002. "On the Emotions of Crime, Punishment and Social Control." *Theoretical Criminology* 6, 3: 243–53.

D'Errico, Peter. 1999. "Restorative Indigenous Justice: States and Communities in Tension." *Contemporary Justice Review* 2, 4: 383–94.

Deci, Edward L., Nancy H. Spiegel, Richard M. Ryan, Richard Koestner, and Manette Kauffman. 1982. "Effects of Performance Standards on Teaching Styles: Behavior of Controlling Teachers." *Journal of Educational Psychology* 74, 6: 852–59.

DeGagné, Michael. 2007. "Toward an Aboriginal Paradigm of Healing: Addressing the Legacy of Residential Schools." *Australian Psychiatry* 15 (Supplement): 49–53.

Dhesi, Autar S. 2000. "Social Capital and Community Development." *Community Development Journal* 35, 3: 199–214.

Diamond, David. 2007. *Theatre for Living: The Art and Science of Community-Based Dialogue.* Victoria, BC: Trafford Publishing.

Dignan, James, Anne Atkinson, Helen Atkinson, Marie Howes, Jennifer Johnstone, Gwen Robinson, Joanna Shapland, and Angela Sorsby. 2007. "Staging Restorative Justice Encounters Against a Criminal Justice Backdrop: A Dramaturgical Analysis." *Criminology and Criminal Justice* 7, 1: 5–32.

Dixon, John, Rhys Dogan, and Alan Sanderson. 2005. "Community and Communitarianism: A Philosophical Investigation." *Community Development Journal* 40, 1: 4–16.

Dobrin, Arthur. 2001. "Finding Universal Values in a Time of Relativism." *The Educational Forum* 65, 3 (Spring): 273–78.

Donziger, Steven R. (ed.). 1996. *The Real War on Crime: The Report of the National Criminal Justice Commission.* New York: Harper Perennial.

Douglas, Cathie, and Larry Moore. 2004. *A Healing River: An Invitation to Explore Restorative Justice Values and Principles.* Kaslo, BC: Heartspeak Productions.

Duguid, Stephen. 2000. *Can Prisons Work? The Prisoner as Object and Subject in Modern Corrections.* Toronto: University of Toronto Press.

Dukelow, Daphne A., and Betsy Nuse. 1991. *Pocket Dictionary of Canadian Law.* Scarborough, ON: Carswell (Thomson Publishing).

Dunedin Study Website. <http://dunedinstudy.otago.ac.nz/index.html>.

Durkheim, Emile. 1933 [1893]. *The Division of Labor in Society.* Toronto: MacMillan.

Dutton, Donald G., and Stephen D. Hart. 1992. "Evidence for Long-Term, Specific Effects of Childhood Abuse and Neglect on Criminal Behavior in Men." *International Journal of Offender Therapy and Comparative Criminology* 36, 2: 129–37.

Dyer, Joel. 2000. *The Perpetual Prisoner Machine: How America Profits from Crime.* Boulder, CO: Westview Press.

Dzur, Albert W. 2003. "Civic Implications of Restorative Justice Theory: Citizen Participation and Criminal Justice Policy." *Policy Sciences* 36, 3–4: 279–306.

Eglash, Albert. 1977. "Beyond Restitution: Creative Restitution." In Joe Hudson and Burt Galaway (eds.), *Restitution in Criminal Justice.* Lexington, MA: Lexington Books.

Eitle, David, and R. Jay Turner. 2002. "Exposure to Community Violence and Young Adult Crime: The Effects of Witnessing Violence, Traumatic Victimization, and Other Stressful Life Events." *Journal of Research in Crime and Delinquency* 39, 2 (May): 214–37.

Elias, Norbert. 1994 [1939]. *The Civilising Process*. Oxford: Blackwells.

Elliot, Jeffrey M. 1993. "The Man and the Symbol: The 'Willie' Horton Nobody Knows." *The Nation* 257, 6 (August 23/30): 201–05.

Elliott, Liz. 2002. "*Con Game* and Restorative Justice: Inventing the Truth about Canada's Prisons." *Canadian Journal of Criminology* 44, 4: 459–74.

Ending Violence Website. n.d. <http://www.endingviolence.org/>.

Erikson, Erik H. 1969. *Gandhi's Truth: On the Origins of Militant Nonviolence*. New York: W.W. Norton.

Falshaw, Louise. 2005. "The Link Between a History of Maltreatment and Subsequent Offending Behavioiur." *Probation Journal* 52, 4: 423–34.

Faulkner, David. 2003. "Taking Citizenship Seriously: Social Capital and Criminal Justice in a Changing World." *Criminal Justice* 3, 3: 287–315.

Feeley, M.M., and J. Simon. 1992. "The New Penology: Notes on the Merging Strategy of Corrections and its Implications." *Criminology* 30, 4: 449–79.

Feigenberg, Luba Falk, Melissa Steel King, Dennis J. Barr, and Robert L. Selman. 2008. "Belonging to and Exclusion from the Peer Group in Schools: Influences on Adolescents' Moral Choices." *Journal of Moral Education* 37, 2: 165–84.

Finkelhor, David. 2008. *Childhood Victimization: Violence, Crime, and Abuse in the Lives of Young People*. Toronto: Oxford University Press.

Fisher, Roger, W. Urry, and Bruce Patton. 1981, 1991. *Getting to Yes: Agreement Without Giving In*. Boston: Penguin. (Second edition, Toronto: Penguin Books).

Flouri, Eirini. 2005. "Post-Traumatic Stress Disorder (PTSD): What We Have Learned and What We Have Still Not Found Out." *Journal of Interpersonal Violence* 20, 4: 373–79.

Foucault, Michel. 1979. *Discipline and Punish: The Birth of the Prison*. New York: Vintage Books.

_____. 1987. "Maurice Blanchot: The Thought from Outside." In Jeffrey Mehlman and Brian Massumi (trans.), *Foucault/Blanchot*. New York: Zone Books.

Freeman, Robert M. 2000. "Planning for Correctional Emergencies: The Need for an Emergency Life Cycle-Based Posttraumatic Stress Disorder Management Component." *Justice Professional* 12, 3: 277–89.

Freiberg, Arie. 1999. "Commercial Confidentiality and Public Accountability for the Provision of Correctional Services." *Current Issues in Criminal Justice* 11, 2 (November): 119–34.

Friscolanti, Michael. 2006. *Maclean's*, May 22 <http://www.macleans.ca/article.jsp ?content=20060522_127339_127339 and source=srch> © Rogers Publishing

Fung, Archon. 2003. "Associations and Democracy: Between Theories, Hopes, and Realities." *Annual Review of Sociology* 29: 515–39.

Galliher, John F. 1991. "The Willie Horton Fact, Faith, and Commonsense Theory of Crime." In Harold E. Pepinsky and Richard Quinney (eds.), *Criminology as Peacemaking*. Bloomington: Indiana University Press.

Garland, David. 2001. "Introduction: The Meaning of Mass Imprisonment." *Punishment & Society* 3, 1: 5–8.

Gaucher, Robert, and Liz Elliott. 2001. "'Sister of Sam': The Rise and Fall of Bill C-205/220." *The Windsor Yearbook of Access to Justice* 19: 72–105.

Gavrielides, Theo. 2005. "Some Meta-Theoretical Questions for Restorative Justice." *Ratio Juris* 18, 1: 84–106.

Gilbert, Paul. 2003. "Evolution, Social Roles, and the Differences in Shame and Guilt." *Social Research* 70, 4: 1206–30.

Gilligan, Carol. 1982. *In a Different Voice: Psychological Theory and Women's Development*. Cambridge, MA: Harvard University Press.

Gilligan, James. 1996. *Violence: Our Deadly Epidemic and Its Causes*. New York: G.P. Putnam's Sons.

_____. 2003. "Shame, Guilt, and Violence." *Social Research* 70, 3: 1149–80.

Glas, Gerrit. 2006. "Elements of a Phenomenology of Evil and Forgiveness." In Nancy Nyquist Potter (ed.), *Trauma, Truth and Reconciliation: Healing Damaged Relationships*. Toronto: Oxford University Press.

Godwin, William. 1976 [1793]. *Enquiry Concerning Political Justice*. New York: Penguin Books.

Goff, Ashley, Emmeline Rose, Suzanna Rose, and David Purves. 2007. "Does PTSD Occur in Sentenced Prison Populations? A Systematic Literature Review." *Criminal Behaviour and Mental Health* 17, 3: 152–62.

Goffman, Erving. 1959. *Presentation of Self in Everyday Life*. New York: Anchor.

_____. 1963. *Stigma*. Englewood Cliffs, NJ: Prentice-Hall.

Gosselin, Luc. 1982. *Prisons in Canada*. Montréal: Black Rose Books.

Govier, Trudy, and Colin Hirano. 2008. "A Conception of Intentional Forgiveness." *Journal of Social Philosophy* 39, 3: 429–44.

Gray, Barbara (Kanatiiosh), and Pat Lauderdale. 2006. "The Web of Justice: Restorative Justice has Presented Only Part of the Story." *Wicazo Sa Review* 21, 1: 29–41.

Green, Bonnie L., Jeanne Miranda, Anahita Daroowalla, and Juned Siddique. 2005. "Trauma Exposure, Mental Health Functioning, and Program Needs of Women in Jail." *Crime & Delinquency* 51, 1: 133–51.

Green, Ross Gordon. 1998. *Justice in Aboriginal Communities: Sentencing Alternatives*. Saskatoon: Purich Publishing.

Greene, Judith A. 2002. "Entrepreneurial Corrections: Incarceration as a Business Opportunity." In Marc Mauer and Meda Chesney-Lind (eds.), *Invisible Punishment: The Collateral Consequences of Mass Imprisonment*. New York: New Press.

Gregory, Maughn. 2000. "Care as a Goal of Democratic Education." *Journal of Moral Education* 29, 4: 445–61.

Gromet, Dena M., and John M. Darley. 2006. "Restoration and Retribution: How Including Retributive Components Affects the Acceptability of Restorative Justice Procedures." *Social Justice Research* 19, 4: 395–432.

Grossman, David. 1995. *On Killing: The Psychological Cost of Learning to Kill in War and Society*. NY: Little, Brown & Company.

_____. n.d. "The Psychological Consequences of Killing: Perpetration-Induced Traumatic Stress." <http://killology.com/art_onkilling_psych.htm>.

Grusec, Joan E., and Jacqueline J. Goodnow. 1994. "Impact of Parental Discipline Methods on the Child's Internalization of Values: A Reconceptualization of Current Points of View." *Developmental Psychology* 30, 1: 4–19.

Gustafson, David L. 2005. "Exploring Treatment and Trauma Recovery Implications of Facilitating Victim-Offender Encounters in Crimes of Severe Violence: Lessons from the Canadian Experience." In Elizabeth Elliott and Robert M. Gordon (eds.), *New Directions in Restorative Justice: Issues, Practice, Evaluation*. Portland,

OR: Willan Publishing.

Gyatso, Tenzin (His Holiness the Dalai Lama). 2000. *Ancient Wisdom, Modern World: Ethics for the New Millenium*. London: Abacus Books.

Hadley, Michael L. (ed.). 2001. *The Spiritual Roots of Restorative Justice*. Albany, NY: State University of New York Press.

Hallett, Michael A. 2002. "Race, Crime, and For-Profit Imprisonment: Social Disorganization as Market Opportunity." *Punishment & Society* 4, 3: 369–93.

Hallett, Michael A., and J. Frank Lee. 2001. "Public Money, Private Interests: The Grassroots Battle Against CCA in Tennessee." In David Schichor and Michael J. Gilbert (eds.), *Privatization in Criminal Justice: Past, Present, and Future*. Cincinnati, OH: Anderson Publishing Co.

Halstead, J. Mark, and Monica J. Taylor. 2000. "Learning and Teaching about Values: A Review of Recent Research." *Cambridge Journal of Education* 30, 2: 169–81.

Hamilton, Hon. A.C. 2001. *A Feather Not a Gavel: Working Towards Aboriginal Justice*. Winnipeg: Great Plains Publications.

Haney, Craig. 2003. "Mental Health Issues in Long-Term Solitary and 'Supermax' Confinement." *Crime & Delinquency* 49, 1 (January): 124–56.

Harding, Richard. 1999. "Prison Privatisation: The Debate Starts to Mature." *Current Issues in Criminal Justice* 11, 2 (November): 109–18.

Harris, M. Kay. 2004. "An Expansive, Transformative View of Restorative Justice." *Contemporary Justice Review* 7, 1: 117–41.

Harris, Nathan. 2003. "Reassessing the Dimensionality of the Moral Emotions." *British Journal of Psychology* 94, 4: 457–73.

_____. 2006. "Reintegrative Shaming, Shame, and Criminal Justice." *Journal of Social Issues* 62, 2: 327–46.

Harrison, Paige M., and Allen J. Beck. 2003. *Bureau of Justice Statistics Bulletin*. US Dept. of Justice, Office of Justice Programs, July, NCJ 200248. At <www.ojp.usdoj.gov/bjs/pub/pdf/siljq.pdf>.

Hay, Carter. 2001. "An Exploratory Test of Braithwaite's Reintegrative Shaming Theory." *Journal of Research in Crime and Delinquency* 38, 2: 132–53.

Hay, Douglas. 1975. "Property, Authority and the Criminal Law." In Douglas Hay, Peter Linebaugh, John G. Rule, E. P. Thompson, and Cal Winslow (eds.), *Albion's Fatal Tree: Crime and Society in Eighteenth-Century England*. New York: Pantheon Books.

Heaney, Seamus. 1961. *The Cure at Troy: A Version of Sophocles' Philoctetes*. New York: Farrar, Straus and Giroux.

Heide, Kathleen M., and Eldra P. Solomon. 2006. "Biology, Childhood Trauma, and Murder: Rethinking Justice." *International Journal of Law and Psychiatry* 29, 3: 220–33.

Hennessy, Peter H. 1999. *Canada's Big House: The Dark History of the Kingston Penitentiary*. Toronto: Dundurn.

Herman, Judith. 1997. *Trauma and Recovery*. New York: Basic Books.

Herrera, Carla, and Judy Dunn 1997. "Early Experiences with Family Conflict: Implications for Arguments with a Close Friend." *Developmental Psychology* 33, 5: 869–81.

Hillyard, Paddy, and Steve Tombs. 2007. "From 'Crime' to Social Harm?" *Crime, Law and Social Change* 48, 1–2: 9–25.

Hoffman, Martin L., and Herbert D. Saltzstein. 1967. "Parent Discipline and the

Child's Moral Development." *Journal of Personality and Social Psychology*. 5, 1: 45–57.

Huesmann, L.R., and C.L. Podolski. 2003. "Punishment: A Psychological Perspective." In Seán McConville (ed.), *The Use of Punishment*. Portland, OR: Willan Publishing

Hulsman, Louk. 1986. "Critical Criminology and the Concept of Crime." In Herman Bianchi, & Rene van Swaaningen (eds.), *Abolitionism. Towards a Non-Repressive Approach to Crime*. Amsterdam: Free University Press.

Human Rights Watch. 2000. "Out of Sight: Super-Maximum Security Confinement in the United States." *Human Rights Watch* 12, 1 (February): 1–9.

Hutchison, Katy. 2006. *Walking After Midnight: One Woman's Journey Through Murder, Justice and Forgiveness*. Vancouver: Raincoast Books.

Hydle, Ida. 2006. "An Anthropological Contribution to Peace and Conflict Resolution Studies." *Contemporary Justice Review* 9, 3: 257–67.

ICPS. 2008. "World Prison Brief of the International Centre for Prison Studies— North America." <http://www.kcl.ac.uk/depsta/law/research/icps/world-brief/wpb_country.php?country=190>.

Jackson Arrick L., Carol Veneziano, and Wendy Ice. 2005. "Violence and Trauma: The Past 20 and Next 10 Years." *Journal of Interpersonal Violence* 20, 4: 470–78.

Jackson, Michael. 2002. *Justice Behind the Walls: Human Rights in Canadian Prisons*. Vancouver: Douglas & McIntyre.

Jacoby, Susan. 1983. *Wild Justice: The Evolution of Revenge*. New York; Harper & Row.

Jamieson, Kathleen Hall. 1993. "The Subversive Effects of a Focus on Strategy in News Coverage of Presidential Campaigns." "Insinuation and Other Pitfalls in Political Ads and News." at <www.pressroom.com/~afrimale/jamieson.htm>.

Jespersen, Per. *Justice*. Randerup, Denmark: SK Publishers. Retrieved at: <http://home12.inet.tele.dk/fil/justice.ht>.

Johnson, Basil. 1984. *Ojibway Heritage*. Toronto: McClelland and Stewart.

Juujärvi. 2006. "Care Reasoning in Real-Life Moral Conflicts." *Journal of Moral Education* 35, 2: 197–211.

Kant, Immanuel. 2003, orig. 1899. *On Education*. Translated by Annette Churton. New York: Courier Dover Publications.

Karr-Morse, Robin, and Meredith S. Wiley. 1997. *Ghosts from the Nursery: Tracing the Roots of Violence*. New York: Atlantic Monthly Press.

Karstedt, Susanne. 2002. "Emotions and Criminal Justice." *Theoretical Criminology* 6, 3: 299–317.

Katz, Rebecca. 2002. "Re-Examining the Integrative Social Capital Theory of Crime." *Western Criminology Review* 4, 1: 30–54.

Kaysen, Debra, Patricia A. Resick, and Deborah Wise. 2003. "Living in Danger: The Impact of Chronic Traumatization and the Traumatic Context on Posttraumatic Stress Disorder." *Trauma, Violence & Abuse* 4, 3: 247–64.

Kelly, Katharine, and Tullio Caputo. 2005. "Case Study of Grassroots Community Development: Sustainable, Flexible and Cost-Effective Responses to Local Needs." *Community Development Journal* 4, 2: 234–45.

Kelly, Russ. 2006. *From Scoundrel to Scholar… The Russ Kelly Story*. Fergus, ON: Russ Kelly Publishing.

Kempinen, Cynthia A., and Megan C. Kurlychek. 2003. "An Outcome Evaluation of Pennsylvania's Boot Camp: Does Rehabilitative Programming Within a Disciplinary Setting Reduce Recidivism?" *Crime & Delinquency* 49, 4 (October): 581–602.

Killian, Kyle D. 2008. "Helping Till It Hurts? A Multimethod Study of Compassion Fatigue, Burnout, and Self-Care in Clinicians Working with Trauma Survivors." *Traumatology* 14, 2: 32–44.

King, Thomas (ed.). 1990. *All My Relations: An Anthology of Contemporary Canadian Native Fiction.* Toronto: McClelland & Stewart Ltd.

Kingwell, Mark. 2000. *The World We Want: Virtue, Vice, and the Good Citizen.* Toronto: Penguin Books Canada.

Klaassen, Johann A. 2001. "The Taint of Shame: Failure, Self-Distress, and Moral Growth." *Journal of Social Philosophy* 32, 2: 174–96.

Kleck, Gary, Brion Sever, Spencer Li, and Marc Gertz. 2005. "The Missing Link in General Deterrence Research." *Criminology* 43, 3: 623–59.

Klein, Lloyd, Joan Luxemburg, and John Gunther. 1991. "Taking a Bite Out of Social Injustice: Crime-Control Ideology and Its Peacemaking Potential." In Harold E. Pepinsky and Richard Quinney (eds.), *Criminology as Peacemaking.* Bloomington: University of Indiana Press.

Koenen, Karestan C. 2005. "Nature-Nurture Interplay: Genetically Informative Designs Contribute to Understanding the Effects of Trauma and Interpersonal Violence." *Journal of Interpersonal Violence* 20, 4: 507–12.

Kohlberg, Lawrence. 1981. *The Meaning and Measurement of Moral Development.* Worchester, MA: Clark University Press.

Kohn, Alfie. 1999. *Punished by Rewards: The Trouble with Gold Stars, Incentive Plans, A's, Praise, and Other Bribes.* Boston: Houghton Mifflin Company.

_____. 2005. *Unconditional Parenting: Moving from Rewards and Punishments to Love and Reason.* New York: Atria Books.

Korn, Richard. 1992. "Excerpts from the Report on the Effects of Confinement in the Lexington High Security Unit." In Ward Churchill and J.J. Vander Wall (eds.), *Cages of Steel: The Politics of Imprisonment in The United States.* Washington, DC: Maisonneuve Press.

Krech, Paul Rock. 2002. "Envisioning a Healthy Future: A Re-becoming of Native American Men." *Journal of Sociology and Social Welfare* 29, 1: 77–95.

Krischer, Maya K., and Kathrin Sevecke. 2008. "Early Traumatization and Psychopathy in Female and Male Juvenile Offenders." *International Journal of Law and Psychiatry* 31, 3: 253–61.

Kristjánsson, Kristján. 2003. "The Development of Justice Conceptions and the Unavoidability of the Normative." *Journal of Moral Education* 32, 2: 183–94.

_____. 2004. "Empathy, Sympathy, Justice and the Child." *Journal of Moral Education* 33, 3: 291–305.

_____. 2006. "Emulation and the Use of Role Models in Moral Education." *Journal of Moral Education* 35, 1: 37–49.

Kruger, Mark H. 2007. "Community-Based Crime Control in Cuba." *Contemporary Justice Review* 10, 1: 101–14.

Kubiak, Sheryl Pimlott. 2004. "The Effects of PTSD on Treatment Adherence, Drug Relapse, and Criminal Recidivism in a Sample of Incarcerated Men and Women." *Research on Social Work Practice* 14, 6: 424–33.

Kucynski, Leon, and Grazyna Kochanska. 1990. "Development of Children's Noncompliance Strategies From Toddlerhood to Age 5." *Developmental Psychology* 26, 3: 398–408.

Kurki, Leena. 2003. "Evaluating Restorative Justice Practices." In Andrew von Hirsch, Julian Roberts, Anthhony E. Bottoms, Kent Roach and Mara Schiff (eds.), *Restorative Justice & Criminal Justice: Competing or Reconcilable Paradigms?* Portland, OR: Hart Publishing.

Lakoff, George. 2002. *Moral Politics: How Liberals and Conservatives Think.* Chicago: Chicago University Press.

_____. 2004. *Don't Think of an Elephant: Know Your Values and Frame the Debate.* White River Junction, VT: Chelsea Green Publishing.

LaMothe, Ryan. 1999. "The Absence of Care: The Core of Malignant Trauma and Symbolization." *Journal of Interpersonal Violence* 14, 11 (November): 1193–210.

Law Commission of Canada. 2003. *Transforming Relationships Through Participatory Justice.* Ottawa: Minister of Justice.

Lemley, Ellen C. 2001. "Designing Restorative Justice Policy: An Analytical Perspective." *Criminal Justice Policy Review* 12, 1: 43–65.

Lerias, Doukessa, and Mitchell K. Byrne. 2003. "Vicarious Traumatization: Symptoms and Predictors." *Stress and Health* 19, 3: 129–38.

Leschied, Alan, Debbie Chiodo, Elizabeth Nowicki, and Susan Rodger. 2008. "Childhood Predictors of Adult Criminality: A Meta-Analysis Drawn from the Prospective Longitudinal Literature." *Canadian Journal of Criminology and Criminal Justice* 50, 4: 435–67.

Lev-Wiesel, Rachel. 2007. "Intergenerational Transmission of Trauma across Three Generations: A Preliminary Study." *Qualitative Social Work* 6, 1: 74–94.

Levrant, Sharon, Francis T. Cullen, Betsy Fulton, and John F. Wozniak. 1999. "Reconsidering Restorative Justice: The Corruption of Benevolence Revisited?" *Crime and Delinquency* 45, 3: 2–27.

Lewandowski, Joseph, and Gregory Streich. 2007. "Democratizing Social Capital: In Pursuit of Liberal Egalitarianism." *Journal of Social Philosophy* 38, 4: 588–604.

Lindner, Robert. 1946. *Stone Walls and Men.* New York: Odyssey Press.

Llewellyn, Jennifer, and Robert Howse. 1998. *Restorative Justice—A Conceptual Framework.* Ottawa: Law Commission of Canada.

Losoncz, Ibolya, and Graham Tyson. 2007. "Parental Shaming and Adolescent Delinquency: A Partial Test of Reintegrative Shaming Theory." *The Australian and New Zealand Journal of Criminology* 40, 2: 161–78.

Lynch, Mona. 2002. "Selling 'Securityware': Transformations in Prison Commodities Advertising, 1949–99." *Punishment & Society* 4, 3: 305–19.

Mahoney, M.J. 1974. *Cognition and Behavior Modification.* Cambridge, MA: Ballinger.

Markel, Dan. 2007. "Wrong Turns on the Road to Alternative Sanctions: Reflections on the Future of Shaming Punishments and Restorative Justice." *Texas Law Review* 85: 1385–412.

Marshall, Tony. 1999. *Restorative Justice: An Overview.* London: Home Office, Research Development and Statistics Directorate.

Mathiesen, Thomas. 1990. *Prison on Trial: A Critical Assessment.* Newbury Park, CA: Sage Publications.

Mauer, Marc. 1999. *Race to Incarcerate.* New York: New Press.

Maxwell, Gabrielle, and Hennessey Hayes. 2006. "Restorative Justice Developments in the Pacific Region: A Comprehensive Survey." *Contemporary Justice Review* 9, 2: 127–54.

McAlinden, Anne-Marie. 2005. "The Use of 'Shame' with Sexual Offenders." *British Journal of Criminology* 45, 3: 373–94.

McCold, Paul. 2000. "Toward a Holistic Vision of Restorative Juvenile Justice: A Reply to the Maximalist Model." *Contemporary Justice Review* 3, 4: 357–414.

_____. 2004. "What is the Role of Community in Restorative Justice Theory and Practice?" In Howard Zehr and Barb Toews (eds.), *Critical Issues in Restorative Justice*. Monsey, NY: Criminal Justice Press.

McCold, Paul, and Benjamin Wachtel. 1998. "Community Is not a Place: A New Look at Community Justice Initiatives." *Contemporary Justice Review* 1, 1: 71–86.

McDonough, Graham P. 2005. "Moral Maturity and Autonomy: Appreciating the Significance of Lawrence Kohlberg's Just Community." *Journal of Moral Education* 34, 2: 199–213.

McKenzie, Kwame, Rob Whitley, and Scott Weich. 2002. "Social Capital and Mental Health." *British Journal of Psychiatry* 181: 280–82.

McKnight, John. 1995. *The Careless Society: Community and its Counterfeits*. New York: Basic Books.

McLaughlin, Eugene, Ross Fergusson, Gordon Hughes, and Louise Westmarland (eds.). 2003. *Restorative Justice: Critical Issues*. Thousand Oaks, CA: Sage Publications.

Mead, George Herbert. 1918. "The Psychology of Punitive Justice." *American Journal of Sociology* 23: 577–602.

_____. 1934. *Mind, Self, and Society*. Chicago: University of Chicago Press.

Meffert, Susan M., Thomas J. Metzler, Clare Henn-Haase, Shannon McCaslin, Sabra Inslicht, Claude Chemtob, Thomas Neylan, and Charles R. Marmar. 2008. "A Prospective Study of Trait Anger and PTSD Symptoms in Police." *Journal of Traumatic Stress* 21, 4: 410–16.

Melossi, Dario, and Massimo Pavarini. 1981. *The Prison and the Factory: Origins of the Penitentiary System*. Toronto: Macmillan.

Messina, Nena, Christine Grella, William Burdon, and Michael Prendergast. 2007. "Childhood Adverse Events and Current Traumatic Distress: A Comparison of Men and Women Drug-Dependent Prisoners." *Criminal Justice and Behavior* 34, 11: 1385–401.

Mika, Harry. 2002. "Evaluation as Peacebuilding? Transformative Values, Processes, and Outcomes." *Contemporary Justice Review* 5, 4: 339–49.

Miller, Shereen Benzvy, and Mark Schacter. 2000. "From Restorative Justice to Restorative Governance." *Canadian Journal of Criminology* 42, 3: 405–20.

Miller, William Ian. 1993. *Humiliation and Other Essays on Honor, Social Discomfort, and Violence*. Ithaca, NY: Cornell University Press.

Minow, Martha. 1998. *Between Vengeance and Forgiveness: Facing History after Genocide and Mass Violence*. Boston: Beacon Press.

Mobley, Alan, and Gilbert Geis. 2001. "The Corrections Corporation of America aka The Prison Realty Trust, Inc." In David Schichor and Michael J. Gilbert (eds.), *Privatization in Criminal Justice: Past, Present, and Future*. Cincinnati, OH: Anderson Publishing.

Monture-Angus, Patricia. 1999. *Journeying Forward: Dreaming First Nations Independence*. Halifax: Fernwood Publishing.

Monture-Okanee, Patricia. 1994. "Thinking about Aboriginal Justice: Myths and Revolution." In Richard Gosse, James Youngblood Henderson, and Roger Carter (eds.), *Continuing Poundmaker & Riel's Quest: Presentations Made at a Conference on Aboriginal Peoples and Justice*. Saskatoon: Purich Publishing.

Morris, Ruth. 2001. *Stories of Transformative Justice*. Toronto: Canadian Scholars' Press.

Morrison, Brenda. 2006. "School Bullying and Restorative Justice: Toward a Theoretical Understanding of the Role of Respect, Pride, and Shame." *Journal of Social Issues* 62, 2: 371–92.

Moulden, Heather M., and Philip Firestone. 2007. "Vicarious Traumatization: The Impact on Therapists Who Work with Sexual Offenders." *Trauma, Violence & Abuse* 8, 1: 67–83.

Mouw, Ted. 2006. "Estimating the Causal Effect of Social Capital: A Review of Recent Research." *Annual Review of Sociology*. 32: 79–102.

Mowbray, Martin. 2005. "Community Capacity Building or State Opportunism?" *Community Development Journal* 40, 3: 255–64.

Muldoon, Orla T., and Ciara Downes. 2007. "Social Identification and Post-Traumatic Stress Symptoms in Post-Conflict Northern Ireland." *British Journal of Psychiatry* 191: 146–49.

Murove, Munyaradzi Felix. 2004. "An African Commitment to Ecological Conservation: The Shona Concepts of *Ukama* and *Ubuntu.*" *The Mankind Quarterly* XLV, 2: 195–215.

Murray, Michael. 2000. "Social Capital and Healthy Communities: Insights from the Colorado Healthy Communities Initiative." *Social Development Journal* 35, 2: 99–108.

Muste, A.J. 1942. *The World Task of Pacifism*. Wallingford, PA: Pendale Hill.

Narvaez, Darcia, and Jenny L. Vaydich. 2008. "Moral Development and Behaviour under the Spotlight of the Neurobiological Sciences." *Journal of Moral Education* 37, 3: 289–312.

Nathanson, Donald L. 1994. *Shame and Pride: Affect, Sex, and the Birth of the Self*. New York: W.W. Norton.

_____. 1997. "From Empathy to Community." In Jerome A. Winer (ed.), *The Annual of Psychoanalysis* Volume 25. Chicago: Chicago Institute for Psychoanalysis.

_____. 2003. "The Name of the Game Is Shame." Report to the Academic Advisory Council of the National Campaign Against Youth Violence. Retrieved at <www.tomkins.org/ PDF/library/articles/thenameofthegameisshame.pdf>.

Neff, Rob. 2004. "Achieving Justice in Child Protection." *Journal of Sociology and Social Welfare* 31, 1: 137–54.

New Penguin English Dictionary. 1986. Markham, ON: Penguin Books Canada.

Nietzsche, Friedrich Wilhelm. 1969 [1885]. *Thus Spoke Zarathustra: A Book for Everyone and No One*. Translated, with contribution, by R. J. Hollingdale. Toronto: Penguin Classics.

Noddings, Nel. 1989. *Women and Evil*. Berkeley, CA: University of California Press.

_____. 1992. *The Challenge to Care in Schools: An Alternative Approach to Education*. New York: Teachers College Press.

Nolen, Stephanie. 2008. "Africa's Unjust Deserts." *Globe and Mail*, Saturday, June

14: F6.

O'Hear, Michael M. 2005. "Is Restorative Justice Compatible with Sentencing Uniformity?" *Marquette Law Review* 89, 2: 305–25.

Oliver, Peter. 1998. *'Terror to Evil-Doers': Prisons and Punishments in Nineteenth- Century Ontario*. Toronto: University of Toronto Press.

Olson, Susan M., and Albert W. Dzur. 2004. "Revisiting Informal Justice: Restorative Justice and Democratic Professionalism." *Law & Society Review* 38, 1: 139–76.

Ontario Ministry of Community Safety and Correctional Services. 2001. "Private Operator Chosen for Penetanguishene" (news release). At <www.corrections.mcs.gov.on.ca>.

Orth, Ulrich, and Andreas Maercker. 2004. "Do Trials of Perpetrators Retraumatize Crime Victims?" *Journal of Interpersonal Violence* 19, 2: 212–27.

Orth, Ulrich, Leo Montada, and Andreas Maercker. 2006. "Feelings of Revenge, Retaliation Motive, and Posttraumatic Stress Reactions in Crime Victims." *Journal of Interpersonal Violence* 21, 2: 229–43.

Packer, Herbert L. 1964. "Two Models of the Criminal Process." *University of Pennsylvania Law Review* 113, 1: 1–68.

Parenti, Christian. 2000. *Lockdown America: Police and Prisons in the Age of Crisis*. New York: Verso.

Parkinson, John, and Declan Roche. 2004. "Restorative Justice: Deliberative Democracy in Action?" *Australian Journal of Political Science* 39, 3: 505–18.

Paton, Douglas. 2005. "Posttraumatic growth in Protective Services Professionals: Individual, Cognitive and Organizational Influences." *Traumatology* 11, 4: 335–46.

Pearlman, Laurie Anne, and Paula S. MacIan. 1995. "Vicarious Traumatization: An Empirical Study of the Effects of Work on Trauma Therapists." *Professional Psychology: Research and Practice* 26, 6: 558–65.

Pemberton, Simon. 2007. "Social Harm Future(S): Exploring the Potential of the Social Harm Approach." *Crime, Law & Social Change* 48, 1–2: 27–41.

Pepinsky, Hal. 2000a. "Empathy Works, Obedience Doesn't." In W. Gordon West and Ruth Morris (eds.), *The Case for Penal Abolition*. Toronto: Canadian Scholars' Press.

Pepinsky, Hal. 2000b. "Making Peace with Shame." *The Red Feather Journal of Postmodern Criminology* 8. Electronic journal retrieved at <http://www.critcrim.org/redfeather/journal-pomocrim/pomocrimindex.html>.

Pepinsky, Hal. 2000c. "Distilling Love and Inclusion." *Contemporary Justice Review* 3, 4: 479–82.

Pepinsky, Harold E., and Richard Quinney (eds.). 1991. *Criminology as Peacemaking*. Bloomington: Indiana University Press.

Perry, Bruce D., and Maia Szalavitz. 2006. *The Boy Who Was Raised as a Dog and Other Stories from a Child Psychiatrist's Notebook*. New York: Basic Books.

Pettigrove, Glen. 2006. "Hannah Arendt and Collective Forgiving." *Journal of Social Philosophy* 37, 4: 483–500.

Police Victim Services Website. n.d. <http://www.policevictimservices.bc.ca/index.php?page=vicserbc&link=victimservices>.

Portes, Alejandro. 1998. "Social Capital: Its Origins and Applications in Modern Sociology." *American Review of Sociology* 24: 1–24.

Powell, Fred, and Martin Geoghegan. 2005. "Beyond Political Zoology: Community

Development, Civil Society, and Strong Democracy." *Community Development Journal* 41, 2: 128–42.

Pranis, Kay, Barry Stuart, and Mark Wedge. 2003. *Peacemaking Circles: From Crime to Community*. St. Paul, MN: Living Justice Press.

Pranis, Kevin. 2003. "Campus Activism Defeats Multinational's Prison Profiteering." In Tara Herivel and Paul Wright (eds.), *Prison Nation: The Warehousing of America's Poor*. New York: Routledge.

Presser, Lois, and Christopher T. Lowenkamp. 1999. "Restorative Justice and Offender Screening." *Journal of Criminal Justice* 27, 4: 333–43.

Putnam, Robert D. 2000. *Bowling Alone: The Collapse and Revival of American Community*. Toronto: Simon and Schuster.

Quinney, Richard. 2000. "Socialist Humanism and the Problem of Crime: Thinking about Erich Fromm in the Development of Critical/Peacemaking Criminology." In Kevin Anderson and Richard Quinney (eds.), *Erich Fromm and Critical Criminology: Beyond the Punitive Society*. Chicago: University of Illinois Press.

Quinney, Richard. 1991. "The Way of Peace: On Crime, Suffering, and Service." In Harold E. Pepinsky and Richard Quinney (eds.), *Criminology as Peacemaking*. Bloomington: University of Indiana Press.

Radosh, Polly F. 2002. "Reflections on Women's Crime and Mothers in Prison: A Peacemaking Approach." *Crime & Delinquency* 48, 2 (April): 300–15.

Ranulf, Svend. 1964 [1938]. *Moral Indignation and Middle Class Psychology: A Sociological Study*. New York: Schocken Books.

Rawls, John. 1999. *A Theory of Justice* (revised edition). Oxford: Oxford University Press.

Redekop, Paul. 2008. *Changing Paradigms: Punishment and Restorative Discipline*. Waterloo, ON: Herald Press.

Regehr, Cheryl, Vicki LeBlanc, R. Blake Jelley, Irene Barath, and Joanne Daciuk. 2007. "Previous Trauma Exposure and PTSD Symptoms as Predictors of Subjective and Biological Response to Stress." *Canadian Journal of Psychiatry* 52, 10: 675–83.

Reiman, Jeffrey. 2007. "The Moral Ambivalence of Crime in an Unjust Society." *Criminal Justice Ethics* 26, 2: 3–14.

Roach, Kent. 2000. "Changing Punishment at the Turn of the Century: Restorative Justice on the Rise." *Canadian Journal of Criminology* 42, 3: 249–80.

Roach, Kent, and Jonathan Rudin. 2000. "*Gladue*: The Judicial and Political Reception of a Promising Election." *Canadian Journal of Criminology* 42, 3: 355–88.

Roberts, Gregory David. 2003. *Shantaram*. New York: St. Martin's Griffin.

Robertson, Noelle, Graham Davies, and Alice Nettleingham. 2009. "Vicarious Traumatisation as a Consequence of Jury Service." *The Howard Journal* 48, 1: 1–12.

Robinson, Gwen, and Joanna Shapland. 2008. "Reducing Recidivism: A Task for Restorative Justice?" *British Journal of Criminology* 48, 3: 337–58.

Roche, Declan. 2001. "The Evolving Definition of Restorative Justice." *Contemporary Justice Review* 4, 3–4: 341–53.

_____. 2004. *Accountability in Restorative Justice*. Toronto: Oxford University Press.

Ross, Rupert. 1992. *Dancing with a Ghost: Exploring Indian Reality*. Markham, ON: Octopus Publishing.

_____. 1994. "Duelling Paradigms? Western Criminal Justice Versus Aboriginal Community Healing." In Richard Gosse, James Youngblood Henderson, and Roger Carter (eds.), *Continuing Poundmaker & Riel's Quest: Presentations Made at a Conference on Aboriginal Peoples and Justice*. Saskatoon: Purich Publishing.

_____. 1996. *Returning to the Teachings: Exploring Aboriginal Justice*. Toronto: Penguin Books Canada.

Rowe, Don. 2006. "Taking Responsibility: School Behaviour Policies in England, Moral Development and Implications for Citizenship." *Journal of Moral Education* 35, 4: 519–31.

Rusche, George, and Otto Kirchheimer. 1968. *Punishment and Social Structure*. New York: Russell and Russell.

Rutsala, Vern. 1988. "Shame." *The American Scholar* 57, 4: 574.

Ryan, Gail. 2005. "Preventing Violence and Trauma in the Next Generation." *Journal of Interpersonal Violence* 20, 1: 132–41.

Ryle, Gilbert. 1949, 2002. *The Concept of Mind*. Chicago: New University of Chicago Press.

Salston, MaryDale, and Charles R. Figley. 2003. "Secondary Traumatic Stress Effects of Working with Survivors of Criminal Victimization." *Journal of Traumatic Stress* 16, 2: 167–74.

Saul, John Ralston. 2008. *A Fair Country: Telling Truths About Canada*. Toronto: Viking Canada.

Savage, Joanne, and Satoshi Kanazawa. 2002. "Social Capital, Crime, and Human Nature." *Journal of Contemporary Criminal Justice* 18, 2: 188–211.

Sawatsky, Jarem. 2009. *The Ethic of Traditional Communities and the Spirit of Healing Justice: Studies from Hollow Water, The Iona Community, and Plum Village*. Philadelphia: Jessica Kingsley Publishers.

Scarpa, Angela, Sara Chiara Haden, and Jimmy Hurley. 2006. "Community Violence Victimization and Symptoms of Posttraumatic Stress Disorder: The Moderating Effects of Coping and Social Support." *Journal of Interpersonal Violence* 21, 4: 446–69.

Scheff, Thomas J., and Suzanne M. Retzinger. 2000. "Shame as the Master Emotion of Everyday Life." *Journal of Mundane Behavior* 1, 1: 1–20.

Schlosser, Eric. 1994. "Reefer Madness: Marijuana Has Not Been De Facto Legalized, and the War on Drugs Is Not Just about Cocaine and Heroin (Mark Young Case)." *The Atlantic Monthly* 274, 2.

_____. 1998. "The Prison-Industrial Complex." *The Atlantic Monthly* 282, 6 (December).

Schore, A.N. 1996. "The Experience-Dependent Maturation of a Regulatory System in the Orbital Prefrontal Cortex and the Origin of Developmental Psychopathology." *Development and Psychopathology* 8, 1: 59–87.

Schroeder, David A., Julie E. Steel, Andria J. Woodell, and Alicia F. Bembenek. 2003. "Justice Within Social Dilemmas." *Personality and Social Psychology Review* 7, 4: 374–87.

Schumacher, E.F. 1974. *Small Is Beautiful: A Study of Economics as if People Mattered*. London: Abacus Books.

Schweigert, Francis J. 1999. "Learning the Common Good: Principles of Community-Based Moral Education in Restorative Justice." *Journal of Moral*

Education 28, 2: 163–83.

_____. 2002. "Solidarity and Subsidiarity: Complementary Principles of Community Development." *Journal of Social Philosophy* 33, 1: 33–44.

Scott, Sheryn T. 2007. "Multiple Traumatic Experiences and the Development of Posttraumatic Stress Disorder." *Journal of Interpersonal Violence* 22, 7: 932–38.

Seiter, Richard P., and Karen R. Kadela. 2003. "Prisoner Reentry: What Works, What Does Not, and What Is Promising." *Crime & Delinquency* 49, 3, July: 360–88.

Sells, Benjamin. 1996. *The Soul of the Law: Understanding Lawyers and the Law.* Rockport, MA: Element.

Sentencing Project Website. n.d. <www.sentencingproject.org>.

Shakespeare-Finch, Jane, Kathryn Gow, and Sandy Smith. 2005. "Personality, Coping and Post-Traumatic Growth in Emergency Ambulance Personnel." *Traumatology* 11, 4: 325–334.

Shapiro, David. 2003. "The Tortured, Not the Torturers, Are Ashamed." *Social Research* 70, 4: 1132–48.

Sharpe, Susan. 1998. *Restorative Justice: A Vision for Healing and Change.* Edmonton, AB: Edmonton Victim Offender Mediation Society.

Shaw, Mae. 2007. "Community Development and the Politics of Community." *Community Development Journal* 43, 1: 24–36.

Sherblom, Stephen. 2008. "The Legacy of the 'Care Challenge': Re-Envisioning the Outcome of the Justice-Care Debate." *Journal of Moral Education* 37, 1: 81–98.

Shercliffe, Regan Jeffrey, and Victor Colotla. 2009. "MMPI-2 Profiles in Civilian PTSD: An Examination of Differential Responses Between Victims of Crime and Industrial Accidents." *Journal of Interpersonal Violence* 24, 2: 349–60.

Sherman, Lawrence W. 2003. "Reason for Emotion: Reinventing Justice with Theories, Innovations, and Research—The American Society of Criminology 2002 Presidential Address." *Criminology* 41, 1: 1–37.

Sherman, Lawrence W., and Heather Strang. 2007. *Restorative Justice: The Evidence.* London: The Smith Institute.

Sieh, Edward W. 1989. "Less Eligibility: The Upper Limits of Penal Policy." *Criminal Justice Policy Review* 3, 2: 159–83.

Sigurdson, Glenn, and Luke Danielson (eds.). 2005. *The Dialogue Forum Handbook.* Vancouver: Centre for Dialogue, Simon Fraser University.

Sims, Barbara, Berwood Yost, and Christina Abbott. 2006. "The Efficacy of Victim Services Programs: Alleviating the Psychological Suffering of Crime Victims?" *Criminal Justice Policy Review* 17, 4: 387–406.

Sinclair, Murray. 1994. "Aboriginal Peoples, Justice and the Law." In Richard Gosse, James Youngblood Henderson, and Roger Carter (eds.), *Continuing Poundmaker & Riel's Quest: Presentations Made at a Conference on Aboriginal Peoples and Justice.* Saskatoon: Purich Publishing.

Smandych, Russell C. 1991. "Beware of the 'Evil American Monster': Upper Canadian Views on the Need for a Pentitentiary, 1830–1834." *Canadian Journal of Criminology* 33, 2: 125–47.

Smeyers, Paul. 1999. "'Care' and Wider Ethical Issues." *Journal of Philosophy of Education* 33, 2: 233–52.

Smith, Polly Ashton. 1998. "William Godwin's Moral Education Theory of Punishment: Is it a Restorative Approach to Justice?" *Contemporary Justice Review*

1, 1: 87–101.

Solomon, Eldra P., and Kathleen M. Heide. 2005. "The Biology of Trauma: Implications for Treatment." *Journal of Interpersonal Violence* 20, 1: 51–60.

Spitz, R.A. 1957. *No and Yes: On the Genesis of Human Communication*. New York: International Universities Press.

Sting. 1987. "Fragile." *Nothing Like the Sun*. Album. A&M Records.

Striblen, Cassie. 2007. "Guilt, Shame, and Shared Responsibility." *Journal of Social Philosophy* 38, 3: 469–85.

Stuart, Barry D. 1998. "Key Differences: Courts and Commu nity Circles." *The Justice Professional* 11: 89–116.

Sub-Committee on the Penitentiary System in Canada, Standing Committee on Justice and Legal Affairs. 1977. *Report to Parliament*. Mark MacGuigan (Chairman). Ottawa: Minister of Supply and Services Canada.

Sullivan, Dennis. 2003. "Facing into the Wind's Teeth: An Interview with Hal Pepinsky." *Contemporary Justice Review* 6, 1: 69–80.

Sullivan, Dennis, and Larry Tifft. 2005. *Restorative Justice: Healing the Foundations of Our Everyday Lives*. Second edition. Monsey, NY: Willow Tree Press, Inc.

Surette, Ray. 1992. *Media, Crime and Criminal Justice: Images and Realities*. Belmont, CA: Wadsworth.

Szmania, Susan J., and Daniel E. Mangis. 2005. "Finding the Right Time and Place: A Case Study Comparison of the Expression of Offender Remorse in Traditional Justice and Restorative Justice Contexts." *Marquette Law Review* 89: 335–58.

Tarnovich, David M. 2004. "Why Race Matters on Sentencing." *Toronto Star*, February 25.

Taylor, Peter. 2008. "Where Crocodiles Find Their Power: Learning and Teaching Participation for Community Development." *Community Development Journal* 43, 3: 358–70.

Tedeschi, Richard G., and Lawrence G. Calhoun. 2004. "Post-Traumatic Growth: Conceptual Foundations and Empirical Evidence." *Psychological Inquiry* 15, 1: 1–18.

Thibaut, J., and L. Walker. 1975. *Procedural Justice: A Psychological Analysis*. Hillsdale, NJ: Earlbaum.

Tifft, Larry L. 2002. "Crime and Peace: A Walk With Richard Quinney." *Crime & Delinquency* 48, 2: 243–62.

Timmerman, Irma G.H., and Paul M.G. Emmelkamp. 2001. "The Relationship Between Traumatic Experiences, Dissociation, and Borderline Personality Pathology among Male Forensic Patients and Prisoners." *Journal of Personality Disorders* 15, 2: 136–49.

Toews, Barb, and Howard Zehr. 2003. "Ways of Knowing for a Restorative Worldview." In Elmar G.M. Weitekamp and Hans-Jürgen Kerner (eds.), *Restorative Justice in Context: International Practice and Directions*. Portland, OR: Willan Publishing.

Tonry, Michael. 1999. "Why Are US Incarceration Rates So High?" *Crime & Delinquency* 45, 4 (October): 419–37.

_____. 1994. "Proportionality, Parsimony, and Interchangeability of Punishments." In Antony Duff and David Garland (eds.), *A Reader on Punishment*. Oxford: Oxford University Press.

Trenczek, Thomas. 2002. "Victim-Offender Reconciliation: The Danger of

Cooptation and a Useful Reconsideration of Law Theory." *Contemporary Justice Review* 5, 1: 23–34.

Tronto, Joan. 1993. *Moral Boundaries: A Political Argument for an Ethic of Care*. New York: Routledge.

Tutu, Desmond. 1999. *No Future Without Forgiveness*. New York: Image Doubleday.

Tyler, Tom. 2006. "Restorative Justice and Procedural Justice: Dealing with Rule Breaking." *Journal of Social Issues* 62, 2: 307–26.

Tyler, Tom R., Lawrence Sherman, Heather Strang, Geoffrey C. Barnes, and Daniel Woods. 2007. "Reintegrative Shaming, Procedural Justice, and Recidivism: The Engagement of Offenders' Psychological Mechanisms in the Canberra RISE Drinking-and-Driving Experiment." *Law & Society Review* 41, 3: 553–85.

Useem, Bert, Raymond V. Liedka, and Anne Morrison Piehl. 2003. "Popular Support for the Prison Build-up." *Punishment & Society* 5, 1 (January): 5–32.

Van der Plaat, Madine, and Gene Barrett. 2005. "Building Community Capacity in Governance and Decision-Making." *Community Development Journal* 4, 1: 25–36.

Van Ness, Daniel W. 1993. "New Wine and Old Wineskins: Four Challenges of Restorative Justice." *Criminal Law Forum* 4, 2: 251–76.

Verity, Fiona, and Sue King. 2007. "Responding to Intercommunal Conflict—What Can Restorative Justice Offer?" *Community Development Journal* 43, 4: 470–82.

Vikan, Arne, Cleonice Camino, and Angela Biaggio. 2005. "Note on a Cross-Cultural Test of Gilligan's Ethic of Care." *Journal of Moral Education* 34, 1: 107–11.

Vinocur, Barry. 1997. "Investors Rush Into a Prison REIT, Though Some View It as Pricey." *Barron's*, July 14: 31.

Von Hirsch, Andrew. 1994. "Censure and Proportionality." In A. Duff and D. Garland (eds.), *A Reader on Punishment*. Oxford: Oxford University Press.

Walgrave, Lode. 2002. "From Community to Dominion: In Search of Social Values for Restorative Justice." In Elmar G.M. Weitekamp and Hans-Jürgen Kerner (eds.), *Restorative Justice: Theoretical Foundations*, Portland, OR: Willan Publishing.

Walker, Lawrence J., and Jon H. Taylor. 1991. "Family Interactions and the Development of Moral Reasoning." *Child Development* 62: 264–83.

Walklate, Sandra. 2005. "Researching Restorative Justice: Politics, Policy and Process." *Critical Criminology* 13, 2: 165–79.

Wall, Barbara E. 2001. "Navajo Conceptions of Justice in the Peacemaker Court." *Journal of Social Philosophy* 32, 4: 532–46.

Walmsley, Roy. 2003. "Global Incarceration and Prison Trends." *Forum on Crime and Society* 3, 1 & 2 (December): 65–78.

Waters, Everett, and E. Mark Cummings. 2000. "A Secure Base from Which to Explore Close Relationships." *Child Development* 71, 1: 164–72.

Way, Ineke, Karen M. VanDeusen, Gail Martin, Brooks Applegate, and Deborah Jandle. 2004. "Vicarious Trauma: A Comparison of Clinicians Who Treat Survivors of Sexual Abuse and Sexual Offenders." *Journal of Interpersonal Violence* 19, 1: 49–71.

Webster, Christopher D., Grant T. Harris, Marnie E. Rice, Catherine Cormier, and Vernon L. Quinsey. 1994. *The Violence Prediction Scheme: Assessing Dangerousness in High Risk Men*. Toronto: Centre of Criminology, University of Toronto.

Weinstein, Lee, and Richard Jaccoma (eds.). 2005. *Prison Voices*. Kingston, ON: John Howard Society of Canada.

Weitekamp, Elmar. 1999. "History of Restorative Justice." In Gordon Bazemore and Lode Walgrave (eds.), *Exploring Restorative Justice for Juveniles*. Monsey, NY: Criminal Justice Press.

Welch, James. 1986. *Fool's Crow*. Toronto: Penguin Books.

Wenar, C. 1982. "On Negativism." *Human Development* 25, 1: 1–23.

Westcott, Scott. 2002. "Jailhouse Shock." *Utne* November–December: 73–75.

Western, Bruce, Jeffrey R. Kling, and David F. Weiman. 2001. "The Labor Market Consequences of Incarceration." *Crime & Delinquency* 47, 3 (July): 401–27.

White, Rob. 2000. "Social Justice, Community Building, and Restorative Strategies." *Contemporary Justice Review* 3, 1: 55–72.

_____. 2003. "Communities, Conferences and Restorative Social Justice." *Criminal Justice* 3, 2: 139–60.

Whitman, James Q. 2007. "What Happened to Tocqueville's America?" *Social Research* 74, 2: 251–68.

Wilson, John P., Boris Drozdek, and Silvana Turkovic. 2006. "Post-Traumatic Shame and Guilt." *Trauma, Violence & Abuse* 7, 2: 122–41.

Witvliet, Charotte V.O., Everett L. Worthington, Lindsey M. Root, Amy F. Sato, Thomas E. Ludwig, and Judy J. Exline. 2008 "Retributive Justice, Restorative Justice, and Forgiveness: An Experimental Psychophysiology Analysis." *Journal of Experimental Social Psychology* 44: 10–25.

Woolford, Andrew, and R.S. Ratner. 2008. *Informal Reckonings: Conflict Resolution in Mediation, Restorative Justice and Reparations*. New York: Routledge-Cavendish.

Wright, Martin. 2002. "The Court as Last Resort: Victim-Sensitive, Community-Based Responses to Crime." *British Journal of Criminology* 42, 3: 654–67.

_____. 2003. "Is it Time to Question the Concept of Punishment?" In Lode Walgrave (ed.), *Repositioning Restorative Justice*. Portland, OR: Willan Publishing.

Wright, Paul. 1998. "Citizen Anti-Crime Initiatives? How the Gun Lobby Bankrolls the War on Crime." In Daniel Burton-Rose, Dan Pens, and Paul Wright (eds.), *The Celling of America: An Inside Look at the US Prison Industry*. Monroe, ME: Common Courage Press.

Yahgulanaas, Michael Nicoll. 2008. *Flight of the Hummingbird*. Vancouver: Greystone Books.

Yazzie, Robert. 1994. "Life Comes from It: Navajo Justice Concepts." *New Mexico Law Review* 24: 175–90.

Yazzie, Robert, and James W. Zion. 1996. "Navajo Restorative Justice: The Law of Equality and Justice." In Burt Galaway and Joe Hudson (eds.), *Restorative Justice: International Perspectives*. Monsey, NY: Criminal Justice Press.

Zehr, Howard. 1990. *Changing Lenses*. Waterloo, ON: Herald Press.

_____. 2002. *The Little Book of Restorative Justice*. Intercourse, PA: Good Books.

Zhang, Lening, and Sheldon Zhang. 2004. "Reintegrative Shaming and Predatory Delinquency." *Journal of Research in Crime and Delinquency* 41, 4: 433–53.

Zion, James W. 1995. "Living Indian Justice: Navajo Peacemaking Today." Paper presented at the Alternative Dispute Resolution Conference, Vancouver, Canada.

_____. 1999. "Monster Slayer and Born for Water: The Intersection of Restorative and Indigenous." *Contemporary Justice Review* 2, 4: 359–82.

Zion, James W., and Elsie B. Zion. 1993. "Hozho'sokee'—Stay Together Nicely: Domestic Violence under Navajo Common Law." *Arizona State Law Journal* 25, 2: 407.

Index

NEW CRIMINOLOGY TITLES
from Fernwood Publishing

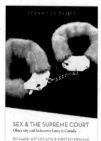

Sex and the Supreme Court
Obscenity and Indecency Law in Canada
Richard Jochelson & Kirsten Kramar
9781552664155 $17.95 112pp Rights: World May 2011 The Basics Series
Canadian laws pertaining to pornography and bawdy houses were first developed during the Victorian era, when "non-normative" sexualities were understood as a corruption of conservative morals and harmful to society as a whole. Today, rather than seeing harm to conservative values, the court sees harm to liberal political values. The authors use Foucault's governmentality framework to show that the liberal harm strategy for governing obscenity and indecency continues to disguise power.

Mr. Big
Exposing Undercover Investigations in Canada
Kouri T Keenan & Joan Brockman
9781552663769 $18.95 138pp Rights: World 2010

"Mr. Big" is a sting operation designed to obtain a confession and other evidence from a suspect targeted by undercover police officers posing as members of the criminal underworld. The authors argue that the Mr. Big procedure encourages a police culture of violence and convictions rather than justice and suggest that this practice must be drastically curtailed if we are to have a legal system that is focused on the pursuit of justice.

Constructing Danger
Emotions and Mis/Representation of Crime in the News, 2nd Edition
Chris McCormick
9781552663820 $29.95 240pp Rights: World 2010
Crime reporting is often thought to be simply an objective and factual description of an event. In *Constructing Danger* Chris McCormick argues that crime is more than simply reported: it is constructed. And sometimes it is distorted, exaggerated and manipulated in order to create certain impressions of and opinions about the world. This book asks the reader to consider the consequences of holding this distorted vision.

Missing Women, Missing News
Covering Crisis in Vancouver's Downtown Eastside
David Hugill
9781552663776 $17.95 112pp Rights: World 2010 The Basics Series

Missing Women, Missing News examines newspaper coverage of the arrest and trial of Robert Pickton, the man charged with murdering 26 street-level sex workers from Vancouver's Downtown Eastside. It demonstrates how news narratives obscured the complex matrix of social and political conditions that made it possible for so many women to simply "disappear" from a densely populated urban neighbourhood without provoking an aggressive response by the state.

visit www.fernwoodpublishing.ca for more criminology titles